Striking Out and Winning!

A music-maker's guide to the HAMMERED DULCIMER
for beginning through intermediate players

Lucille Reilly

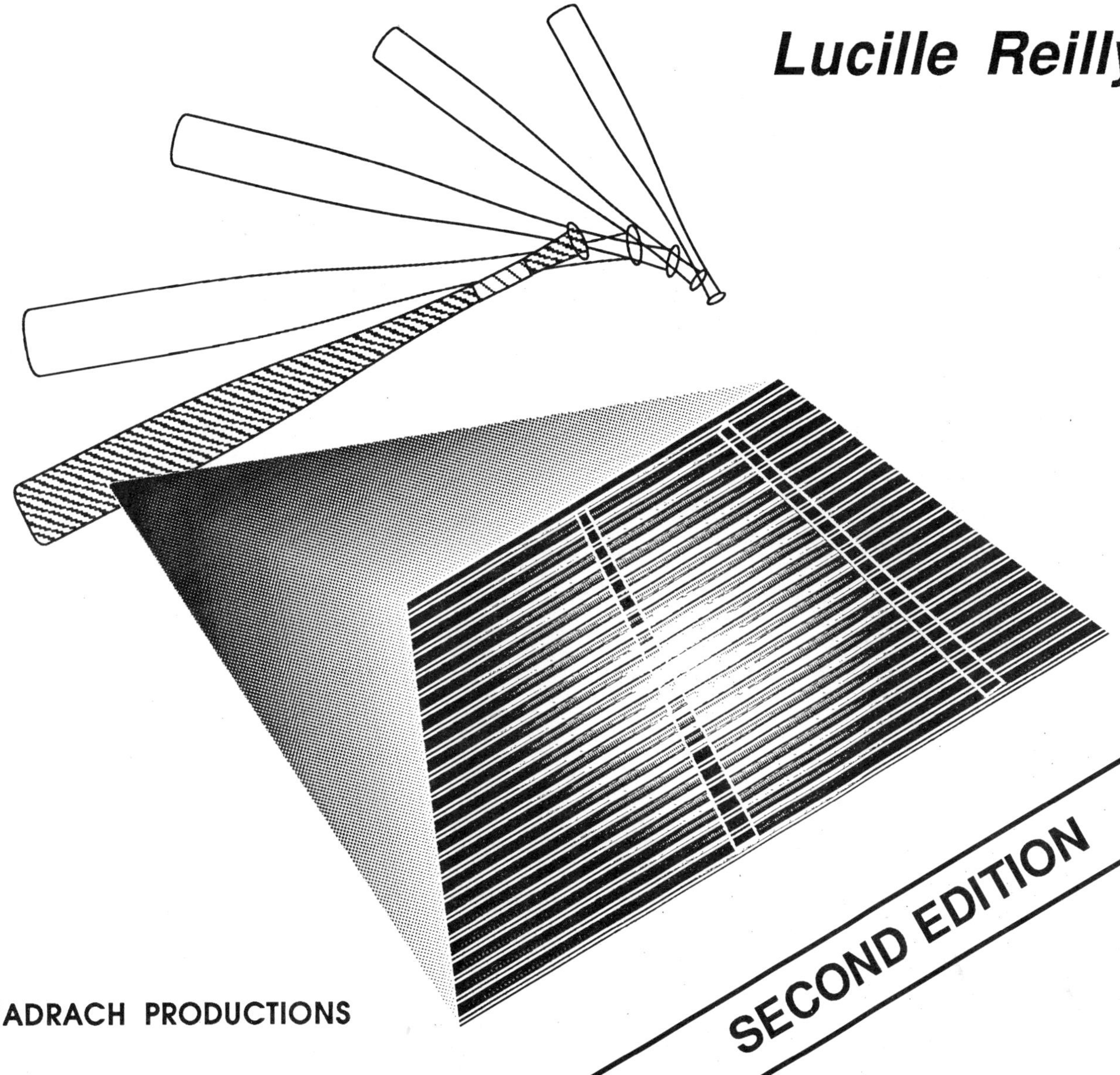

SHADRACH PRODUCTIONS

SECOND EDITION

*To the glory of God
and in memory of
Florence Hollis,
social worker, professor, student and friend*

Copyright ©1984, 1992 Lucille Reilly
All rights reserved. No part of this book may be reproduced mechanically
    or photocopied without permission in writing from the author.
First printing: July 1984
First printing of the second edition: June 1992

Cover and book design, typesetting, technical drawings and music
    autography by Lucille Reilly
Editor: Sarah Winston Christmyer
Photo credits: Janet Bryan: back cover; David Rewick: pg. 16; all others by
    Bill Lindsey
Illustrations on pp. xiv, 8, 22, 42, 116, 124, 128, 139, 144, 152, 158, 178
    © 1992 Lucille Reilly

Printed in the U.S.A.

Library of Congress Cataloguing-in-Publication Data:
Reilly, Lucille.
Striking out and winning! : a music-maker's guide to the hammered
dulcimer for beginning through intermediate players /
Lucille Reilly. —2nd ed.
p. of music
Includes bibliographical references and index.
ISBN 0-9613356-4-5
1. Dulcimer: Methods.   I. Title
MT717.2.R   92-8527

Published by: Shadrach Productions
               P. O. Box 49
               Basking Ridge, NJ 07920

Introduction

When some *Striking Out and WINNING!* fans heard I was rewriting the book, they asked, "How can it get any better?" While the book taught thoroughly how tuning set-up and stroke order worked together to keep from tying one's arms in knots, it still didn't teach adequately how to *play* the dulcimer. My own students were proof! They struck the strings with the same series of right and left strokes as I, but their music sounded weak and labored where mine floated and zipped! What else was I doing? And could I teach what I seemed to be born with, whatever it was? As I was self-taught and musically intuitive, answers were hard to come by.

On November 13, 1985 (a very lucky Wednesday), I was demonstrating for a student and suddenly saw what was missing in her playing—and everyone else's: a smoothness and buoyancy in her moves. With them, she relaxed and her dulcimer resonated like it never had before! Best of all, that missing link *could* be taught! That day, I stopped teaching the dulcimer and started teaching how to make music *through* it. (What a relief! Listening for "right notes" was awfully boring.) This discovery was only the beginning: Over the next four-plus years, I taught backwards to find "square one" (the beginner's very first step) and all the things that can make music played on the dulcimer sound either flowing and resonant or encumbered and brittle. All the missing links turned out to be basic not only to dance tunes (to me, the easiest music to start with) but also for playing variations and arrangements of any other style of music.

This new edition is more of a beginner's book than the original book ever was, but it's also for the experienced player who wants to streamline current habits. The 50 dance tunes remain the same as before, as does my premise of a rhythm-based stroking molded to the dulcimer's tuning set-up, rather than the other way around. What's new?

- A step-by-step method, starting from "square one."
- How to enhance "that sound" so your dulcimer sings (and zings!).
- How to develop an "inner vision" of the dulcimer's tuning.
- How to play easily and *fast* while mistake-proofing your playing.
- An improved step-by-step approach for rolls.
- The exercises teach techniques and the tunes they come from at the same time, complete with stroking and positions for right- *and* left-handed players.

A newly revised set of the original three companion cassettes is available, and now you can see it all in living color on a video, too!*

With all this going for you, you can't help but strike out and win! Have fun!

Lucille Reilly
May 15, 1992

---

* See the *Order Form* on the last page for more details.

Acknowledgements

If Lynn McCabe hadn't been in the right place at the right time, and if Connie Waring hadn't made a curious observation, I would never have seen the need to write a new edition. But they did, and my life as a musician and teacher changed. Lynn, Connie and another dozen or so regular private students taught from 1985 to 1988 in Moorestown, New Jersey, opened my eyes and were invaluable. I learned much from them.

In June of 1988, I moved 80 miles north to marry the man I love. Although now too far away for most of my students to continue lessons, I caught up with numerous, mostly anonymous players at workshops and festivals who asked either directly or through their playing for clearer answers to the questions "How?" and "Why?" They're here.

I relived my Moorestown days with more recent students' help. Linda Sepe was my first student to play the dulcimer from scratch using this edition, her hammers sending signals for more information. Carol Kerr, a "retired" music editor, taught herself from the text as a leftie, offering advice where words or exercises didn't quite "make it." My 1991 summer class at Westminster Choir College unwittingly presented still more interpretations and problems of playing that the text had yet to address. When they asked why my solutions weren't in print, I spilled the beans and told them this edition was on the way. They then made emphatic, good suggestions of things they wanted to see included.

Melva Johnson was my right arm. A student since 1989, she'd picked up "missing" tips from the original book in her lessons and was eager to see what I'd written this time. However, Melva's real job was to pretend she was back home in Wisconsin without a teacher, learning jigs and hornpipes from the new lessons. She played each exercise *exactly* as I described, giving us both some good laughs whenever we met for "check-ups" which often sent me back in search of better words. Melva held me up in the tougher times and I'm sure she must have kept praying.

Louise McClure, a Suzuki violin specialist, served as a sounding board of my discovery process since it began in 1985. Over the years, I've seen a striking link, if you will, between hammers and violin bows (and I think when this is done, I'll ask Louise to teach me how to fiddle). Louise is always on the lookout for new ways of teaching, and I'm grateful that she's always been there to inspire, confirm and encourage.

Once all of the above had their say, Sarah Winston Christmyer got the final word. Though not a dulcimer player herself, Sarah shared enthusiasm as she "saw" my words in action in her mind. (Elation!) Bettie Scott then followed up with one last check of the text before the printer made it a reality.

Finally, my husband David gave me encouragement to go for quality, to settle for something better, to give you the best I can. This is it.

L. R.

(Note: To the best of my knowledge, all of the tunes are in the public domain. If I've missed one that wasn't written by Anonymous, I will acknowledge the composer in future editions.)

Table of Contents

Introduction iii
Acknowledgements iv
Alphabetical Listing of Tunes viii
Tunings Used for This Book ix
How to Use This Book x
The Hammered Dulcimer xii

1. Create a Winning Team 1
The hammered dulcimer 1 ★ Hammers 2 ★ Stands 3 ★ Written music 4 ★ The Position System 5 ★ The singing voice 6 ★ Miscellaneous equipment 7

2. Spring Training 9
On your mark,... 9 ★ ...Get set,... 9 ★ ...Play! 12 ★ How are you holding your hammers? 14 ★ Simple songs 19 ★ Testing one, two... 21

3. The Playing Field 23
Major scales 23 ★ Unisons 29 ★ Octaves 31 ★ A Challenge 35 ★ Which scale is best? 35 ★ Minor scales 35 ★ Modes: The Mixolydian mode 38 ★ The Dorian mode 40

4. Batter Up! 43
About this chapter 43

REELS 44 ★ The basic principle of stroke order for reels 44

Lesson 1: Alternating strokes, etc. 44 ★ "Spotless" playing 46 ★ How to learn a tune 48 ★ Should you think about note names while you play? 50 ★ A mini-lesson on shifting positions 51 ★ Your first reel 51 ★ It's play time! 55

Lesson 2: Building your pattern vocabulary 56 ★ Postscript: The comedy of errors 58

Lesson 3: The basic rhythm in reels 60

Lesson 4: Easy rhythmic sequences 66 ★ A position-shift puzzle 67

Lesson 5: "Aerobic" sequences 68

Lesson 6: Hiccups and the art of dulcimer playing 72 ★ A true confession 73 ★ Keeping the magic 73

Lesson 7: "Blackberry" in reverse 74

Lesson 8: "3D" sound 75

Lesson 9: Multiple-bounce strokes and rolls 78 ★ How to play multiple-bounce strokes 78 ★ May we have a drum roll, please? 79 ★ Two-stroke rolls: The *reel* reason for this lesson! 80 ★ Adding rolls to reels 82

Lesson 10: Rolls within the "going up" rhythm 83

(continued)

Lesson 11: Ginger snaps 84 ★ When to ginger snap 86 ★ Ginger snaps with rolls 87
Lesson 12: Rolls 201 88 ★ Rolls passing the bar (line, that is!) 88 ★ "Rapid-fire" rolls 89 ★ Downbeat rolls 91
Lesson 13: Syncopation 92 ★ Another mini-lesson on stroke order 94

JIGS 96
Lesson 14: Alternating strokes 96
Lesson 15: Quick, two-note pick-ups 99 ★ Another mini-lesson on shifting positions 101
Lesson 16: The most common rhythm in jigs 102
Lesson 17: Rolls 107

HORNPIPES 109
Lesson 18: The dotted rhythm 109
Lesson 19: Triplets 111

SPECIAL EFFECTS WITH MULTIPLE-BOUNCE STROKES 112
Lesson 20: Descending triplets 112
Lesson 21: Ascending pick-up triplets 114 ★ Other tunes to which you may add ascending triplets 115

5. Time Out: Tuning and Maintenance 117
Tuning the dulcimer 117 ★ Other tuning tips 118 ★ Keeping your dulcimer in tune 118 ★ If the treble bridge needs adjusting 119 ★ Replacing a broken string 119 ★ How to make loop-end strings 122 ★ T. L. C. 123

6. The Grand Slam: Fifty Dance Tunes 125
Striking Out... 126

Soldier's Joy 126
How to build speed and accuracy 127
Cincinnati 127
Golden Slippers 128
Galopede 129
My Love Is But a Lassie Yet 129
Successful Campaign 130
Liberty 131
Staten Island 131
Petronella 132
St. Anne's Reel 132
Over the Waterfall 133
On the Road to Boston 133

Arkansas Traveller 134
The Rose Tree 134
Turkey in the Straw 135
The Irish Washerwoman 135
Tobin's Favorite 136
Kitty McGee 136
Smash the Windows 137
Swallowtail Jig 138
Keel Row 138
Boys of Bluehill 139
Swallowtail Reel 140
Fisher's Hornpipe 140
The Breakdown 141

...and WINNING! 142

Pretty Little Dog 142
The Devil's Dream 143
Hull's Victory 143
MacIlmoyle Reel 144
The White Cockade 145
Reel de Montréal 145
Red-Haired Boy 146
College Hornpipe 146
Swinging on a Gate 147
La Bastrangue 147
Gaspé Reel 148
Old Grey Cat 148
Temperance Reel 149

Whiskey Before Breakfast 150
Top of the Cork Road 150
Tenpenny Bit 151
Shandon Bells 151
Maggie Brown's Favorite Jig 152
The Quaker's Wife 153
Old Rosin the Beau 153
When Daylight Shines 154
Black Joke 154
Drowsy Maggie 155
Flowers of Edinburgh, The 156
Larry O'Gaff 156

Conclusion (or, Where do you go from here?) 157

7. Appendix...159

Music symbols in this book 159 ★ Other symbols 159 ★ Position symbols 160 ★ Note values 160 ★ Addendum to Fig. 1-4a 161 ★ About the lettering on page xiv 162

Chapter 3 diagrams: Unisons 162 ★ Octaves: In neighboring positions 164 ★ Spanning second and bass positions 166 ★ In one position 168 ★ Answers to *A Challenge* 170

How to count measures 171 ★ How to find the first note of a tune 171 ★ Form 172 ★ Why aren't the chords with the tunes? 173 ★ Position shifts for Ex. 22 173 ★ About the footnotes with the tunes 173 ★ How to transpose a melody 174 ★ Going beyond: Creating variations of tunes 175 ★ The history of the dulcimer 175 ★ Tunebook sources 176 ★ Glossary 176

8. Index..179

Notes...188

Striking Out and Winning!

Alphabetical Listing of Tunes

Arkansas Traveller 134
Black Joke 154
Boys of Bluehill 139
Breakdown, The 141
Cincinnati 127
College Hornpipe 146
Devil's Dream, The 143
Drowsy Maggie 155
Fisher's Hornpipe 140
Flowers of Edinburgh, The 156
Galopede 129
Gaspé Reel 148
Golden Slippers 128
Hull's Victory 143
Irish Washerwoman, The 135
Keel Row 138
Kitty McGee 136
La Bastrangue 147
Larry O'Gaff 156
Liberty 131
MacIlmoyle Reel 144
Maggie Brown's Favorite Jig 152
My Love Is But a Lassie Yet 129
Old Grey Cat 148
Old Rosin the Beau 153

On the Road to Boston 133
Over the Waterfall 133
Petronella 132
Pretty Little Dog 142
Quaker's Wife, The 153
Red-Haired Boy 146
Reel de Montréal 145
Rose Tree, The 134
St. Anne's Reel 132
Shandon Bells 151
Smash the Windows 137
Soldier's Joy 126
Staten Island 131
Successful Campaign 130
Swallowtail Jig 138
Swallowtail Reel 140
Swinging on a Gate 147
Temperance Reel 149
Tenpenny Bit 151
Tobin's Favorite 136
Top of the Cork Road 150
Turkey in the Straw 135
When Daylight Shines 154
Whiskey Before Breakfast 150
White Cockade, The 145

Tunings Used for This Book

The instruction in this book is based on regularly-tuned, fifth-interval, 12-11 and 15-14 dulcimers.

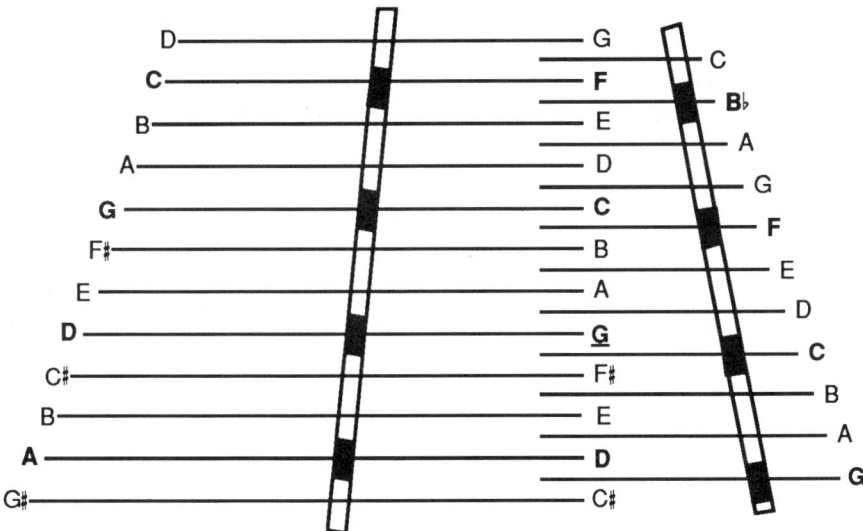

Fig. 1 Tuning and bridge mark locations for a 12-11 dulcimer

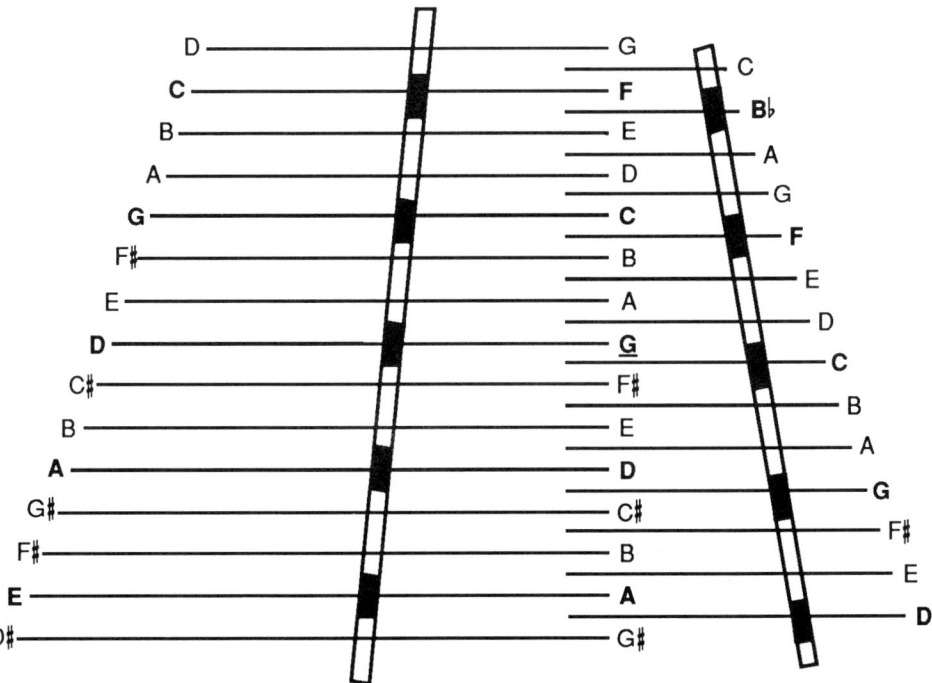

Fig. 2 Tuning and bridge mark locations for a 15-14 dulcimer

These tunings are common to most dulcimers, despite the addition in recent years of extra sharped and flatted tones which render certain instruments "chromatic." (If you have a chromatic dulcimer, you will experience some limitations *and* extensions of range at the upper—and possibly also lower—end of your instrument.)

Striking Out and Winning!

If your dulcimer's bass strings sound one octave instead of a fifth below the first-position courses (a tuning found on dulcimers constructed by some Michigan builders), concentrate your playing on the treble strings.

Your dulcimer *must* have bridge marks as shown in Fig. 1 or 2 because you'll be referring to them constantly. If you don't have bridge marks, ask your builder about adding them. White and black Delrin® is the bridge-mark material of choice, but some older instruments may not be able to accept it without alteration. Paint, stain or dark nail polish brushed on both sides of the bridges at the spots shown in Fig. 1 or 2 are other ways to mark them if you're handy. If you're undecided about how to mark your bridges permanently, a temporary solution is small, cut-to-fit "Post-It Notes®" pieces on those bridge saddles needing the marks.

The bridge marks on your dulcimer are all you need for this book. *Do not* affix letter names and/or any other identifying "crutches" to it. (If you already have them, remove them. This goes for aesthetic reasons, too. The soundboard will darken with age *except* where the strips are!) You'll be learning to recognize striking locations *as they relate to each other and to the bridge marks.* Any additional markings will only get in your way.

How to Use This Book

One of the music shops selling *Striking Out* gives the best advice: "Start at the beginning and keep going." How can I improve on that? Well, just a few more words:

There isn't anything in this new edition that my students and I haven't tried out a lot. That goes for what works and what doesn't. From it, I draw one conclusion: When striking the strings feels easy, the dulcimer sounds great! Any "success tips" toward easy playing and resonant sound are preceded by the symbol "★" throughout this book. Certain techniques may be difficult to play without them.

Some of what's here may seem incovenient or even crazy, but after you've practiced a technique, I present other ways people approach it. Compare the differences in sound and feel of these functional variations wherever the symbol "♪" appears. I've found that "comparison shopping" is the best way to learn to play the dulcimer. When you know what you're doing and why, you'll have more fun. Isn't that what it's all about?

To that end, take the instruction as it comes. In Chapter 4, the longer lessons are divided into sections, providing convenient stopping points. Don't jump around or skip something because it looks too easy, even if you've been playing for a while. (I'm training your arms, body and ears as well as your mind.) And most of all, don't even think of changing the strokes shown for the exercises and tunes! I don't want you to miss the music! (More about that in Chapter 4.)

If something here still mystifies you despite all my best analogies and "buzzwords," get the companion video, or better yet, ask a knowledgeable teacher in your area to guide you in person.

If you're just starting out,...

there's nothing more I can say but "have at it" and enjoy yourself!

If you've been playing long enough to form your own ideas,...

try to approach what's here as if you never played the dulcimer before. You're about to see how some small changes can make big improvements in your sound and ease of playing. You'll hear and feel a difference immediately with simple one- to three-note patterns; however, applying these new ideas to any tunes you know may be more than a little challenging. You'll think so much about *how* you're playing you'll forget about the notes and goof more than you'd like. Don't give up; the mistakes will pass! (I and my students still know what that's like from time to time, so you're in plenty of good company.) Remember: new habits feel hard *because* they're new. The week or two of inconvenience you invest for a lifetime of great music-making is a small price to pay. Once the new habits are second nature, you'll barely have to think about them and your tunes will come back better than before. Hang in there; these basic things are *extremely* important if you want to explore the creative realm of music-making which knows no limits.

If you're a teacher,...

I invite you to become a purveyor of resonant sound instead of an administrator of "right notes." Good musicianship is not a stroke of luck, but a deliberate act; if I can teach it, you can. Let this book start your students off. In the meantime, train your ears and eyes to help sharpen theirs (they still need you despite the companion cassettes or the video). If a problem arises, chances are good that you'll find a solution here. To look up solutions fast, familiarize yourself with the text. Better yet, apply the techniques to your own playing! As to weekly assignments, don't feel that you have to assign a whole lesson and all of the tunes given with it. How about the first one or two sections of a lesson and one tune? I've even assigned only half a tune if it's tricky. And feel free to invent your own exercises to suit specific needs; Chapter 4 and the tunes are loaded with ideas in this regard. Knowing each student's capacity is important, especially when complicated by a 9-to-5 job or raising a family. (And don't inflict *Golden Slippers* on students from Philadelphia! See page 128.) If you need more help, try to attend one of my week-long summer workshops. It's a fast way to grasp what's here first-hand until there are enough of you out there to gather together for a teachers' seminar.

Striking Out and Winning!

The Hammered Dulcimer

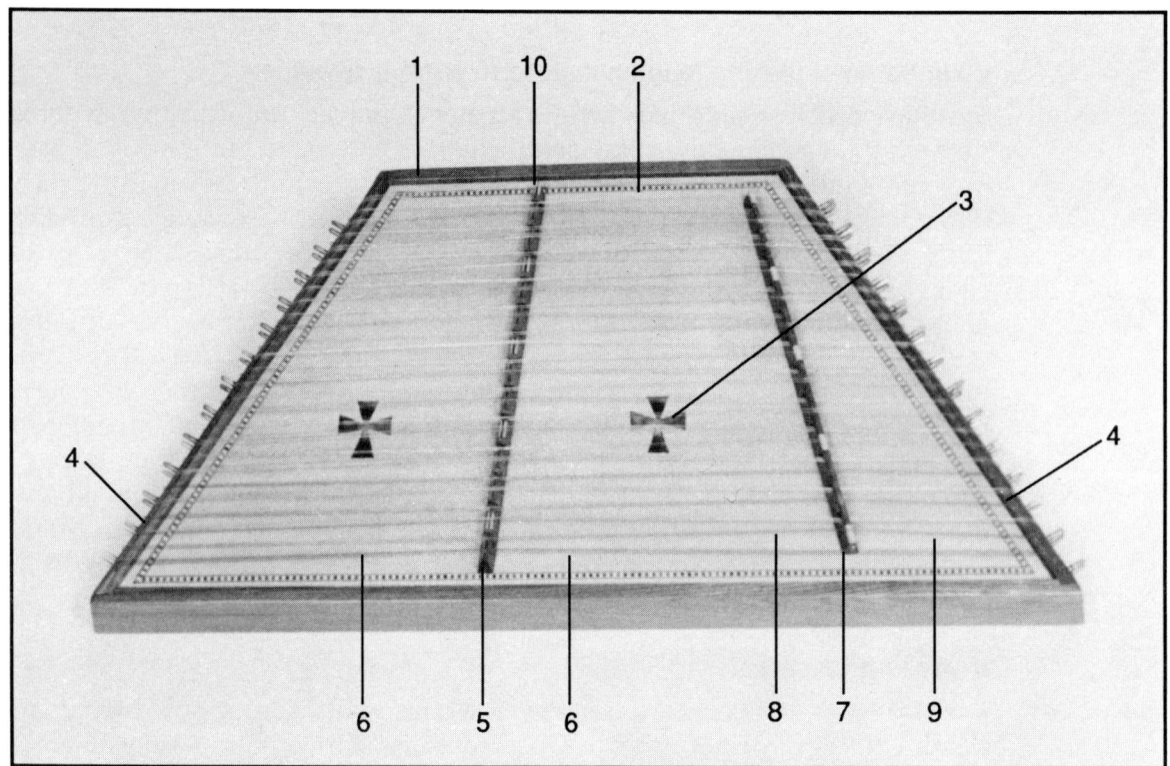

Fig. 3 Front view

1. frame
2. soundboard
3. soundhole
4. side rail
5. treble bridge
6. treble course
7. bass bridge
8. bass course
9. unplayable part of bass course
10. bridge mark

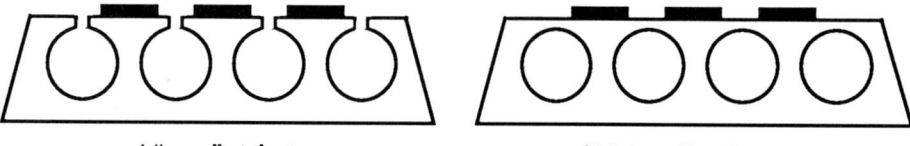

a) "open" at the top   b) "closed" at the top

Fig. 4 The two most common types of bridges

Striking Out and Winning!

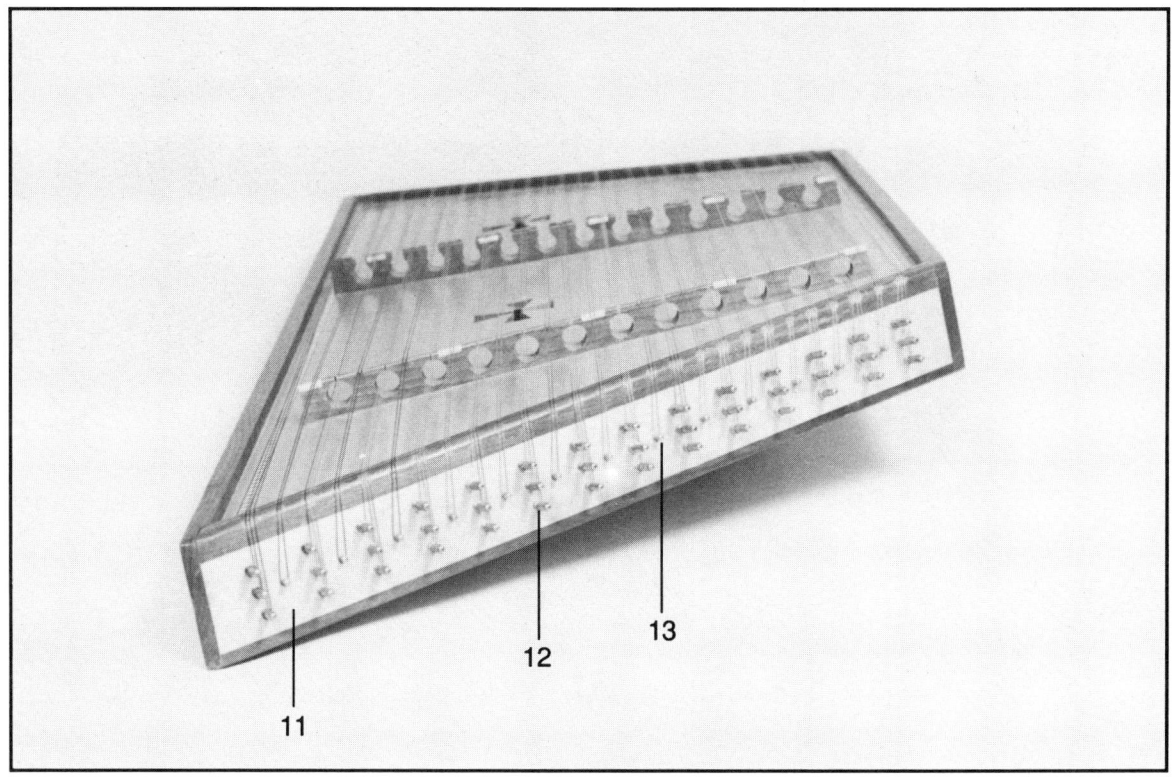

Fig. 5 Side view

11. pinblock
12. tuning pin
13. hitch pin

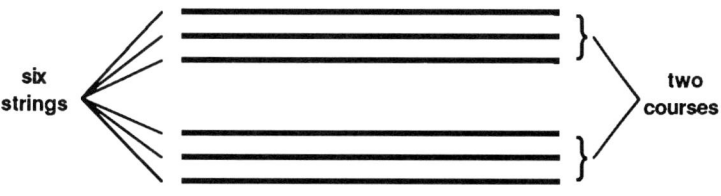

Fig. 6 Strings vs. courses

A list of music symbols and note values appears in the *Appendix*.

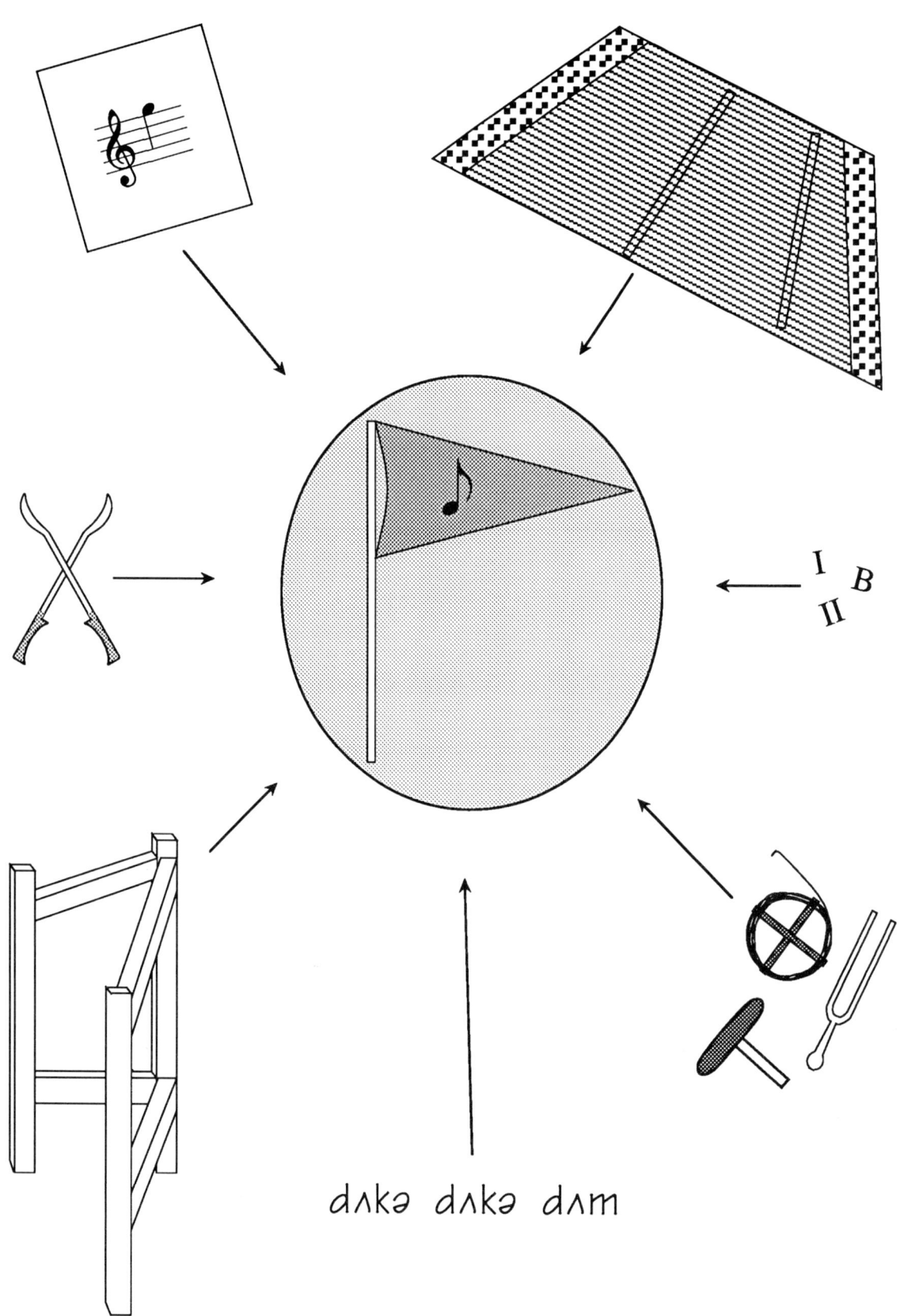

Create a Winning Team

Every year, major-league baseball teams draft rookies and trade players in hopes of creating a winning team all the way through the next season and the World Series. You, too, need to put together a "team" of tools and skills for winning dulcimer playing. Here is what you'll need:

The hammered dulcimer

Of course! Hammered dulcimers have improved in construction, design and sound over the years, so virtually any make should serve you well. (Be sure you have at least a 12-11 dulcimer; see page ix.)

Familiarize yourself with the dulcimer's parts on pp. xii-xiii. Note the treble and bass bridges and the diagram showing courses versus strings.

By now you've noticed (and may be a little boggled by) all the strings. Did you also notice that some courses sit lower than others? Do you strike them or are they there just for effect? Stoop down or lean over so you can look across the strings at eye level. This is what you'll see:

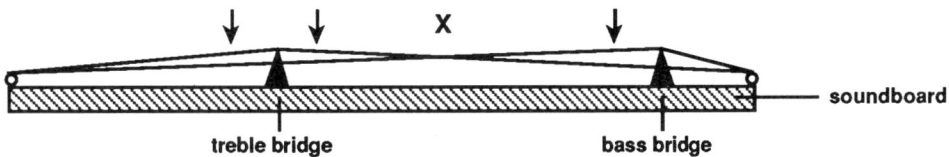

Fig. 1-1 Side view of the dulcimer from the low strings up

The strings crisscross and trade planes so all are playable. ★ Strike them near the bridges (at arrows) to avoid the crossover point at "**X**."

I've divided the dulcimer's strings into three vertical *positions*. Rest your hand on the bass courses to the left of the bass bridge. (The right side is not playable.) This is *bass position* (B). Slide your hand left until it's on the courses to the right of the treble bridge. This is *first position* (I). Slide your hand to the left of the treble bridge, and this is *second position* (II).

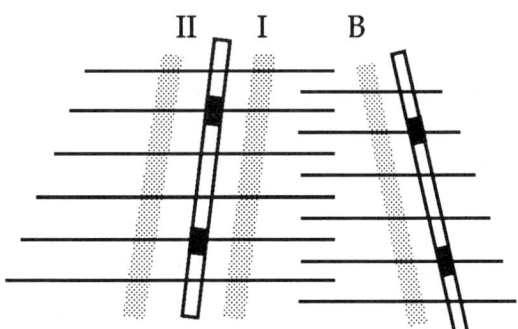

Fig. 1-2 Positions on the dulcimer

All of the tunes in this book can be played in these positions.

Some "chromatic" dulcimers have smaller bridges at the upper end. Include these in the above positions. If yours has one or two bridges at the extreme left of the soundboard, call it/them third position (III).

1

Striking Out and Winning!

Hammers

Your hammers are perhaps more of an instrument than your dulcimer (after all, without them you don't have a *hammered* dulcimer). They must function as an extension of your arms to complement your every move (more in Chapter 2). Not all do.

★ Here is the design I've found to be the most complementary. (You'll understand why in Chapter 2.)

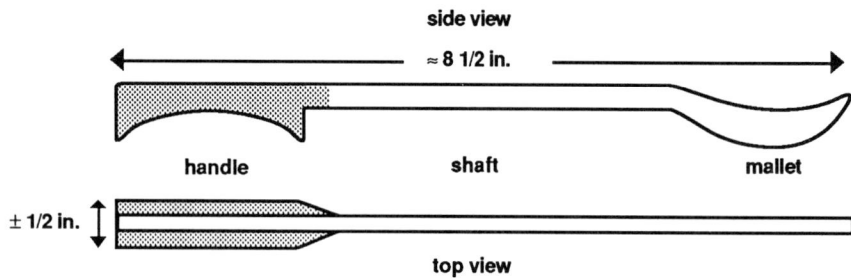

Fig. 1-3 My recommended hammer design

Look for these features:

1. An overall length of about 8½ inches. If they're too short, they'll feel "like toys," as one of my students puts it. If they're too long, your dulcimer may feel far away to you.

2. The handle is flat on top with a long curve underneath; its width from ³/₈–⁵/₈ inches. Any wider and it may not fit in your hand well; any thinner and it could flop sideways (more in Chapter 2).

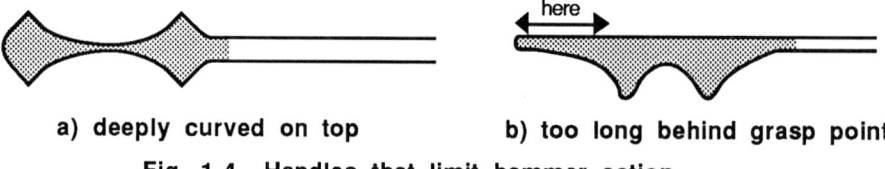

a) deeply curved on top   b) too long behind grasp point

Fig. 1-4 Handles that limit hammer action

Note: I've met some nice-working hammers without handles. (But not all are; check yours in Chapter 2.)

3. A curve in the mallet's striking surface. Those with a point may cause the mallet to slide down between two courses and strike both, depending on where it is.

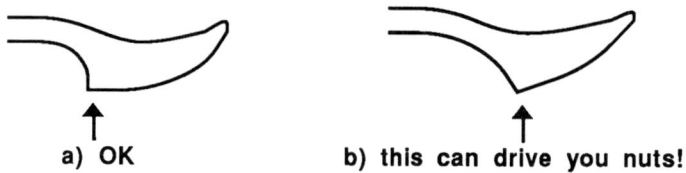

a) OK   b) this can drive you nuts!

Fig. 1-5 Mallets with a point on the striking surface

4. A rigid shaft. If it's even a little flexible, it may oppose your best efforts to play rolls and other neat licks.

5. The overall weight should be neither too heavy nor too light. You should never feel like your hammers are taking you for a ride or like you have to push them along (more in Chapter 2). The best balance is somewhere in between. Try before you buy.

   Hammers with "flip-over" mallets (wood on one side and leather on the other; I affectionately call them "double whammies!") are a convenient two-in-one style, but they tend to be topheavy and often come with the handle in Fig. 1-4a. Forget convenience; balance and ease of playing are higher priorities! Buy two pairs of well-balanced, single-sided hammers and back the mallets of one with leather.

6. Miscellaneous: Avoid hammers made of rosewood or ebony (some trim in the handle is okay). They tend to feel like bricks on the strings and may wander on the rebound. Hammers of cherry, walnut and maple seem to be the best.

   Some hammers may produce a loud-ish "thud" on the dulcimer. (All dulcimers have thud, but some more than others.) A lighter-weight pair can decrease, though not eliminate it.

   Emergency hammers: Toothbrushes (with straight shafts) and Sweetheart® plastic spoons (the forks are topheavy and sluggish).

★ Use hammers with wooden (not leather-backed) mallets for jigs, reels and hornpipes, as they speak with more definition.* Wooden mallets have an unwarranted reputation for producing a brash sound— but they don't have to! (Yes, more in Chapter 2 *and* 4!) Save the leather backed hammers for lush harp tunes, hymns, etc.

Hammers that work with you really do make all the difference!

Stands

★ Look for a stand with a set angle of 10-30°. I like a 30° angle for dances so I can look at the band and caller for cues, but prefer 10° for concerts so my audiences can watch the hammers fly! (A note of interest: ♪ The smaller the angle, the fuller the dulcimer's sound.)

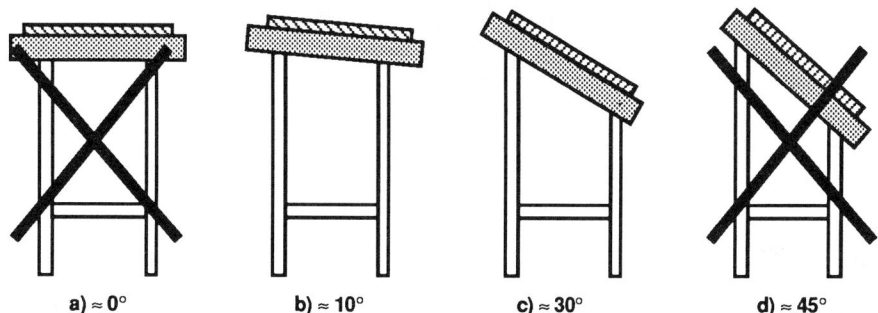

a) ≈ 0°   b) ≈ 10°   c) ≈ 30°   d) ≈ 45°

Fig. 1-6 Dulcimers on stands of different angles

---

* For an explanation of the symbols "★" and "♪," see page x.

Striking Out and Winning!

Avoid any stand with an obvious 45° angle; it'll make you feel like you're climbing Mt. Everest, ♭ give your dulcimer a weak sound, and, as one student reports, will decrease your accuracy. Also, avoid stands with no angle; they make the highest strings difficult to see and strike.

A stand adjustable in height lets you stand or sit, and is great for festivals or any place where chairs are at a premium. ★ Make sure it's not too high for sitting when it's at its lowest height, as this will hamper your playing (more in Chapter 2). And as long as you plan to lug pounds of stuff around, make sure your stand is lightweight as well as strong. (Stands with adjustable *angles* as well as legs tend to be heavy and bulky.) Shop carefully. An adjustable stand would be wonderful to use as you go through this book so you can ★ stand to play the tunes and exercises.

Some dulcimers are equipped for a screw-in leg, or monopod, supporting the upper end of the instrument when you sit. The lower edge of the dulcimer then leans against your lap. Although the monopod is very portable, it limits your ability to dance along with your music-making (see Chapter 4) and makes striking the lowest strings difficult.

If you don't have a stand, you can put your dulcimer on a table and raise the far end with a thick book or two (Fig. 1-7). But get one soon! ★ My students improved their playing instantly once they had a reliable height and angle to play on.

Fig. 1-7 Setting up the dulcimer on a table

Written music

If you read music, staff notation is a natural music-learning tool, but if you don't, is it beyond you? Not a bit! In fact, playing solely by ear may be harder! I suggest you cheat by ★ *listening* to a tune while *following* the "spots" on the five-line staff like a road map. My non-music-reading students, including some related to Doubting Thomas, have learned to play notey jigs and reels with written music, with nary a word from me about note names or types, ever since I discovered some of them couldn't hear the ups and downs in the melody! When they saw and heard a tune using this book with its companion cassettes (see the *Order Form*), the ups and downs in sound made sense, and then they played tunes in no time. You, too, can pick up a lot by osmosis.

The Position System

The music in this book is marked with the dulcimer's positions over the notes, making it a more useful road map. (I borrowed the symbols from guitar and violin music.) For example, look at this scale:

Fig. 1-8 The D major scale notated with positions

You play the first four notes in first position (first position is assumed when nothing is written over the music) and the last four notes in second (shown by II·······). A series of notes in bass position will have B········ over them. Play the notes under the dashed line in that position until it ends with a downward "hook" (·······⌐).

The stroke mark under the first note (R or L) shows which hammer to strike. After this alternate hammers until other strokes appear.

Listed below are some exceptions to these basics:

1. Occasionally a "I" appears over a single note. This symbol appears whenever a passage is played mostly in second position but with one or two first-position notes thrown in. (See the A section of *On the Road to Boston*, page 133.)

2. When a position mark appears in parentheses—(II), (B)—play the note(s) in that position or first position, whichever you prefer.

3. For long passages of music in second position, the dotted line after "II" is cut short and *"sim."* is added (Fig. 1-9). This is an abbreviation for the Italian word *simile* (pronounced SEE-mee-ley) and means "continue in the same fashion." Stay in that position until the end of the tune or until a position shift is noted.

Fig. 1-9 *Soldier's Joy* (excerpt), played in second position

Striking Out and Winning!

4. *Double stops,* or two courses struck simultaneously, appear in one of three ways (Fig. 1-10). In Fig. 1-10c, the bracket ([) next to the upper note shows that only that note is played in second position; the lower note is played in first. In all three cases, there are two stroke marks underneath. The upper letter corresponds to the note on top while the lower letter goes with the lower note.

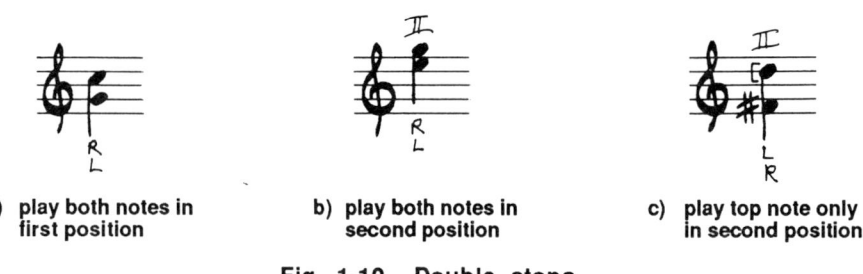

a) play both notes in first position

b) play both notes in second position

c) play top note only in second position

Fig. 1-10 Double stops

5. The symbol "LR" under a note means more than my initials; they tell you to strike with both hammers together (not separately).

The singing voice

Your first-grade teacher told you you had a terrible voice, so you haven't warbled a note since. Shame on that teacher! I've seen singing help so many players, I've been saying, "Singing is the medicine for *all* your musical ills." I know it can work for you. ★ When coupled with written music, singing gets tunes in your ear and head faster than eye/hand *un*coordination and with fewer errors than any other method. (Even proficient music readers find looking at the music and playing all at once too difficult to be practical.) And on its most sophisticated level, ★ singing also can greatly influence how sensitively you'll play. How your voice ties in to playing the dulcimer is described in Chapter 4.

You don't have to sound like a Metropolitan Opera star; matching pitch will do! And just in case *that's* tough: One of my students plays the dulcimer quite well despite the fact that his voice seldom cooperates with his ear (or mine), and another *found* his singing voice after a few weeks of playing. So dust off those vocal cords and forget the past! If you're sensitive about someone hearing you, find a private place where you can wail to your heart's content. (Bring back the outhouse!)

Miscellaneous equipment

1. A tuning wrench. The tuning pins on one of my dulcimers (see pp. xii-xiii) stick out the sides. For it I prefer a gooseneck wrench. It's great for fine tuning and replacing broken strings fast. However, on my other dulcimer (see the back cover), the pins stand vertically. I find the "T" wrench is better for tuning this dulcimer and absolutely essential for stringing up. (The gooseneck doesn't give enough clearance for my hand to hold onto the string.)

   Whichever style you use, ★ make sure the wrench fits on the pins snugly. If the wrench moves a lot before the pin turns, the wrench could grind the pin corners down over time.

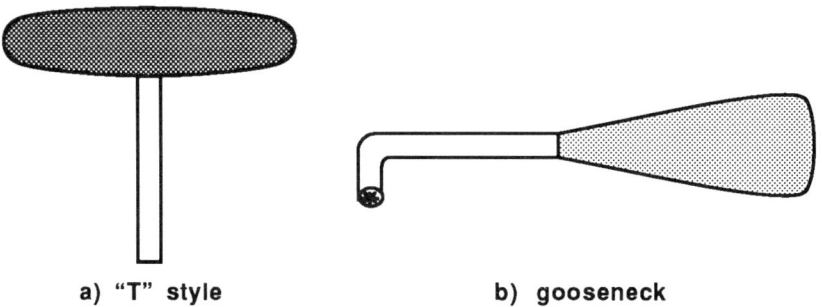

a) "T" style   **b) gooseneck**

Fig. 1-11 Tuning wrenches

2. An electronic tuner or a tuning fork? See Chapter 5.

3. A string replacement kit. (A list appears on page 119.)

4. A case. If you plan to carry your dulcimer anywhere, a heavily padded gig bag is lightweight and surprisingly protective.
   Some dulcimers come with a hinged lid, but they still remain subject to scratches and bumps in the night. If yours is built this way, ★ make a cover to fit around the dulcimer and lid with machine quilted fabric having a *woven* cloth backing (a knit backing catches and snags on everything). To draw the pattern: Hold a pencil straight up and add a one-inch seam allowance when it's sewn. This little bit of thickness is worth the extra weight and will spare the dulcimer a lot of minor scratches.

5. ★ A mirror to check your playing periodically. It's the cheapest video device available, and a great at-home instructor.

6. Extra leather for leather-backed hammers (it flattens down in time) and a spool of thread. (I apply leather with thread to avoid glue and weight build-up.)

7. A sturdy container for your hammers if your case doesn't already have a place to store them.

8. A music stand and a chair. You'll need your lap sometimes.

Looks like you're ready to play ball!(?)

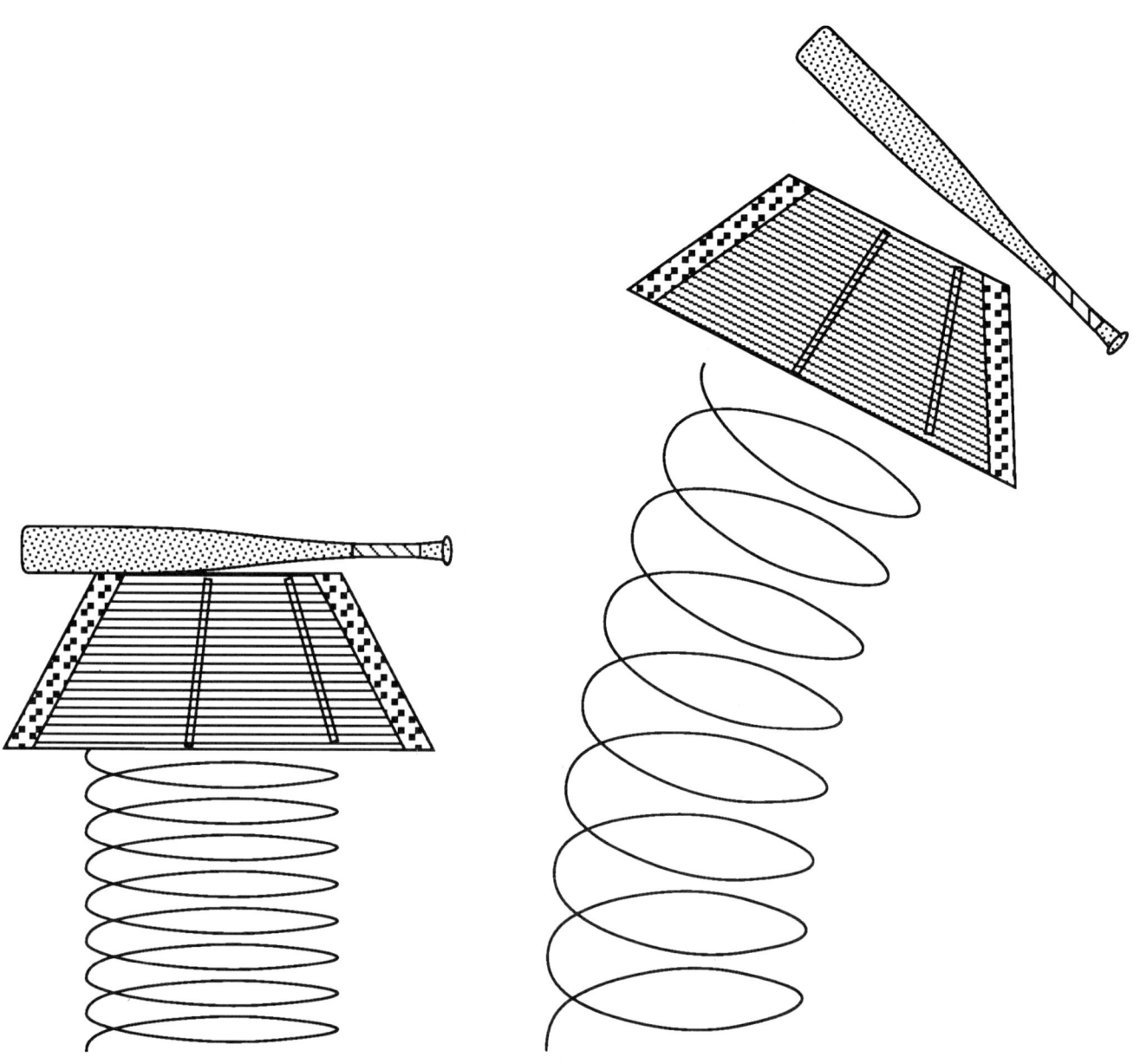

Spring Training

I love teaching first lessons. That's when the biggest improvements occur. Students come into my home playing with a "tinny" sound and they leave producing a full, confident sound—even if they don't know what they're doing! (That's for the second lesson!)

What accounts for the change? Some little things that together make a big difference. Apply them now and your music-making experiences will be more satisfying later. If you've been playing for a while, expect what follows to take some getting used to (see page xi). Whatever your status, if you want results, starting with or backing up to "square one" will help you get them, just as it has for many other players.

On your mark,...

Set up your dulcimer in front of a mirror for either sitting or standing so you can see yourself from the side. ★ Stand to play if you can, as this will free you to move with your music and reach all the strings easily.

Find a course named G in the middle of first position (the right side of the treble bridge). It's underlined in Figs. 1 and 2 on page ix. Notice in the diagram that it's on a bridge mark. Put your index finger on this course.

With one hammer, strike G ★ 1-1½ inches from the bridge a few times (see Fig. 1-1, page 1). Strike some other courses in first position, then in second and bass positions, too, always striking near the bridges. Finally, strike any course at the crossover point. What do you hear? (Whoops!) Strike G once more so you know where it is. This will be a reference course throughout this chapter.

...Get set,...

How high should your dulcimer be and how far should you stand or sit from it? That depends on how tall you are, your arm length, the stand's angle and the key and range of the tune. While I can't give specific measurements, I can offer guidelines to help you determine what will be most comfortable. And you need to know this, because ★ height and distance contribute to the dulcimer's sound and your ease of playing.

Stand in front of first position (not the treble bridge) about eight inches from the bottom end of the dulcimer with ★ your feet about a foot apart and your torso erect (Fig. 2-1a & b). ★ Bend your knees forward slightly. Hold your hammers by the handles (Fig. 1-3), then rest the mallets on G on a 12-11 dulcimer, or on first-position D (at the next bridge mark below G; see page ix) on a 15-14 dulcimer, *or*

Sit on the ★ front four inches of the chair seat with ★ your feet under your knees (Fig. 2-2, page 11), then position your body eight inches from the dulcimer. Careful; some chairs may topple over when you sit this way. Speaking of knees, don't hold them together. Doing so causes tension and makes playing harder (ladies, wear pants or a long skirt). Dining-room chairs and most greyish-beige metal folding chairs are

Striking Out and Winning!

a) front view   b) side view

Fig. 2-1 Standing at the dulcimer

usually sturdy enough. ♪ If you sit on the front four inches rather than against the back of the chair: a) you'll sit taller; b) you'll reach all the strings easily; c) you'll have more mobility; and d) you'll look beautiful. Rest your hammers' mallets on the course suggested for your instrument size.

Now look at your forearms in the mirror. A dulcimer angled closer to 30° will make your forearms level with the floor (Fig. 2-2). If its angle approaches 10°, your forearms will droop a little (Fig. 2-1b). If your forearms droop or bend more than shown, you'll overwork to fight gravity and add unwanted overtones that will muddy your dulcimer's sound.

Raise or lower your stand to position your forearms like the photo nearest your dulcimer's angle. If you're sitting and the chair is too low, make it higher with a cushion or pillow on the seat. If the chair is high, extend the stand's adjustable legs (if it has them) an inch or two.

Two final comments on height: 1) High-heeled shoes or bare feet may require a change in stand height. 2) The steeper the stand angle, the higher the stand (but not by much!).

Spring Training

Fig. 2-2 Sitting at the dulcimer

Now find what I call your *playing distance*. Before you begin, wear a sleeveless shirt or a snug knit turtleneck, or roll up the sleeves on a T-shirt. You'll need to see the contours of your upper arms clearly.

Step away from the dulcimer and hold your hammers in playing position (Fig. 2-3). ★ Let your elbows hang at your sides. Look at your upper arm in the mirror. Its front and back should look symmetrical (Fig. 2-3a). Imagine a vertical line running from the end of your shirt's shoulder seam to your elbow.

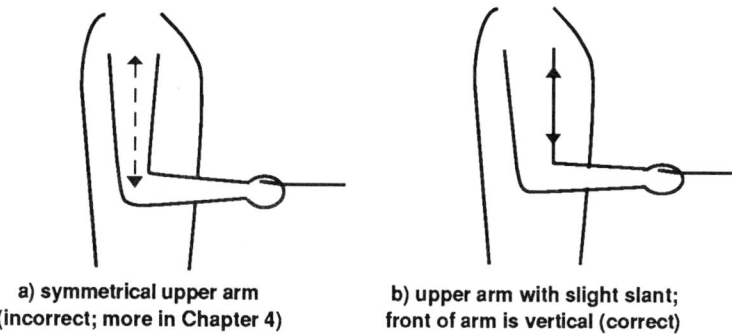

a) symmetrical upper arm
(incorrect; more in Chapter 4)

b) upper arm with slight slant;
front of arm is vertical (correct)

Fig. 2-3 Establishing upper-arm slant to determine playing distance

Now move your elbows forward an inch or two until the *fronts* of your upper arms are vertical (Fig. 2-3b). The resulting upper-arm slant ★ opens your arms just enough to free them so you can play anywhere on the dulcimer easily. ★ Open arms also mean open, resonant sound.

With the forward slant in place, rest the mallets again on G or D. If you're sitting, you may have to push your chair back. If you've been playing for a while, you're probably further away from the dulcimer now, but ♩ this new distance really will help you relax and play effortlessly.

Striking Out and Winning!

Finally, look down at your elbows. ★ Mine stick out a little in Fig. 2-1a, but this isn't on purpose. ★ They're just hanging; what you see is the result of upper-arm slant. Don't try to push your elbows in or you'll feel excessive tension that will inhibit speed and accuracy in your playing. ★ Let your elbows hang where they may!

Your playing distance will change whenever a tune requires a shift from one area of the dulcimer to another. When that happens, ★ move your body toward the new strike area to maintain your upper-arm slant. How to do it: Hold your hammers over (not on) G. ★ Lean forward an inch or two from your heels (not hips) to feel your weight on the balls of your feet if you're standing (heels remain on the floor), or from your hips if you're sitting. Now you can strike the highest courses comfortably without stretching your arms a lot. (♭ Stretching can tire you fast.) From here, ★ sway a little from side to side (waltz with your feet glued to the floor or with your rump stuck on the seat). Finally, ★ pivot body and arms about an eighth of a turn to the left (to second position) and back to a "12-o'clock" position, then pivot to the right (to bass position).

★ Standing to play lets you adjust your playing distance instantly when necessary. If you're sitting, you'll need to move your chair to maintain arm slant for tunes played solely on the lowest or highest courses.

If your playing distance changes your forearm position, readjust your stand's height if you can. Once it's where you want it (you may need more time to decide), mark the stand's legs with a pencil so you can set up your dulcimer at the same height every time.

Now you're ready to…

…Play!

Start off with a simple five-note scale. (Do this even if you're an experienced player, as I will also show you *how* to strike the strings.)

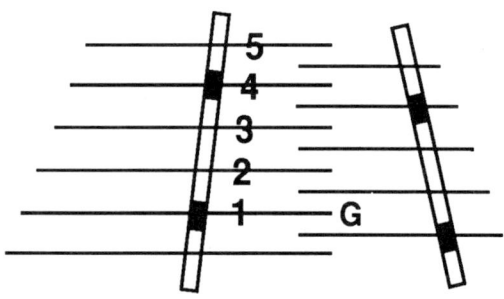

Fig. 2-4 Finding a five-note scale

Look at the scale on your dulcimer with your eyes *and* ★ fingers. Place the thumb of either hand on first-position G and the other fingers on the four courses above it. This is your first ★ *visual pattern*. To spot it immediately every time, ★ focus on steps #1 and #5. Step #1 is on a bridge mark. Where is step #5? It's one course above a mark. ★ Use the bridge marks to find your way; that's what they're there for!

Spring Training

Strike G ★ 1-1½ inches from the treble bridge with *both* hammers together 8 times (shown by "LR" in the music below) about twice as fast as the second hand on a watch, then go to step #2 and repeat. Do this up to step #5 and then back down to step #1. (I didn't write out the whole exercise because ★ you should look at your dulcimer to play.) ★ Let your body lean forward and back as you go up and down the scale. If you hear more than one note per strike, check your aim and make sure your right hammer is well to the left of the crossover point.

How did that feel? Easy? Labored? Striking the strings should always feel easy, so let's find out what makes it that way. All you have to do is ★ loosen up and keep your arms moving. To loosen up, ★ drop your shoulders and let your elbows hang at your sides.* To keep your arms moving, ★ bounce your hands up and down in one, *continuous* six-inch-high motion between strikes† using your ★ *forearms* (think bouncing balls; bend your elbows, not your wrists). A ball bouncing downstairs doesn't stop in midair to find the next step; neither should your hands!

Six inches may seem like a lot, but you'll be amazed how high your hammers can go without missing. That's because your arms are relaxed. (♪ You miss more when they can't move.) Plus, ★ bouncing makes your playing sound more confident and audible. You can play it like you mean it!

If you bounced your hands but stopped them in between, like this,...

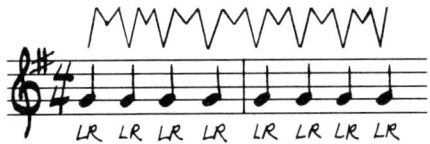

Fig. 2-5 The "stop-and-search method" of dulcimer playing
(not recommended)

---

* Can't tell if your elbows are relaxed? "Push" them out sideways so your upper arms are at 45° angles from your body. Feel the pressure under your upper arms. Conversely, squeeze your elbows against your body for a few seconds, then let go so they "dangle" alongside your body. *That's* where your elbows need to be so you can play relaxed.
† Bounce height increases the slower you play and decreases as you play faster.

Striking Out and Winning!

...the extra "jerks" created tension. You know where to strike, so take out the extra moves. ★ Single, continuous bounces from strike to strike are essential, no matter how fast or slow you play.

The more I observe dulcimer players at workshops and festivals, the more convinced I become that excess tension, not mistakes, is the #1 playing problem!* (It's often the cause of mistakes, too.) When you're tense, you have to work harder to play to overcome stiffness, and the result you get is extra overtones that make the dulcimer sound "tinny." ★ The dulcimer is only a mirror; it'll reflect back whatever you put into it. If you want a pure, *magical* sound (who wouldn't?) and at the same time be able to *zip* when you want to (yes!), you've got to let go and relax.

Play the five-note scale once more to practice bouncing your hands. When you return to step #1, don't stop! Go on into:
1) 4 strikes per course (up and down the scale once)
2) 2 strikes per course (up and down 2-3 times)
3) 1 strike per course (up and down 4 or more times)

In the future, I'll call this reduction process "8-4-2-1."

You're on your way to playing with a singing sound, but you can still do more. Now I must ask:

How are you holding your hammers?

Strike G eight times with both hammers together, then stop and hold that pose. Look down at your hands and answer these questions:

1. Are you holding both hammers the same? (If not, don't match them up; leave them as is.)
2. Are your fingers apart or together?
3. On what part of your index finger is the hammer sitting? The first segment (where the fingernail is)? The first joint? The middle segment? The second joint?
4. Are your thumbs in line with the hammer shafts? Or are they at an angle to them?
5. Are your wrists bent or straight?
6. Are your hammers parallel or do they "pigeon-toe" toward each other?
7. What is the size and shape of the opening in your hand next to your thumb?

All of the above variables affect the quality of your dulcimer's sound. Which ones will work to your advantage? Let's find out.

---

* You do need a certain amount of *good* tension for musical expression. I'm talking about excess physical tension that gets in your way.

Spring Training

I hold the hammers identically. (I'm sure you guessed that much!) They sit on the middle segments of my index fingers. My fingers are together and my thumbs are in line with the hammer shafts, with wrists straight and hammers pigeon-toed. This hold frees my arms to sail over the strings, curbs any fear of hammers flying from my grasp (a real fear of some players; I'll show you why later) and eliminates those overtones that make the dulcimer sound tinny.

What does my hold *look like?* Here it is in words and pictures. (It may feel strange if you've been playing a while. Hang in there; it will get easier the longer you stick with it.)

1. Find the fleshy pad of your thumb, a large area midway between the tip and the joint (Fig. 2-6).

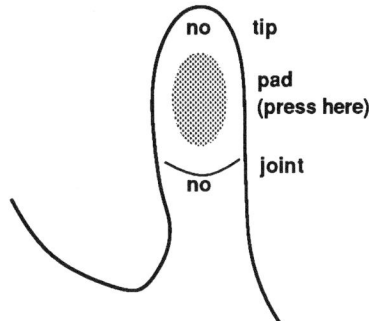

Fig. 2-6 The pad of your thumb

2. ★ Put your fingers together and curl them into a relaxed, open curve (Fig. 2-7a). ♪ Don't close your hand into a fist; ★ an open hand means open sound!

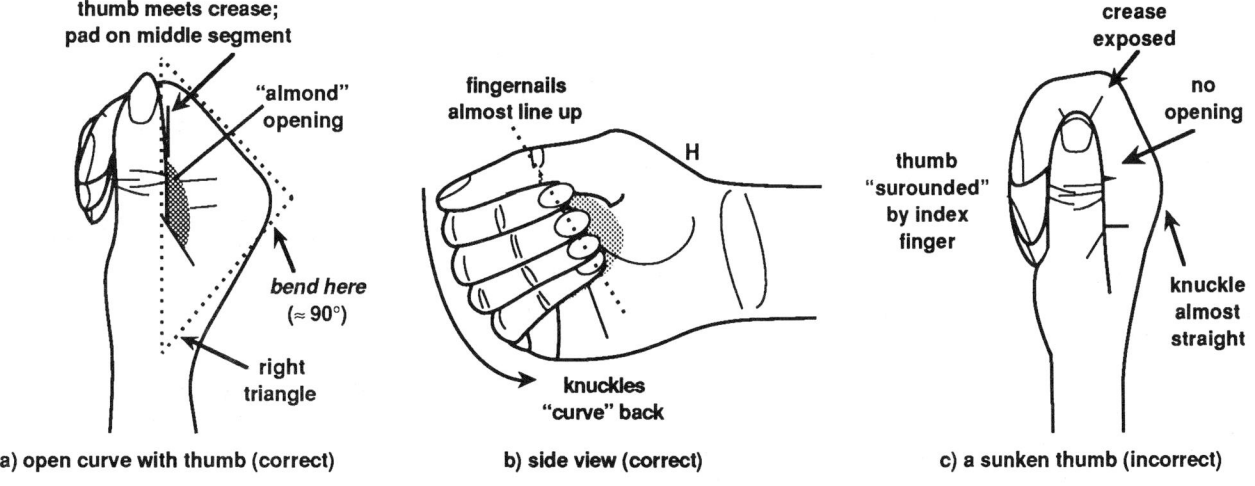

Fig. 2-7 Hand position for holding hammers

Your fingers are relaxed when a friend can uncurl them without resistance (think jellyfish!). ♪ They need to be together to support and relax your thumb. This ensures a clear, full sound.

Striking Out and Winning!

2. ★ Rest the pad of your thumb on top of the *middle* segment of your index finger so its side runs along the crease in the joint (Fig. 2-7a). ★ This will bend your hand at the base of your fingers about 90°. Don't bend your thumb over; let it lay on your index finger. Look for an almond-shaped opening next to your thumb *and* a right triangle running down the inside edge of your thumb, up the side of your hand and along the outside of your index finger as shown.

Your index finger must sit directly on top of your middle finger. If the index-finger knuckle juts out more than the others, the back of your hand will straighten, your thumb will sink into your hand, the other fingers will close into a fist and the almond-shaped opening will disappear (Fig. 2-7c).

Once your hand is ready to hold a hammer, catch a side view of it in a mirror (don't raise your hand to eye level; it'll change your finger positions). Notice that the knuckles of all your fingers "slope" back (Fig. 2-7b).

★ Like your fingers, your thumb is relaxed when a friend can lift it without resistance.

3. Raise and lower your thumb about two inches several times, like you're opening and closing a toilet-seat lid(?!). Don't bend your thumb back as you lift it; keep it straight and relaxed. Look at your hand. Where is the "hinge" in this action? Surprise! It's not at the base of your thumb; it's down near your wrist (at "H" in Fig. 2-7b). ★ Watch the entire fleshy part of your hand below the thumb's base move with your thumb.

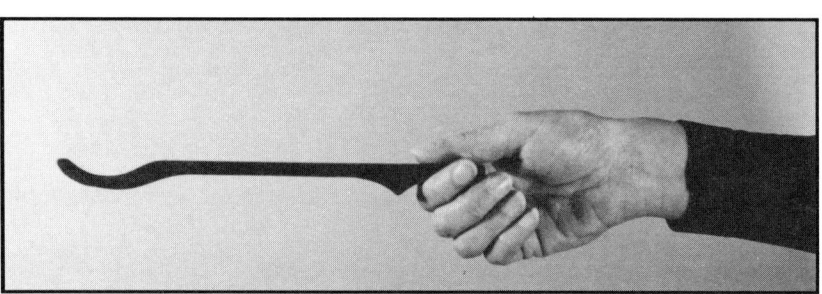

Fig. 2-8 Holding the hammer (side view)

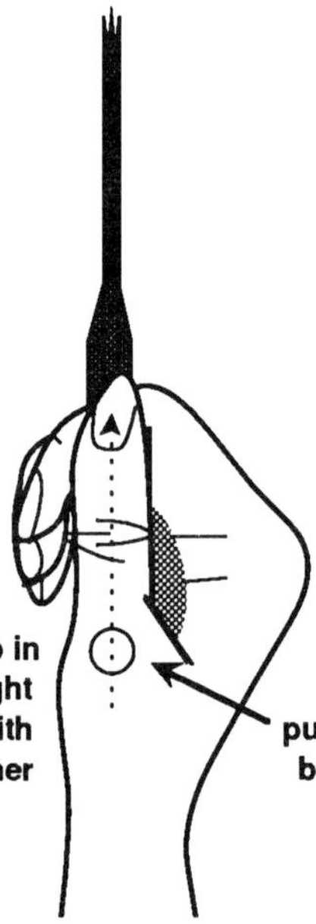

3. Lift your thumb, sit the hammer handle on the ★ middle segment of your index finger, then rest the *entire* first segment of your thumb on the handle (Fig. 2-8) ★ so it's in a direct line with the shaft (Fig. 2-9). Don't change the curve in your fingers!

Fig. 2-9 Holding the hammer (top view)

The pad of your thumb is the "pressure point" but you should have enough pressure if it *lays* there. (If you need more weight, ★ press on the handle from the "hinge." Pressing the thumb alone will bend it over into a hook.)

For handle-less hammers, ★ sit the shaft on your index finger with the end under the thumb's entire first segment (Fig. 2-8).

If your thumb is truly loose, the tip of the hammer should "swing" up and down freely when you press the "button" joint at

16

the base of your thumb a few times. (Slightly loose wrists help loosen your thumbs so your hammers can swing freely.)

4. ★ "Pigeon-toe" your hammers slightly so the tips are about an inch apart, *without* pushing your elbows out (Fig. 2-10a). Look for straight lines from the hammer shafts to your *elbows*. Your hammers are now natural extensions of your forearms.

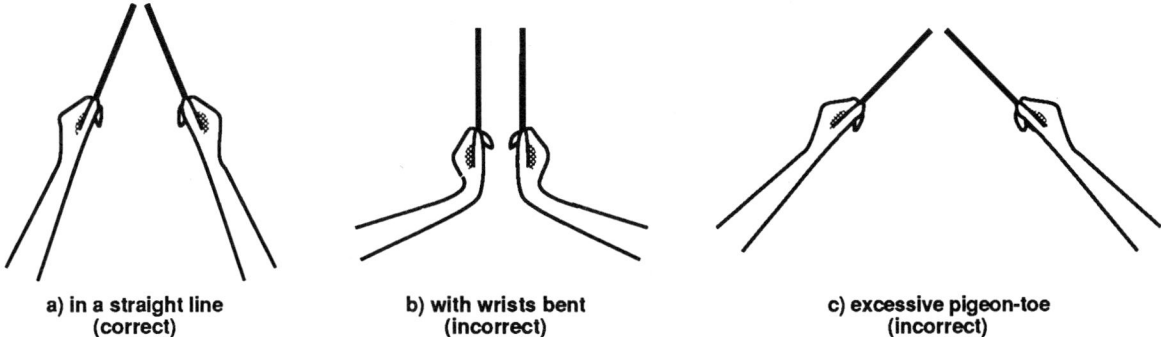

a) in a straight line
(correct)

b) with wrists bent
(incorrect)

c) excessive pigeon-toe
(incorrect)

Fig. 2-10 The hammers-to-arms relationship

Don't hold your hammers parallel (Fig. 2-10b). ♪ Your wrists will bend and tense up, and make your playing frantic.

If your hammers pigeon-toe too much (Fig. 2-10c), ★ drop your elbows so they and your upper arms dangle at your sides. If your elbows are already dangling, ★ bend your wrists away from each other very slightly (this won't be enough to tense them).

4. ★ Drop your shoulders and elbows and rest the mallets of both hammers on first-position G. ★ Don't bend your wrists; let your hammers pigoen-toe symmetrically.

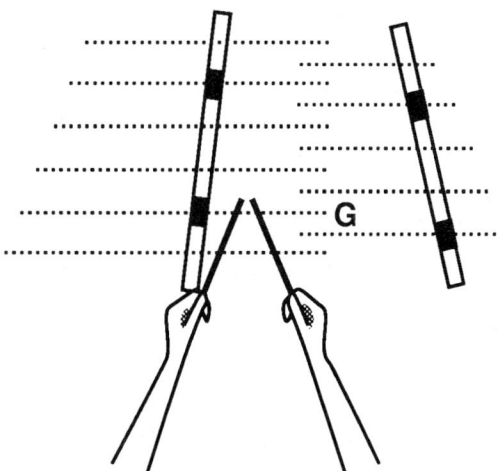

Fig. 2-11 Playing in first position (symmetrical arms and "straight" wrists)

If your hammers are parallel to each other, your wrists are bent. Step away from the dulcimer to straighten them and to maintain upper-arm slant. (If you're sitting to play, you may need to push your chair back yet a little further.)

Striking Out and Winning!

3. Press the hammer handles firmly ★ with the pads of your thumbs (thumbs remaining straight). ★ Without striking the strings, bob your forearms up and down together gently by bending your *elbows* (not wrists; upper arms are quiet). Bounce your hands 2-3 inches. The firm hold makes the hammers rigid. Strike first-position G with both hammers together and hear the hammers "buzz" on the strings. Yuck!

   Obviously, you don't want your dulcimer to sound like a buzz-saw! However, this is a good starting place to find out how much thumb weight you need to produce a clear sound. Bob your forearms over the dulcimer at a moderate pace without striking the strings and ★ *very* slowly lighten your thumbs' weight from the "hinges" until the handles "see-saw" between your thumb and index finger and the mallets "swing" up and down 5-6 inches. At the same time, ★ loosen your wrists so your hands remain level at their highest point (Fig. 2-12a). This helps loosen your thumbs and lets your hammers swing close to level so they're ready to strike anywhere. Watch your hands and hammers in a mirror. (Not sure how your hands can stay level? Shake hands with someone. You may hurt the other party—or yourself—if your wrists are stiff!)

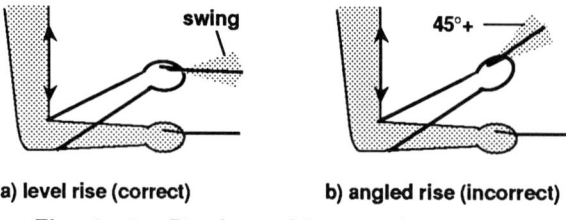

a) level rise (correct)   b) angled rise (incorrect)

Fig. 2-12 Playing with level hammers

You may feel like you're losing control, but ★ you've got to lose it to gain it! If your hammers angle 45° or more at their highest point, your wrists are either stiff or bending upward. Let go of them.

★ As the hammers swing, project their weight toward the mallets. If they pigeon-toe more than they did originally, your thumb tips or joints are on the handles. Unbend them so the *pads* sit on them (Fig. 2-6). Lightening your thumbs may help, too.

4. Strike each course of the five-note scale once, both hammers striking together. Bounce your hands about six inches high, ★ strike steadily and continuously to keep your arms relaxed, wrists loose and hammers level. Now what do you hear? If your hold and strike action are free enough, the hammers will bounce once each time they strike the strings and you'll hear "that sound!" It may sound louder if you've been playing for a while, but it should sound rounder and fuller, too. (★ To play softer, lighten your thumbs very slightly. Don't decrease the bounce height.) If they bounce twice, lighten the thumb weight from the hinges just a tad or strike with a little more *oomph* until the sound is clear.

   If your hammers pigeon-toed more than they should, do your arms look like chicken wings? Are your thumbs flat? Drop your elbows, step away from the dulcimer a little and flatten those thumbs! Check your hammers, too. Do they feel balanced in your hands? If they feel top-heavy or too light, try another pair. (Don't choke up on the shafts of long, handle-less hammers to correct balance; the ends will butt against your palms and prevent swing. Cutting them down may worsen balance.)

★ A clear, full sound comes from an easy hold combined with a forearm action originating from your elbows, *not* your thumbs or wrists! (You wouldn't throw a ball from your thumb or wrist because you know it won't go very far. Neither will your hammers!) ♪ Playing from your wrists or thumbs adds tension and overtones while tiring you quickly.

The handles shown in Fig. 1-4 on page 2 won't let the hammers swing enough (if at all), as the ends will butt up against your thumbs or palms. ♪ Changing your hold to make them swing (as in Fig. 2-14 on page 21) will add unwanted overtones to the sound, making it sound "nasal." Try another pair of hammers with handles like those in Chapter 1.

Great playing! Now try some songs!

Simple songs

Play the songs from the following tune list by ear with both hammers together. They will give you more practice with bouncing hammers and help you understand the dulcimer's tuning set-up in the next chapter:

Twinkle, Twinkle Little Star	*Joy to the World*
Skip to My Lou	*Amazing Grace*
O Susanna	Anything else you can think of

Need help or just some good tips? Refer to the how-to below for *Twinkle*.

Twinkle, Twinkle Little Star

1. Sing the tune (first line, second line, repeat first line and stop):

2. Play *Twinkle* in first position. The first note is G. (Some songs will begin on a non-bridge-mark course, and may involve two positions.) You may have to play the song a few times to find all the

Striking Out and Winning!

notes. Don't let mistakes bother you; they're better teachers than the right notes! ★ Sing along; your voice can help you find your way.

3. Nearly everyone misses the third note of *Twinkle*. Any time you miss a course, ★ play the song from the beginning up to the mistake. Find the right course, ★ put a finger on it, then put another finger on the course you struck immediately before it. Where are both courses in relation to each other and to the bridge marks? Once you know, you'll always remember where to strike.

4. Play the song again. Bounce your hands and ★ loosen your wrists so your hammers are level and ready to strike at all times. ★ Refer to the bridge marks to find your way. Listen for "that sound!"

5. Now play *Twinkle* in second position from the same bridge mark. The song will look the same, but will sound in a different, higher key. To play in second position, hold your hammers over G, then ★ pivot your torso to the left (page 12) and ★ lean a little in that direction to help your hammers clear the treble bridge (Fig. 2-13a). ★ Your left hammer will be almost perpendicular to the strings and your right hammer will angle more.

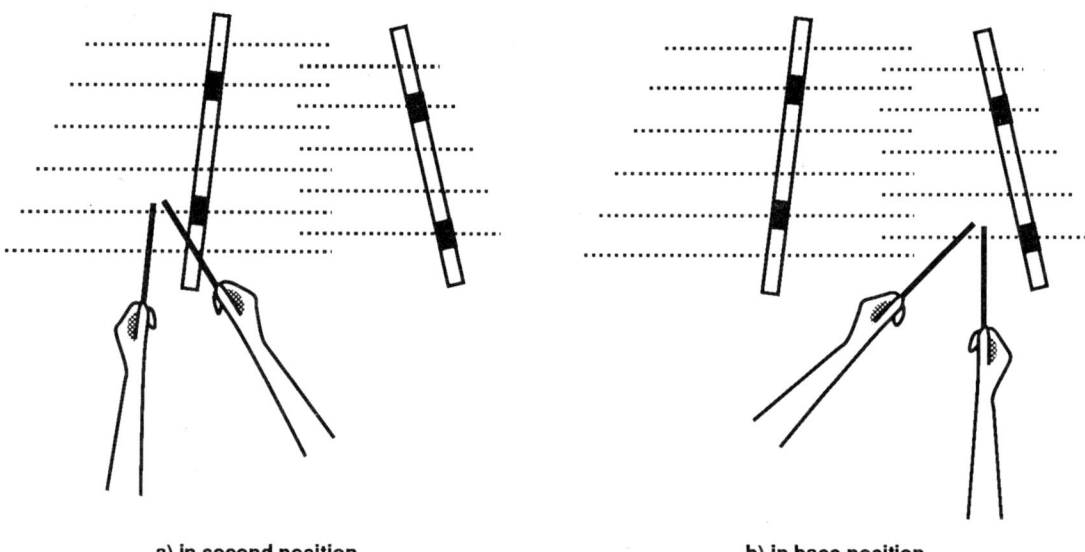

a) in second position   b) in bass position

Fig. 2-13 Pivoting the forearms to play in second and bass positions

You've just *transposed* the song from G to D major. Transposing to other keys on the dulcimer is easy—as long as you have the key you need to transpose to! (See Chapter 3 and page 174.)

Now pivot and ★ lean a little to the right toward the corresponding bass-bridge mark (Fig. 2-13b) and and play *Twinkle* on the bass courses (in C major). ★ Your right hammer will be perpendicular to the strings and your left hammer will angle. ★ Always look for straight lines from elbows to mallets no matter what position you play in; this is a sign that your wrists are relaxed.

6. Play the rest of the songs on the list by ear. To avoid persistent mistakes, ★ sing each one first, then sing along while you play,

★ noting where the notes fall on the dulcimer in relation to the bridge marks.

Testing one, two...

Now that you know the basic playing skills, run these sound tests:

1. Play any song from your wrists and listen to your dulcimer's sound. Then play it from your forearms. ♪ Can you hear the difference?

2. ♪ Hold your hammers between the first segments of your thumbs and index fingers, as shown in Fig. 2-14. (Maybe you used to hold them this way?) Your thumbs will be at an angle to the hammer shafts.

Fig. 2-14 A common (but unstable) hammer hold

Feel the tension in your thumbs. Swing the hammers and feel the pressure in your arms and shoulders *and* how unsteady the hammers feel. Several players have admitted to me that they feel like their hammers will go flying off at any moment with this hold. Playing anything, especially a fast reel, is risky when your hammers are shakily balanced on the ends of your fingers.

♪ Play a song with the fingertip hold and listen to your dulcimer. It's a rigid sound with more overtones, and it feels a little painful (why bother?). Now hold your hammers on the middle segments of your index fingers so your thumbs line up with the shafts and play. ★ The overtones disappear, and the sound floats around the room. That's my kind of sound!

Sounds like you've got it. On to Chapter 3!

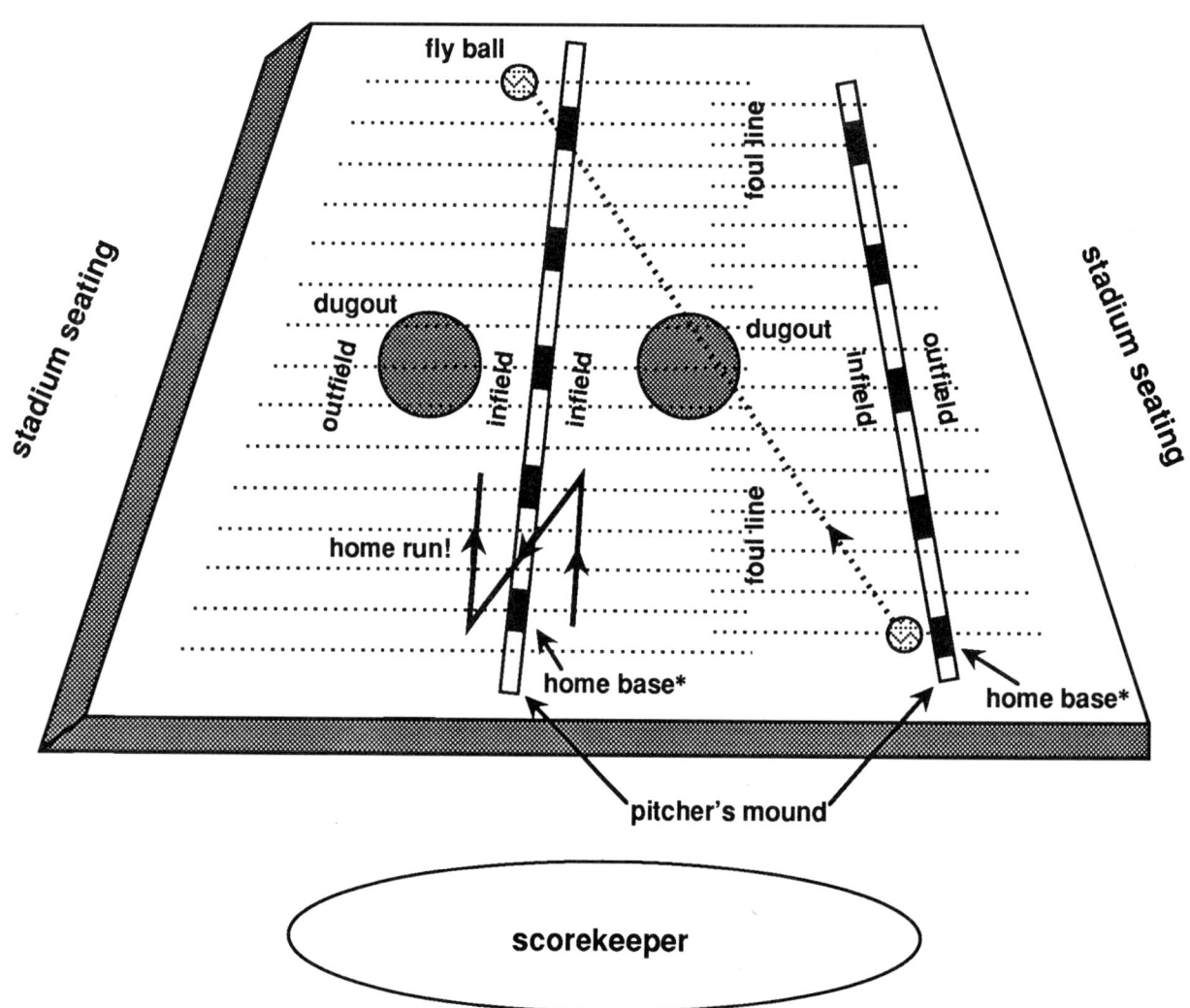

*two out of ten home bases

The Playing Field

The Playing Field

This chapter will increase your awareness of the dulcimer's tuning arrangement, where the various scales are, etc. It's designed to expand upon anything you've already discovered on your own. You'll see how everything fits together in Chapter 4 and in the music you play. (Don't make memorizing what's here a priority, but do keep your eyes open!)

Make sure your dulcimer is in tune before you begin. Have a pencil handy to mark the diagrams most nearly matching your instrument size. (Tunings for "regular" 15-14 and 12-11 dulcimers appear on page ix.)

If you just bought your dulcimer and haven't played it yet, please play the song list on page 19 first. (Those of my students who dove into this chapter without making initial discoveries on their own always found it more difficult than it needs to be. Striking out some simple songs first really does help.)

Major scales

The hammered dulcimer's tuning is a series of major scales in different keys. Loosely defined, a scale is made up of a number of consecutive ascending or descending tones set at predetermined intervals (the major scale has eight tones). By knowing how to play the major scale several ways, you'll discover other things about your dulcimer's tuning which will help you see your way clearly around the strings.

The most easily recognized scale pattern on the dulcimer is the *4/4 scale*. On the treble strings, you begin at any bridge mark and strike four courses in first position (to the right of the treble bridge) followed by four courses in second position (Fig. 3-1).

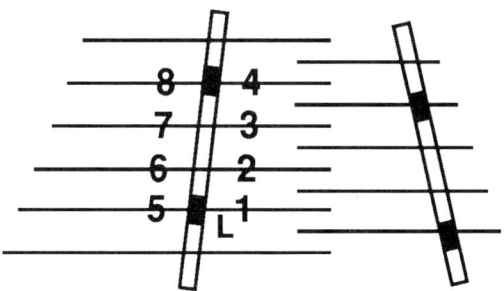

Fig. 3-1 The treble 4/4 scale

Set your playing distance to the lowest treble-bridge mark (step #1) and play the lowest possible 4/4 scale on the treble courses, using Fig. 3-2a or b on the next page as a guide. Begin with your left hand and alternate strokes thereafter. Count aloud one number for each tone of the scale.

What scale did you just play? The answer is the letter opposite step #1.

Now look at step #4 of that scale. It's on a bridge mark. This course is also step #1 of a new 4/4 scale. Lean forward a little to reset your playing distance and play it, beginning with your left hand once again and alternating strokes. The scale will look the same as Fig. 3-1, but will occur higher on the soundboard. Then go up to the next bridge mark and play a third 4/4 scale. You may have to step forward to keep your arms at a comfortable angle (see page 12). This will be the last one on a 12-11 dulcimer, but 15-14 dulcimers have one more above that. Be sure to play them all!

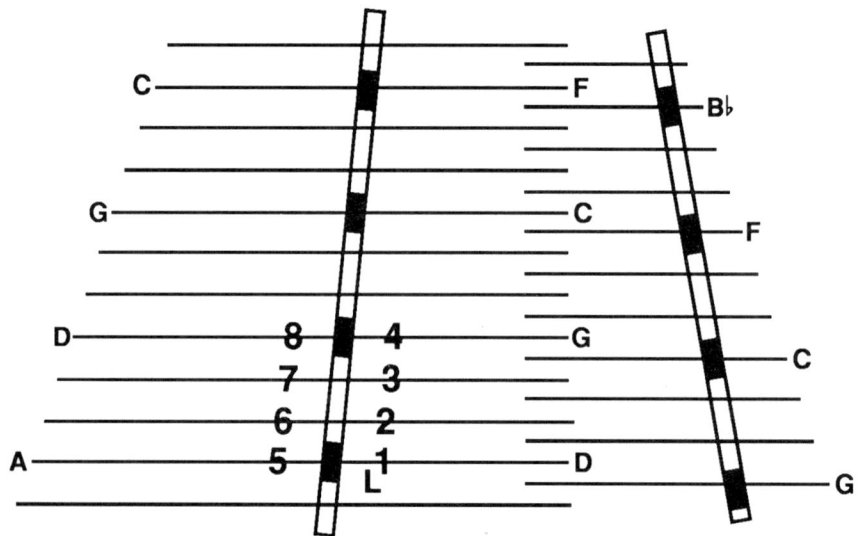

Fig. 3-2a The lowest treble 4/4 scale on the 12-11 dulcimer (D major)

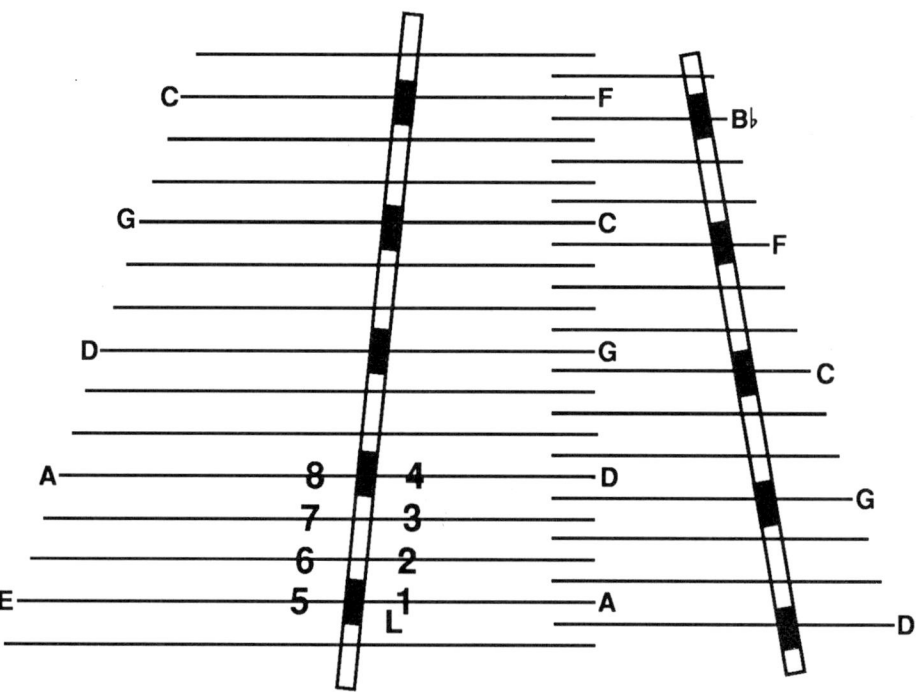

Fig. 3-2b The lowest treble 4/4 scale on the 15-14 dulcimer (A major)

If your dulcimer has bass courses, you may also play major scales by starting at any bridge mark on the bass bridge and striking four bass plus four first-position courses (Fig. 3-3, next page). Pivot your body to the right to help your hammers reach the bass strings (see page 20).

The Playing Field

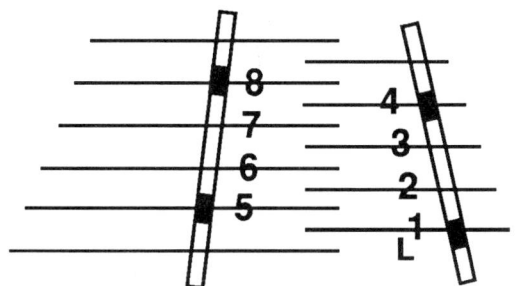

Fig. 3-3 The bass 4-4 scale pattern*

As you can see, you strike the first tone to the left of a bass-bridge mark. The right side of the bass bridge is not playable.

Back away from your dulcimer to set your playing distance to the bottom of the dulcimer again and turn your body so you can play the lowest bass scale on your dulcimer, using Fig. 3-4a or b as a guide. What is the key of this scale? Now play the remaining bass scales, naming each one without looking at the diagram. Begin each one with your left hand and alternate strokes, counting one number aloud for each tone as you play. Lean or step forward with each new scale to maintain upper-arm slant.

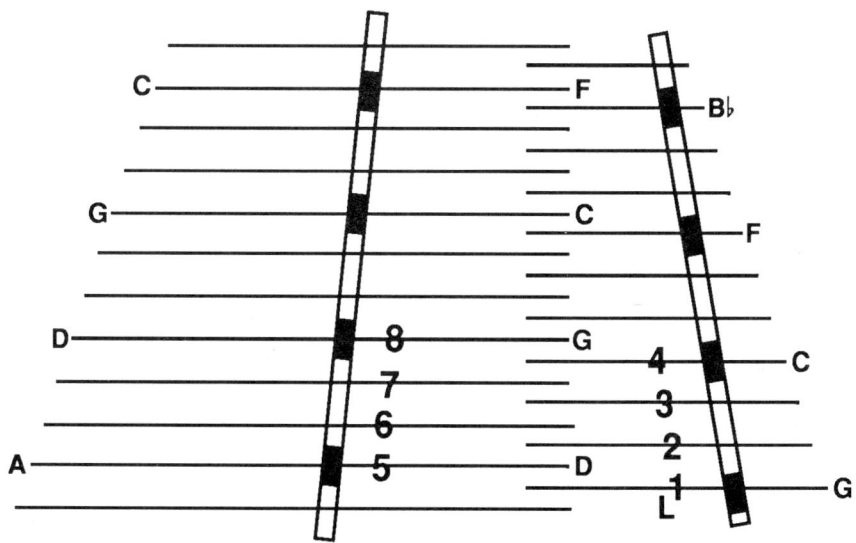

Fig. 3-4a The lowest bass 4-4 scale on the 12-11 dulcimer (G major)

---

* When bass courses are part of a scale, the numbers are hyphenated.

Striking Out and Winning!

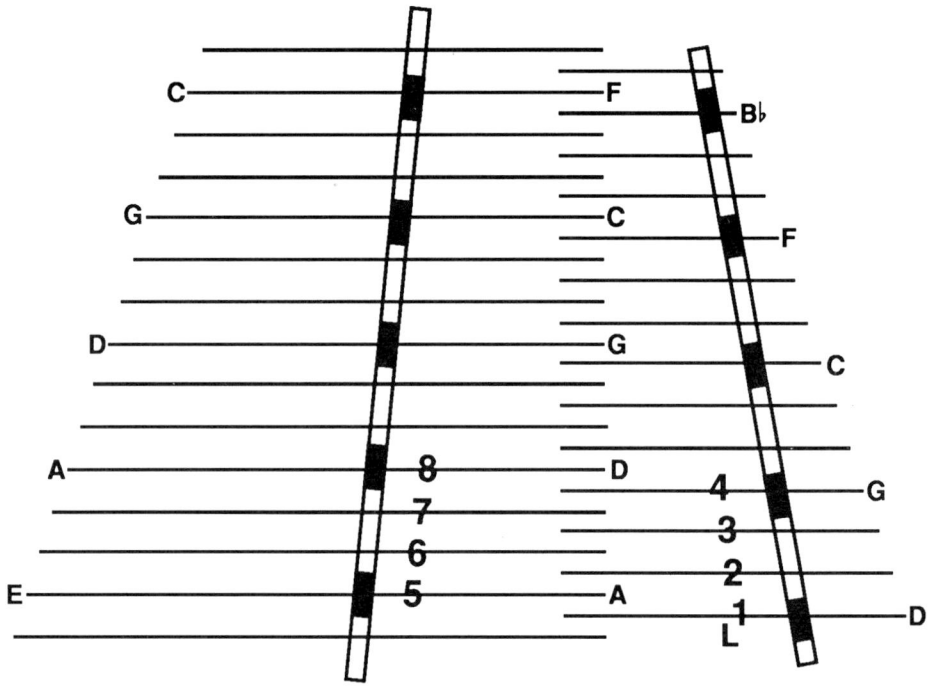

Fig. 3-4b The lowest bass 4-4 scale on the 15-14 dulcimer (D major)

Fig. 3-5 shows all the 4/4 treble and 4-4 bass major scales you played on either the 12-11 or 15-14 dulcimer. (It's good to know the names of each scale area. You'll learn this mostly by playing tunes, but here's a help: For 12-11 dulcimers, remember the word <u>D</u>O<u>G</u>; for 15-14's, spell the word <u>A</u>N<u>D</u>. The underlined letters are the lowest treble and bass scale keys. Find the other keys by going through the musical alphabet: ABCDEFG.)

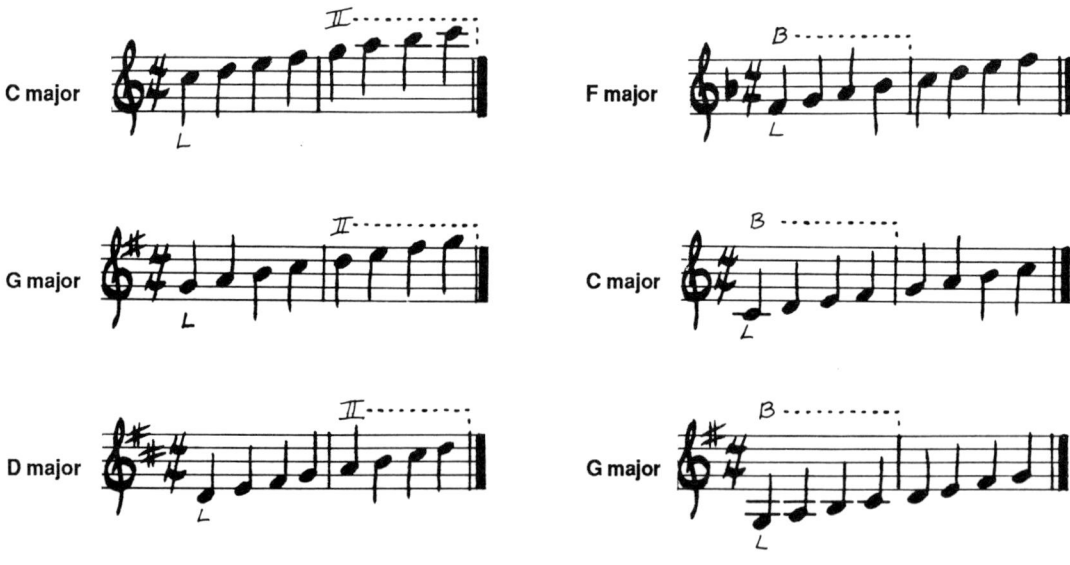

Fig. 3-5a The 4/4 scales on the 12-11 dulcimer

26

The Playing Field

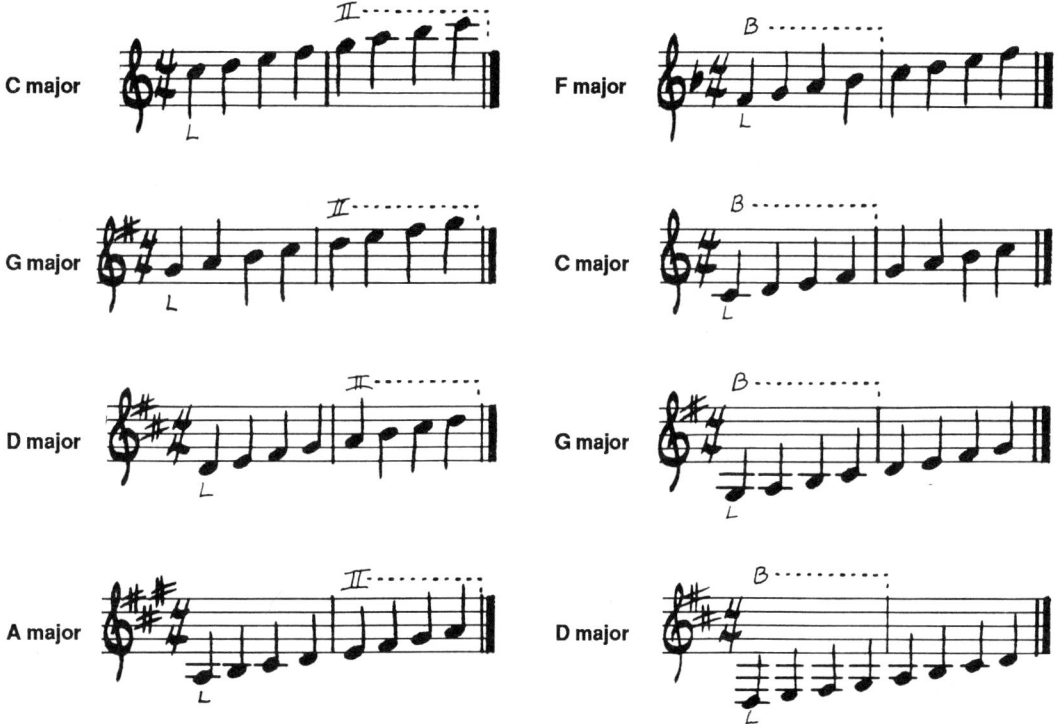

Fig. 3-5b The 4/4 scales on the 15-14 dulcimer

Let's play the 4/4 scale a little differently. Play the lowest treble scale again (12-11: D major; 15-14: A major), but this time begin with your *right* hand and alternate strokes, counting as you go (Fig. 3-6).

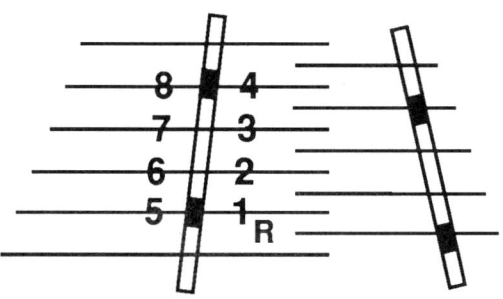

Fig. 3-6 The 4/4 scale begun with the right hand

Did something look or feel awkward between steps 4 & 5? You may have shoved your left hand out of the way to strike step #5, or crossed your right hand over your left. Play the scale both ways again if you need to.

This hammer crossing will encumber your playing, especially at fast tempos. If you must alternate strokes, how will you avoid the cross? *Change the scale pattern on the dulcimer!*

Four plus four equals eight. What other numbers add up to eight? Five and three. Ah! Play a 5/3 scale (Fig. 3-7) beginning with your *right* hand. Now you'll be able to alternate strokes without crossing hammers!

Striking Out and Winning!

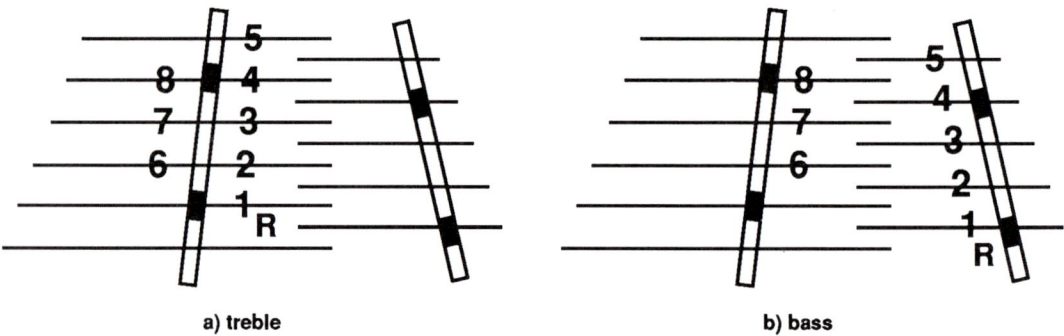

Fig. 3-7 The treble and bass 5/3 scales

Dulcimer players often don't see the 5/3 and other scale patterns in this chapter, yet you've got to be aware of all the options your dulcimer offers if you want to get around all the strings easily.

Play all the remaining treble 5/3 major scales. The keys will be the same as for the 4/4 scales shown in Fig. 3-5a and b. Strike the first note of each scale with your right hand, alternate strokes and count aloud as you play. Lean or step forward with each scale.

If you keep missing the shift to second position, start the 5/3 scale and stop at step #6. Place your index finger on this course and look at it. Where is it in relation to a bridge mark? It's one course above a mark. Remember this spot and you'll find it every time. Use the bridge marks for all they're worth!

When you've played all the 5/3 treble scales, play the 5-3 bass scales, too. Again, pivot your body to the right to strike the bass strings.

What other numbers add up to eight? Six and two. Hey, that works, too! Start with your left hand once again and alternate strokes.

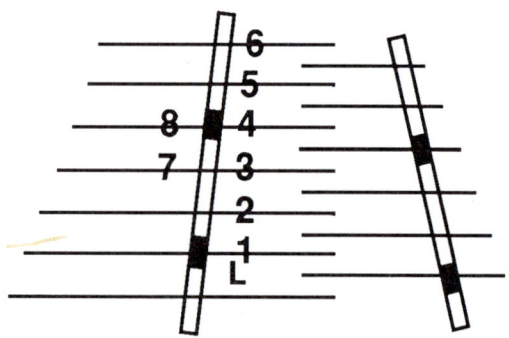

Fig. 3-8 The 6/2 scale

Play this pattern in as many keys as possible. (You won't be able to play the C treble and F bass scales unless you own a 16-15 dulcimer.)

How about a 7/1 scale? Play it, starting at the lowest treble bridge mark with your right hand. Oops! It isn't a major scale (neither is 8/0), but it *is* something. I'll tell you more about it later on in this chapter.

Some scale keys are in both treble and bass. You can play *two*-octave scales of some keys. Before you look, can you play a two-octave C major scale without crossing hammers to shift? Start it with your right hand.

The Playing Field

Fig. 3-9 Two-octave major scales

The first octave is a 5-3 scale and the second can be either a 4/4 or 6/2 scale. When you begin a two-octave scale with your left hand, reverse the patterns: Start with 4-4 or 6-2 and finish with 5/3.

Unisons

Unisons are identical tones. Pluck the individual strings of any course on the dulcimer and you'll hear unisons. This section, however, will deal with locating unisons on different courses throughout the dulcimer's range.

Count and play the lowest 4/4 treble scale beginning with your left hand (12-11: D major; 15-14: A major). Then play the same scale in the 5/3 pattern beginning with your right hand.

Which number in your count appeared in different positions? (If you're not sure, play both scale patterns again.)

Step #5 is in both first and second positions. Strike these courses once together (Fig. 3-10; the first-position course is one above a bridge mark). If they don't sound alike, watch your aim. (Is your dulcimer in tune?)

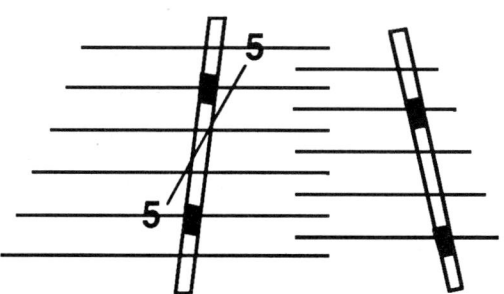

Fig. 3-10 Playing the Step #5 unisons

Striking Out and Winning!

This unison is shown for your instrument size below:

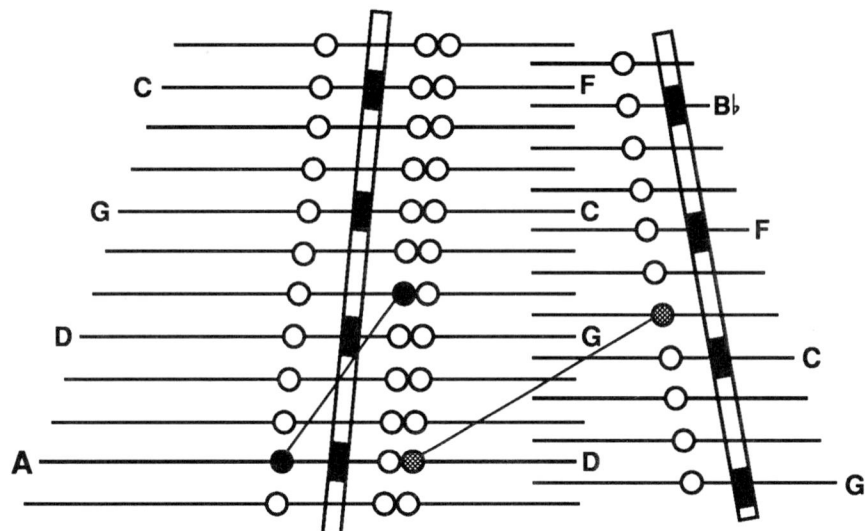

Fig. 3-11a The lowest treble unisons on the 12-11 dulcimer

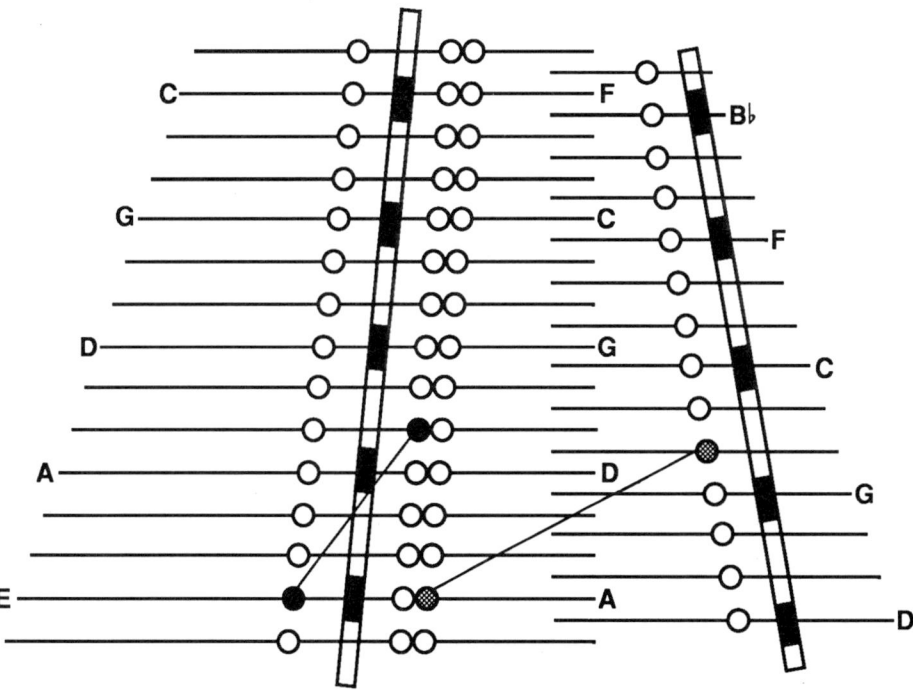

Fig. 3-11b The lowest treble unisons on the 15-14 dulcimer

Play this unison pair together once more. Now move each hammer up *one* course and strike this new pair once together. Do they sound alike? (Maybe, but not all will.) Continue up the dulcimer one course at a time until your right hand runs out of courses and find all the unisons. Fill in the circles of *only* the unisons in Fig. 3-11a or b.

Did you see a pattern in the locations of the unisons?

The Playing Field

Of course, you also have unisons in the 4-4 and 5-3 bass scales. Play the lowest bass scale both ways (if you need to) and then strike just the #5 unisons. They look like this:

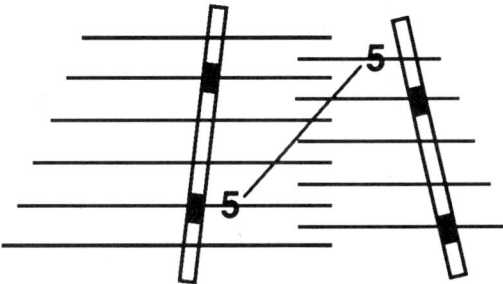

Fig. 3-12   The unison on bass- and first-position courses

Find and mark all the bass/first unisons in Fig. 3-11a or b.

Why are unisons important? I call them the hammered dulcimer's "escape valves." Unisons let you shift positions without changing your stroke order or crossing hammers, as you'll see in Chapter 4.

Octaves

Octaves are tones which are eight scale steps apart. In music they have the same letter name.

The simplest way to find an octave on the dulcimer is to play the lowest treble 4/4 scale on your dulcimer and then to strike only steps 1 and 8 together (Fig. 3-13).

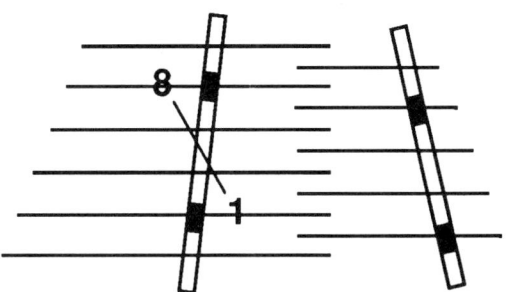

Fig. 3-13   One way to play the octave

Notice that both courses fall on bridge marks. This won't be true for all octaves, but we'll use the marks as points of reference to find them all.

Go up the dulcimer *one* course at a time as you did for the unisons to find all the treble and bass octaves, then mark them in Fig. 3-14a or b on the next page. (Play the lowest bass 4/4 scale to find the first octave if you need to.)

Striking Out and Winning!

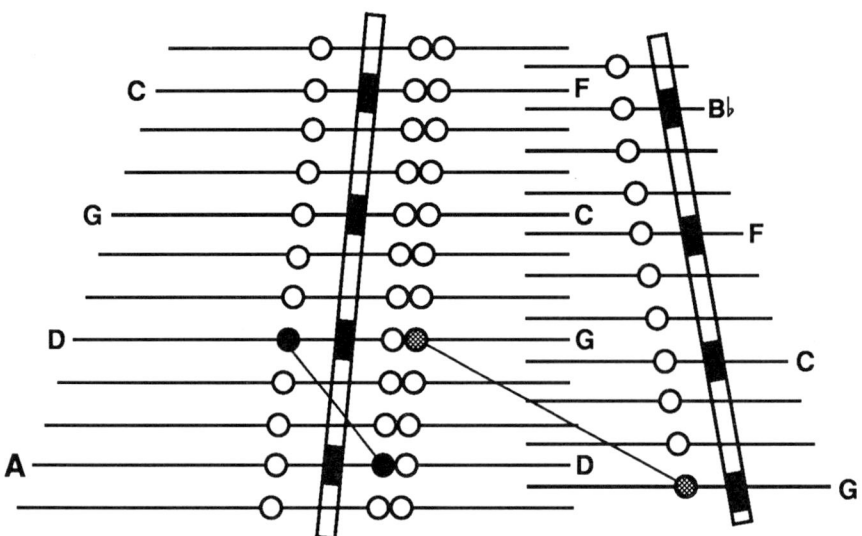

Fig. 3-14a A two-position octave on the 12-11 dulcimer

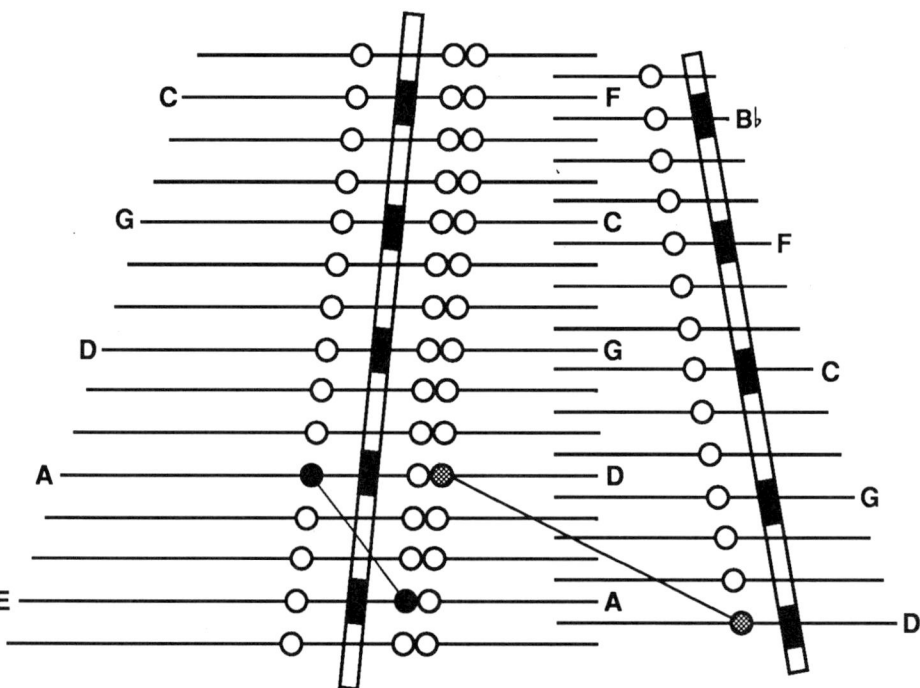

Fig. 3-14b A two-position octave on the 15-14 dulcimer

(Oh: Those first eight octaves you played weren't quite a major scale, but a *Mixolydian mode;* more in *Modes* later in this chapter.)

Now look at your answers and notice two things. First, there's a treble octave below the octave I filled in. Did you catch that? And second: Did you notice that some tones are two octaves apart? (And if your dulcimer is a 15-14 or larger, you'll find at least one *three*-octave interval!) Before you go on, play all the two- and three-octave intervals.

The Playing Field

Just as with scales, the dulcimer gives us more than one way to play octaves. To find the next pattern: Rest your left hammer on the lowest bridge-mark course in second position. Look at the bass course immediately above it. Rest your right hammer on that course and strike the octave (Fig. 3-15a or b).

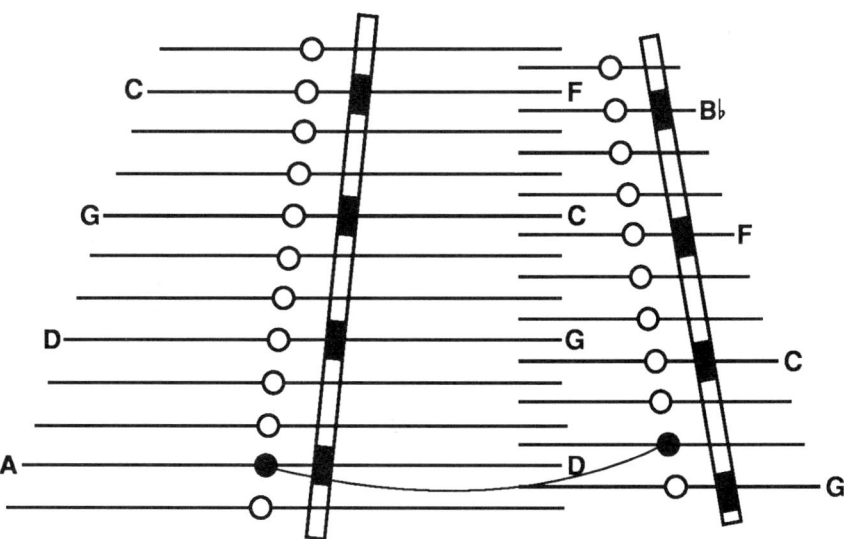

Fig. 3-15a The lowest bass/second-position octave on the 12-11 dulcimer

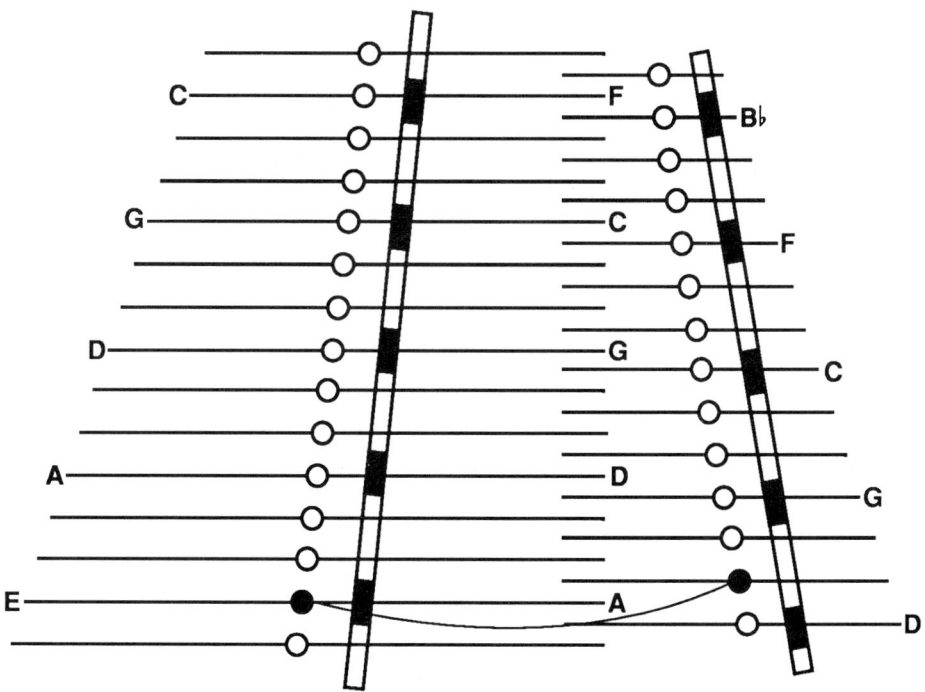

Fig. 3-15b The lowest bass/second-position octave on the 15-14 dulcimer

Move both hammers up one course at a time to find all of these octaves, too (not all will be), and mark them on Fig. 3-15a or b.

33

Striking Out and Winning!

You have one more way to play octaves. Starting at the lowest bridge mark in first position, play and count up eight courses (you'll play a Mixolydian mode again) and then strike both tones of the octave together (Fig. 3-16a or b).

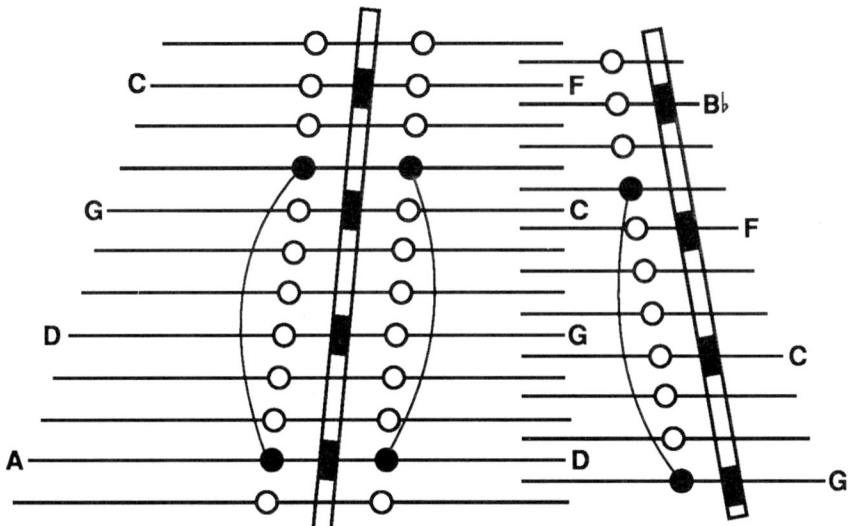

Fig. 3-16a The lowest one-position octaves on the 12-11 dulcimer

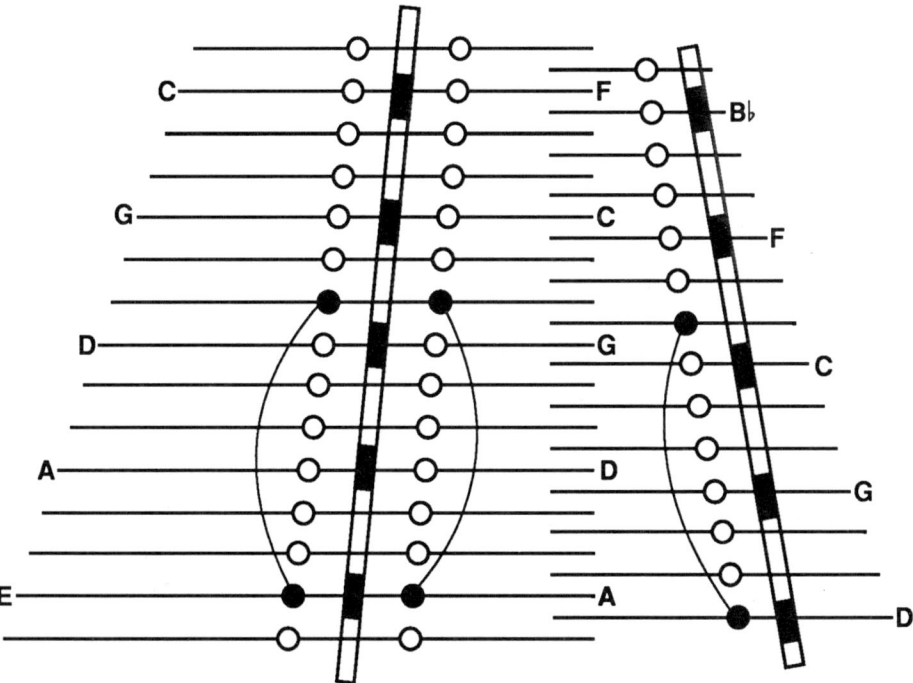

Fig. 3-16b The lowest one-position octaves on the 15-14 dulcimer

Now move both hammers up one course at a time and mark the octaves you find in Fig. 3-16a or b.

See all the options you have? How will you make sense of it all? That's where Chapter 4 comes in. But first...

A Challenge

In the beginning of this chapter you played the same one-octave major scale in the 4/4, 5/3 and 6/2 patterns. You began with either hand and alternated strokes without crossing hammers to shift positions. There are three more scales on the dulcimer encompassing *all three* positions. Find these patterns with the D major scale. Use what you know about unisons and octaves to help you. Each pattern could begin with either hand; as before, alternate strokes without crossing hammers.

Fig. 3-17 Find three more ways to play a D major scale

The answers to these and all the diagrams are in the *Appendix*.

Which scale is best?

Of all six scale patterns, which one is best to follow when you're playing a tune? Any of them! It's common for a dance tune to meander through two or three different scale patterns. Let it happen. If you restrict a tune to any one scale pattern, you'll cross hammers a lot or change the stroke order in a way that will prevent the dulcimer from singing its best. It's just plain clumsy. I'll explain the logic of patterns and position shifts fully in Chapter 4.

Speaking of Chapter 4, you can leave this chapter and go there now. Return here when you're ready to play minor and modal tunes.

Minor scales

Music is composed in minor as well as major keys. Here's how to find and play minor scales on the dulcimer.

Every major scale shares its key signature (the number of sharps—♯—and flats—♭—at the beginning of each line of music) with a minor scale called the *relative minor scale*. Step #1 of the relative minor scale is a minor third below step #1 of the major scale.

For example, find step #1 of the 4/4 G major scale on your dulcimer (G). Beginning with this course, count down three courses to E (Fig. 3-18, next page).

Striking Out and Winning!

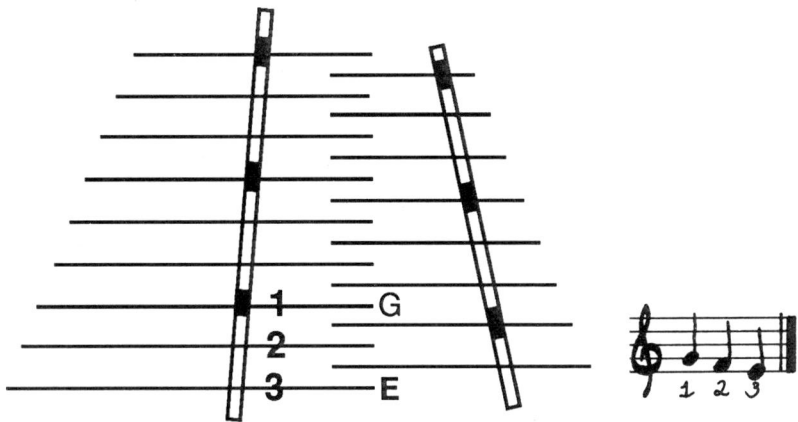

Fig. 3-18 Finding Step #1 of the relative minor scale

E minor is the relative minor key of G major; both scales have one sharp in their key signatures.

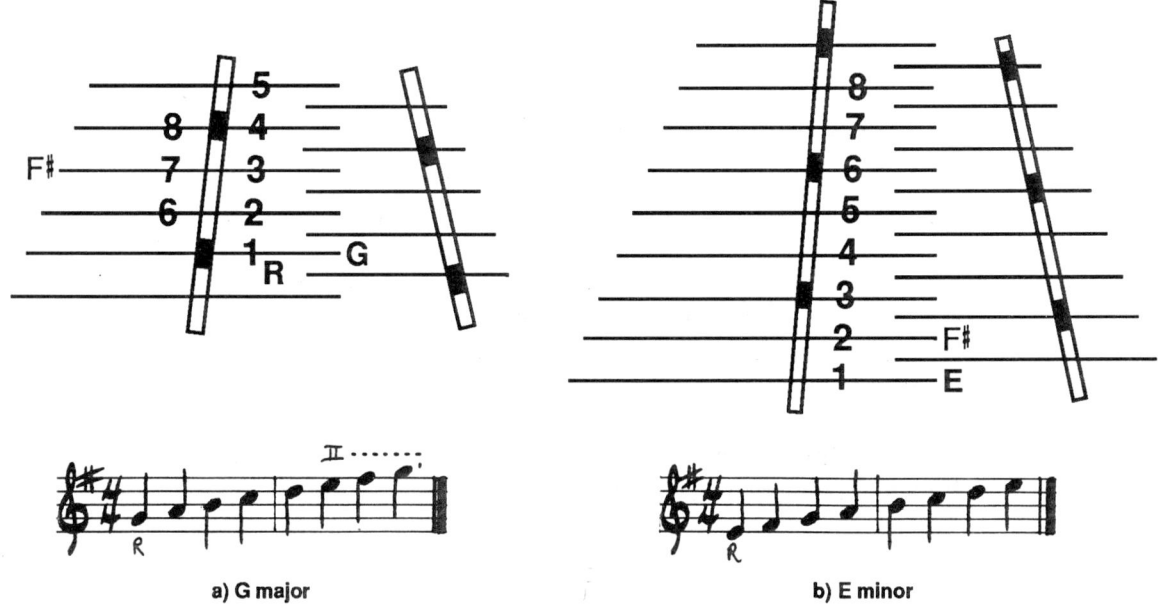

a) G major

b) E minor

Fig. 3-19 Comparing the G major scale to its relative scale in E minor

Setting your playing distance for minor keys is no different than it is for major keys: Set it to the first step of the scale. It won't be on a bridge mark this time, but that doesn't matter.

Minor scales are played in one position, and you can resort to the alternate patterns in Fig. 3-20 when you run out of courses at the high end of your dulcimer.

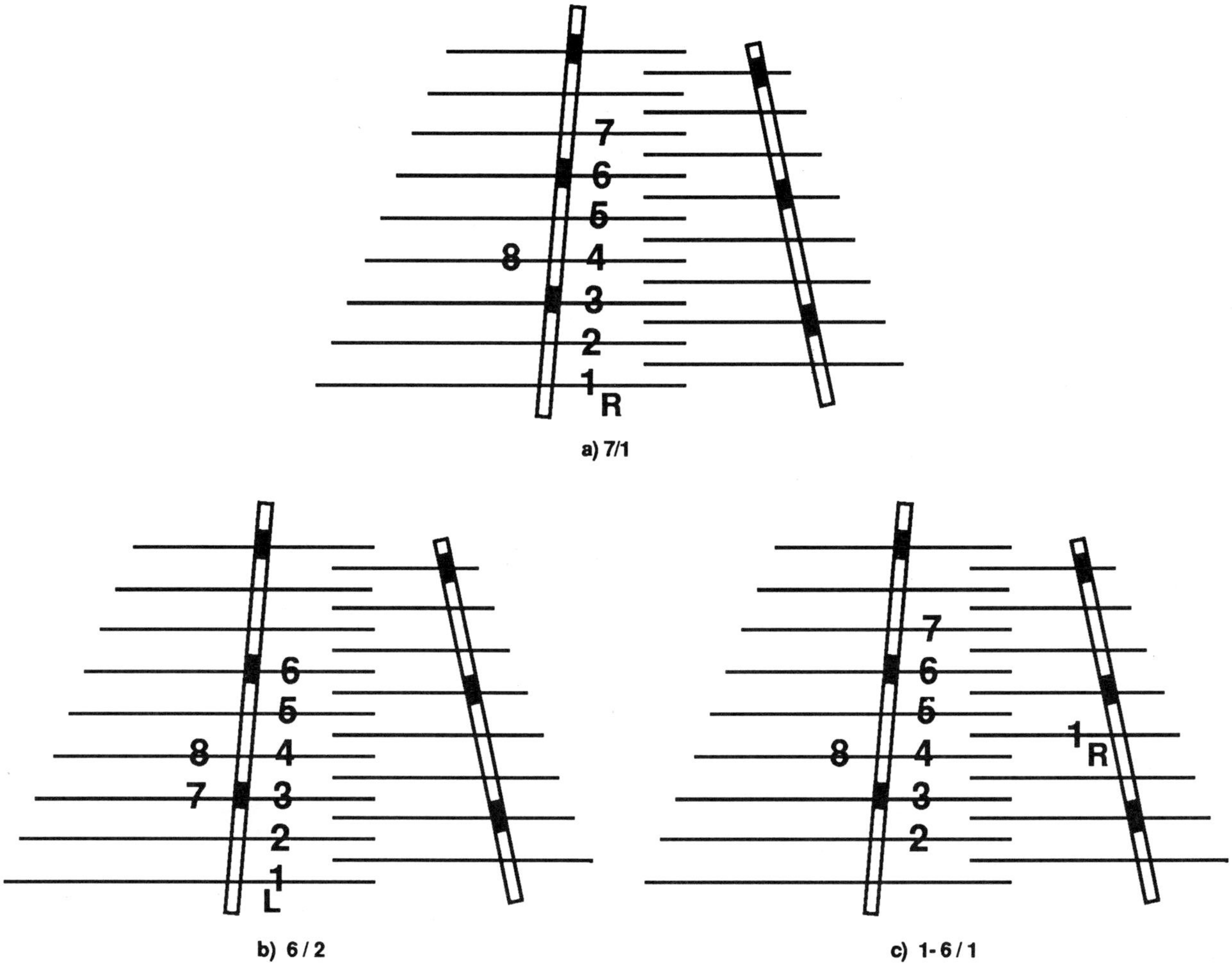

The Playing Field

a) 7/1

b) 6/2

c) 1-6/1

Fig. 3-20 Alternate minor scale patterns

Fig. 3-21 shows all of the dulcimer's relative minor scales:

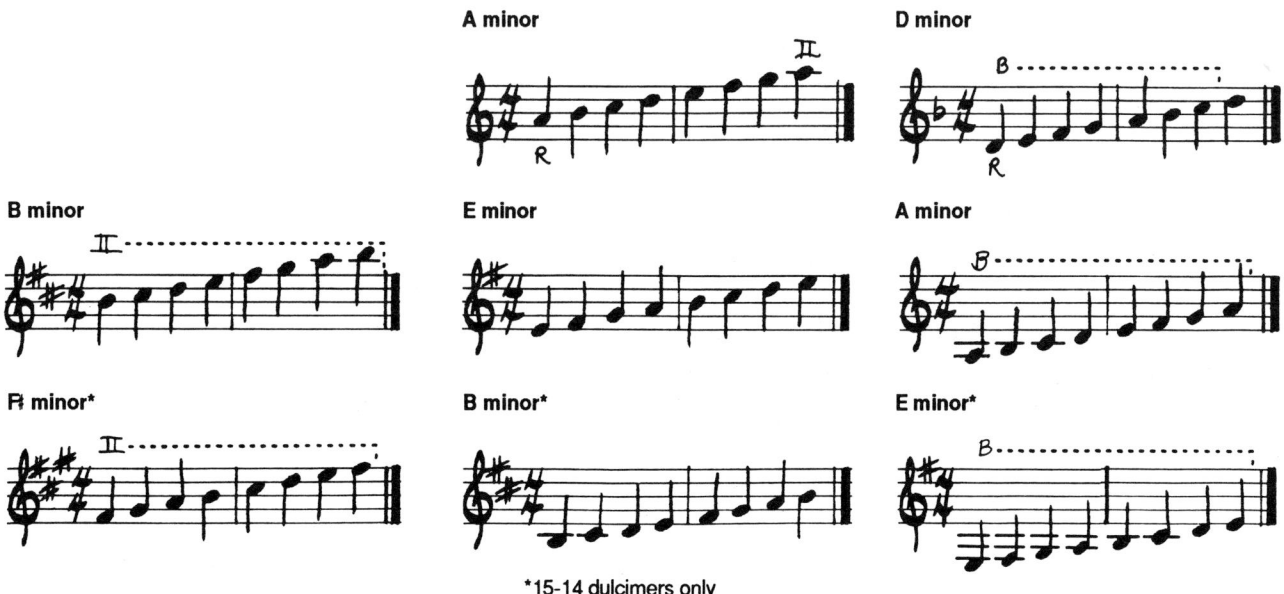

*15-14 dulcimers only

Fig. 3-21 Minor scales on the dulcimer

Striking Out and Winning!

Modes

Modes are scales composed on each tone of the C major scale, which uses only the white keys of the piano. Some of the existing modes were created as early as the ninth century and formed the basis for Gregorian chant. Today, modes are used in modern composition and are familiar to mountain dulcimer players who tune their instruments in different ways to obtain each mode's peculiar tonal flavor.

You were briefly introduced to modes earlier in this chapter. They're encountered in jigs and reels, so they're good to know about. Let's explore the characteristics of each.

The Mixolydian mode

The Mixolydian mode is almost like the major scale except step #7 sounds one half-tone flat. It's played on eight consecutive courses in one position, beginning at a bridge mark. (At last! The 8/0 pattern!) Play the D major 4/4 scale and the D Mixolydian mode. Listen to the differences in their sounds.

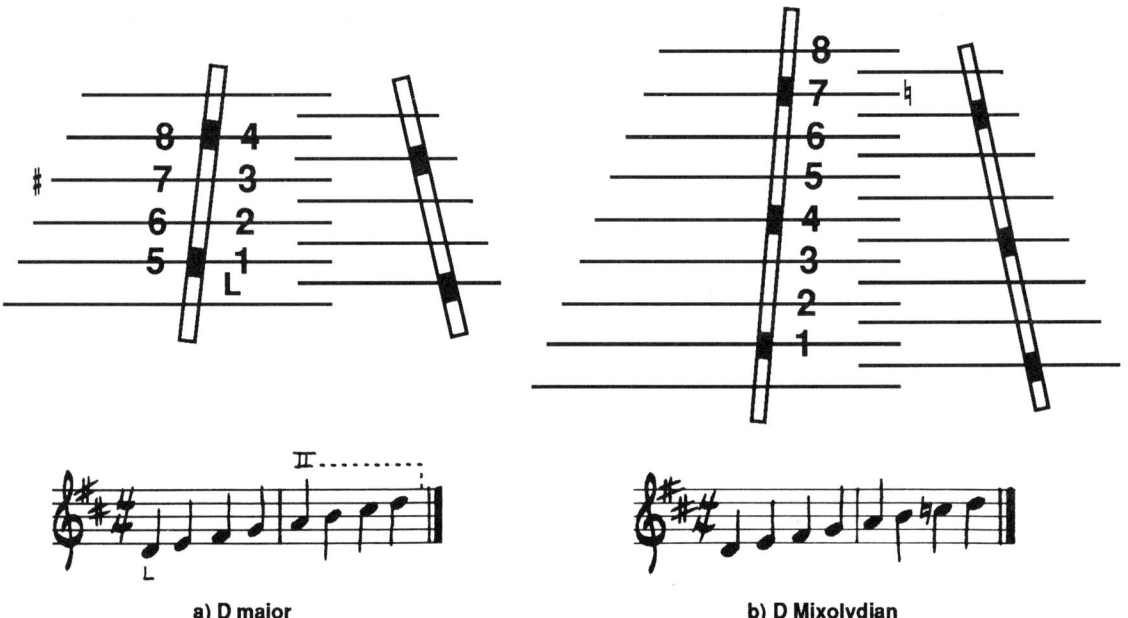

a) D major   b) D Mixolydian

Fig. 3-22 The D major scale and the D Mixolydian mode

Set your playing distance for each Mixolydian mode from step #1.

Fig. 3-23 on the next page lists all the Mixolydian modes on the dulcimer. Each one begins at a bridge mark and is played in one position.

Fig. 3-23 The Mixolydian modes

*15-14 dulcimers only
†may or may not be playable on dulcimers of other course numbers

If you have a 15-14 dulcimer, look diagonally from the top left to the bottom right of Fig. 3-23 and you'll see that you can play a three-octave D Mixolydian mode. The entire scale is written out below. To play all three octaves without crossing hammers, begin with your right hand and play the lowest octave in a 7-1 pattern, the middle octave entirely in first position and the top one in 1/7.

Fig. 3-24 The three-octave D Mixolydian mode (15-14 only)

What patterns would you need to play Fig. 3-24 beginning with your left hand? Try it, then check your answer at the bottom of page 41.

You can also play two octave's worth of A and G Mixolydian with the same visual scale patterns as the first two octaves of D Mixolydian.

Red-haired Boy, page 146, is the only truly Mixolydian tune in this book, although *Over the Waterfall*, page 133, and *MacIlmoyle Reel*, page 144, hint at it a little.

Striking Out and Winning!

The Dorian mode

The Dorian mode is almost like the minor scale, but step #6 is a half-tone higher, giving it a tonal quality all its own. Find step #1 the same way you found it for minor scales (pages 35-36) and play a 4/4 scale from that course.

Compare the E minor scale with the E Dorian mode.

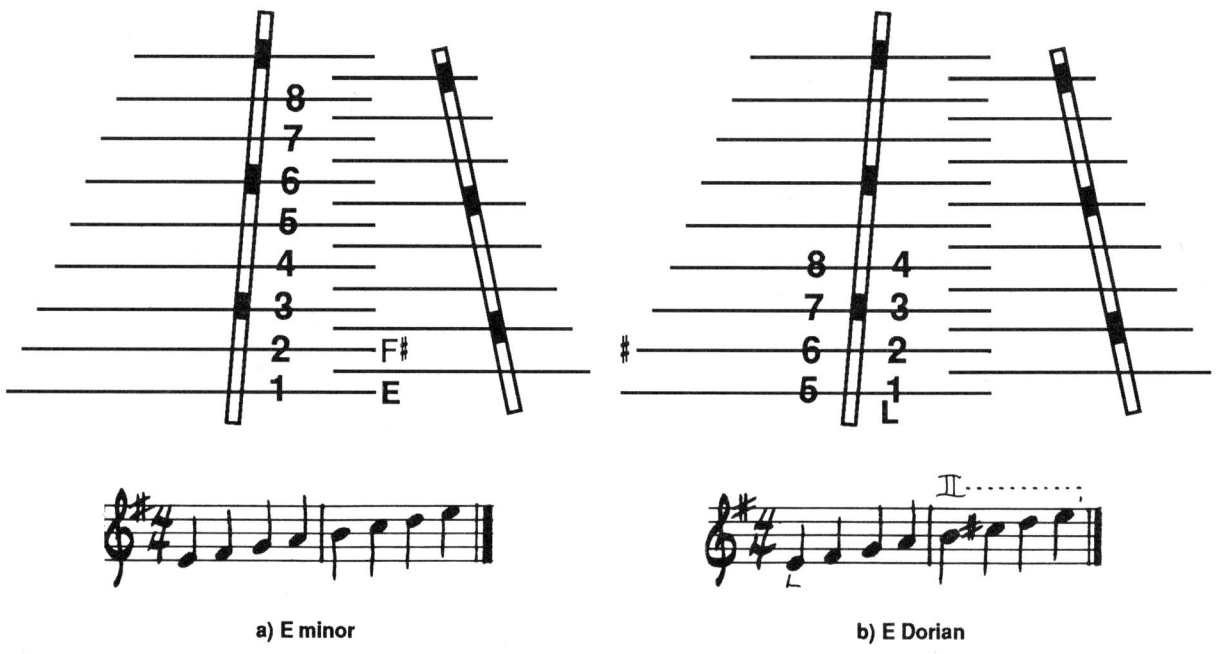

Fig. 3-25 Comparing the E minor scale with the E Dorian mode

Alternate visual patterns for the Dorian mode are:

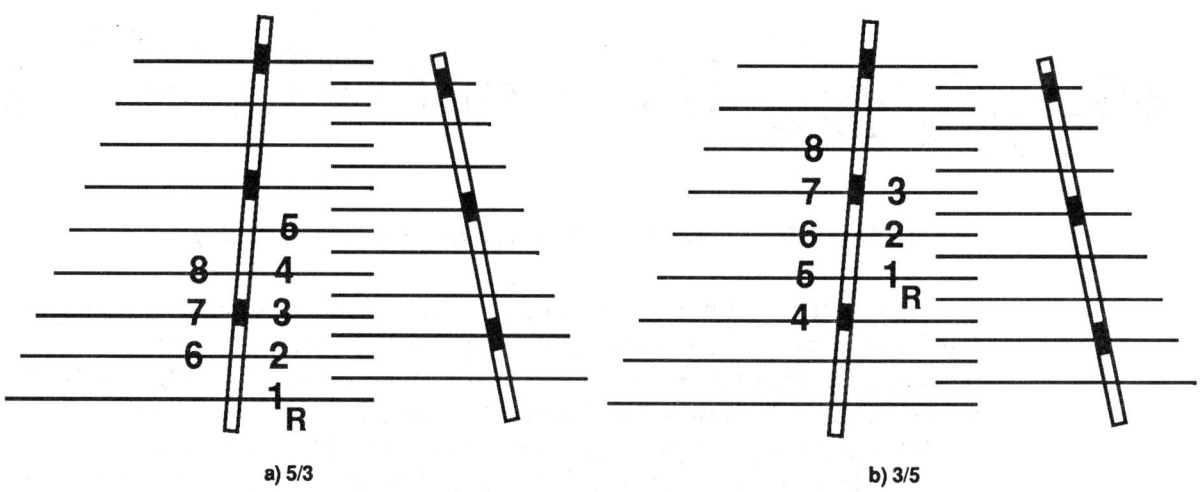

Fig. 3-26 Alternate Dorian mode patterns

Set your playing distance for each Dorian mode from step #1, just as you have with all the other scale types.

Fig. 3-27 shows all the possible Dorian modes on the dulcimer:

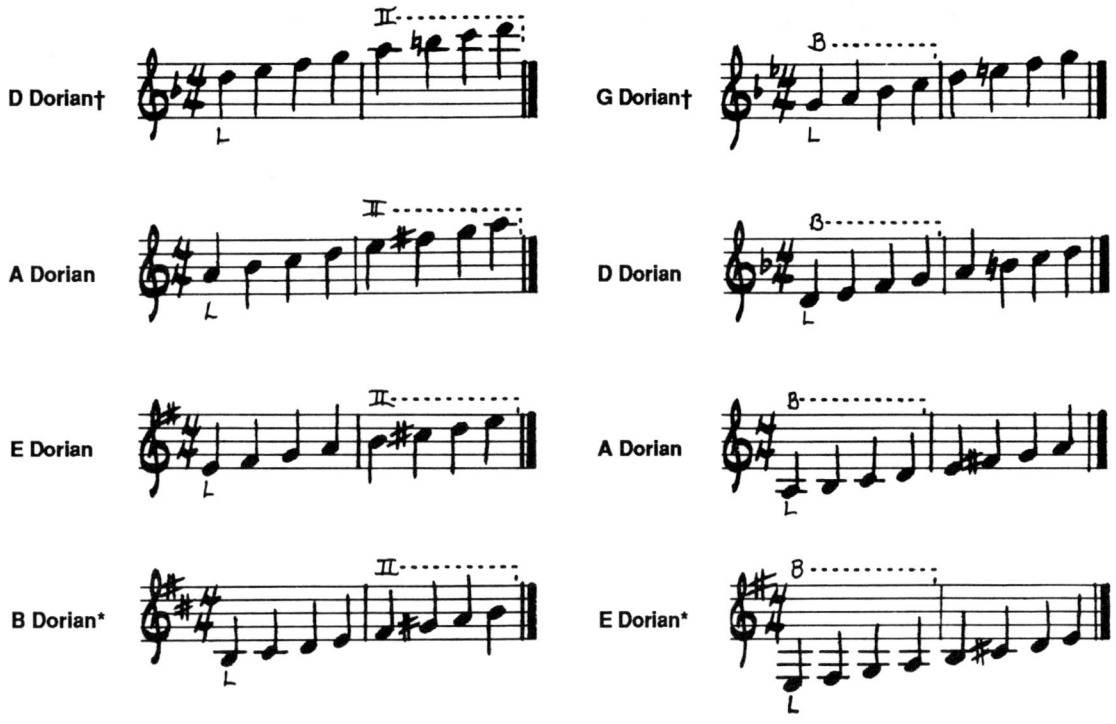

*15-14 dulcimers only
†may or may not be playable on dulcimers of other course numbers

Fig. 3-27 The Dorian modes on the dulcimer

Play a two-octave Dorian mode the same way as the two octave major scale: 4-4 to 5/3 beginning with the right hand, or 5-3 to 4/4 on the left.

Swallowtail Jig, page 138, *Swallowtail Reel,* page 140, *Old Grey Cat,* page 148, *Tenpenny Bit,* page 151, and *Drowsy Maggie,* page 155 are tunes in the Dorian mode.

Before we leave modes and this chapter, you already know two others: *Ionian* (the major scale) and *Aeolian* (the minor scale).

For three octave's worth of the Mixolydian mode, play 8-0, 7/1 and 8/0.

TEAMS	1	2	3	4	5	6	7	8	9	R	H	E
2/4 TIMERS	0	0	0	0	0	0	0	0	3	3	32	6
ZOIDS	0	0	0	1	0	0	1			2	16	4

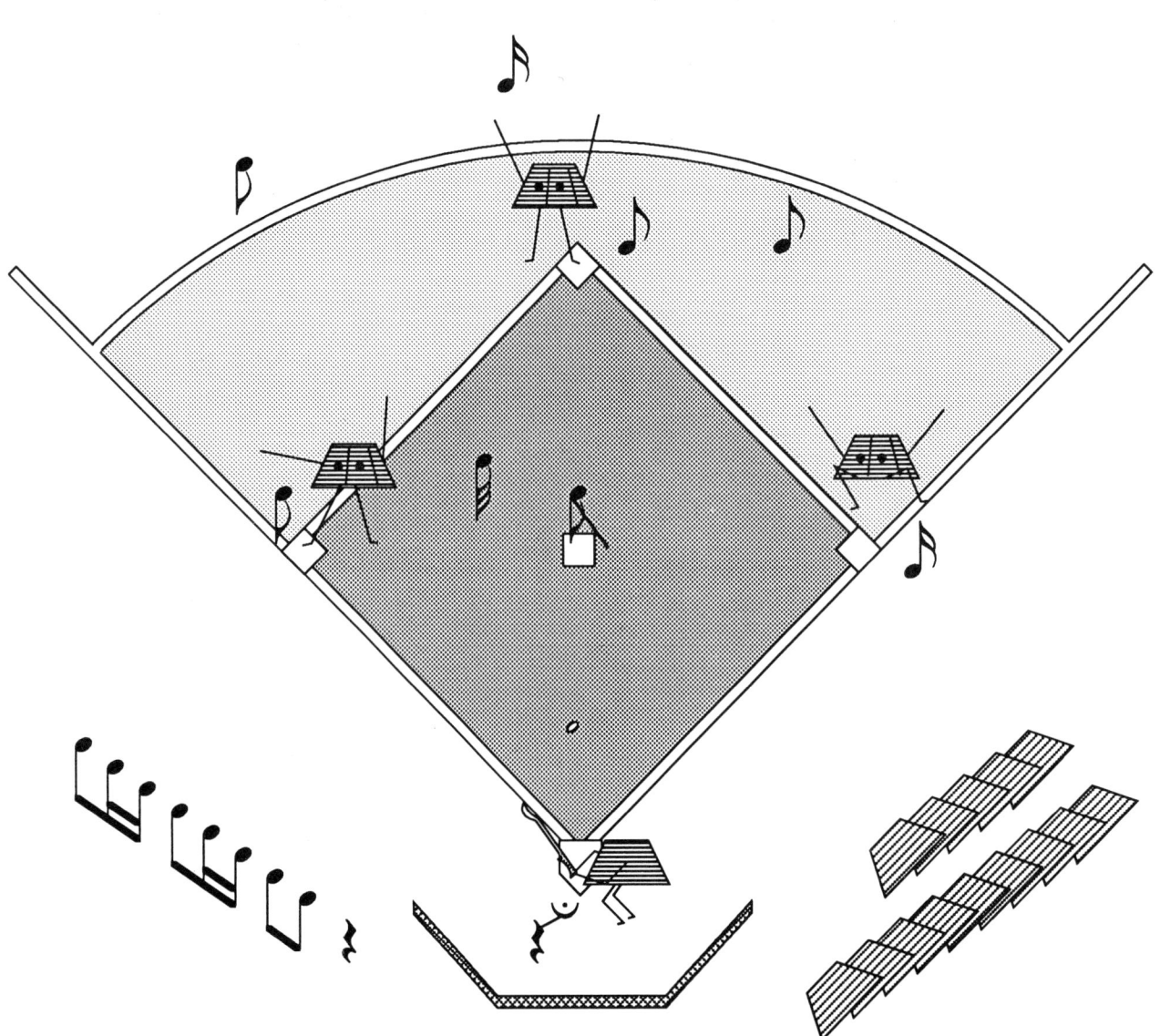

Batter Up!

About this chapter

The combination of right and left strokes you use is by far the most important part of playing the dulcimer. Nothing—absolutely *nothing* else—affects how easily you'll play and what you and your listeners will hear as much as stroke order will.

I let the *rhythm* set the stroking for a tune, *not* the dulcimer (the unisons make it terribly indecisive) or the melody (it can't tell a right stroke from a left). Physically, mentally and musically, taking your stroke cues from the rhythm is the easiest, least taxing way to play. You'll think less about when to hit what where with which hammer, your arms and body will be free to move and your dulcimer will thank you with a resonant sound. And if that isn't enough, I *know* I couldn't spin out variations on tunes off-the-cuff without having the rhythm to hang my hat on. Having let the dulcimer and the melody dictate my moves when I first began playing, I can tell you: this method is a relief!

Most of the exercises here are short melodic patterns taken from the tunes in the back of this book. Thumb through this chapter and you'll see how brief and easy they are. As you play a pattern, you'll immediately learn its stroking and what it looks like on the strings. That's a great start, but don't stop, because there's more! Go on to ★ *feel* the rhythm's natural motion (described in the text and shown by arrows and curved lines over the music) until you're on "automatic pilot." Most of the time, this will take 60 seconds or less. When you barely have to think about strokes, motion and patterns, you'll be able to play dance tunes—and later on, anything else—easily. If you've been playing for a while and find you need to do some "technical house-cleaning," approaching each tune through the exercises will help you change old habits with minimum hassle.* (Note: Be sure you've gone over everything in Chapters 2 and 3.)

Some exercises are in parts, each one serving as a warm-up to the next. Repeat the first part until you're on automatic pilot, then continue. Don't stop for mistakes unless you're really blundering; keep the momentum going! Some exercises can't be finished off neatly, and that's okay. Sight, strokes and motion count more.

Stroke marks are shown for right- and left-handed players (RH on top, LH below; if you're left-handed, notice that the strokes for both exercises *and* tunes are exactly the opposite of those for righties). Positions over the music are for righties only. Lefties will find position shifts in the text or next to the exercise number (sometimes they're the same as for righties). Exception: I sometimes leave out position symbols because showing feel with arrows is more important; when this happens, "no positions shown" is written next to the exercise number. ★ Be sure to read any exercise-number notes; they will save you time.

---

* You may get a strong itch every now and then to play a tune *before* going over the exercises to grasp the techniques within them. You *can* do that, but I've found that students who put the cart before the horse always end up travelling backwards! A *Patterns, etc.* paragraph shown with each tune in Chapter 6 will invariably send you back to related exercises for how-tos and general loosening up, so why not reach your destination sooner and put the horse first? (Have a carrot handy!)

Striking Out and Winning!

REELS

What can I say about reels? They run! Here's how.

The basic principle of stroke order for reels

To play reels rhythmically on the dulcimer, *always play the accented (strong) part of the beat with your strong hand and the unaccented (weak) part with your weak hand, regardless of the rhythm in the music.* In other words, ★ maintain a *strong-hand lead.*

The first note of each pair in Fig. 4-1 (at ">") is the accented part of the beat. In groups of four notes, the first and third are accented. The first note in a group of four is also called the *downbeat*.

Fig. 4-1 Notes of equal value

Your strong hand is the one you write with, even if you say you're ambidextrous. (We all are!) Don't play left-handed if you're a righty or vice versa for the sake of "building up your weak hand;" your playing won't be as solid. ★ The weak hand is exactly that, *and therein lies its strength!* I'll tell you more about its special function in Lessons 3 and 8.

Lesson 1: Alternating strokes, etc.

This lesson is all about alternating strokes, how to learn your first dance tune, seeing patterns in the melody as visual patterns on the dulcimer's courses and playing your first reels. Along the way, I'll train your ear to listen for "that sound" and explain what helps or hinders it.

Set your dulcimer up for standing if you can.

Alternating strokes

Alternating strokes are a series of right/left strokes if you're right-handed (RLRL), or left/right strokes if you're left-handed (LRLR). ★ Your strong hand always strikes the downbeat.

Check your hammer hold and playing distance (Chapter 2) from first-position G and play Ex. 1. Strike both hammers together as shown. Listen for single bounces on the strings; if you hear more, lighten your thumb weight from the "hinge" mentioned on page 16. When you hear a clean sound, alternate strokes twice as fast by "scissoring" your forearms: ★ One hand goes up while the other goes down, like the pistons in a car engine; they don't stop in between. ★ Bounce your hands about six inches high.

Batter Up!

Strike G ★ evenly (don't "dot" the rhythm; see page 110 at "➤") for at least eight counts (16 strikes in all), then do the same up and down a five-note scale, as shown by the curvy line at the end.

Avoid bending your wrists or twisting your forearms to strike the strings. Relax your wrists so your hammers can stay level and over the strings at all times (see Fig. 2-12 on page 18) and scissor from your elbows only. ♪ Bouncing your hands relaxes you, improves your aim and helps the dulcimer sing. ★ Finally, let go of your shoulders and elbows. If they drop substantially, any extra overtones in the dulcimer's sound will disappear, enabling "that sound," full and pure, to emerge!

Oh, one more thing: Smile!

Repeat Ex. 1 from the same bridge mark in second position, then in bass. ★ Turn your body and angle your hammers (see page 20). No matter what position you play in, ★ always alternate strokes with the downbeat in your strong hand. That goes for tunes as well as exercises.

New players often tell me the weak hand doesn't play as easily as the strong hand. You, too? Watch your playing in a mirror. If your weak shoulder is shrugged, no wonder your arm won't behave: It's frozen! ★ Drop your shoulder, please. (Thanks!)

Now run these experiments and listen to your dulcimer's response:

1. ♪ Scissor from your *wrists* and listen to your dulcimer. What do you hear? Did you feel your arms stiffen up, too? Wrist-playing cramps your style *and* sound. It's not worth the trouble.

2. Check your upper-arm slant and scissor on G. While you're playing, ♪ lean or step closer to the dulcimer so your arms slant *backwards*. Feel your shoulders jiggle, like you're driving on a bumpy dirt road. Back away until your upper arms slant forward again. The jiggling disappears (ah! a newly paved road!), and scissoring feels streamlined. ★ Just as you can drive more comfortably on smooth roads, playing the dulcimer is easier when you slant your upper arms forward just a little.

3. Scissor and ♪ lock and unlock your knees at the same time. Did you hear the sound become tinny when your knees locked? Knees are the dulcimer player's "MacPherson struts!"

Striking Out and Winning!

"Spotless" playing

Now alternate strokes on a five-note scale:

2 (LH: all in I)

Did you look at the "spots" (notes) while you played? If so, do you really want to lug this book around to every jam session you go to? How *awful!* You'll be much better off looking at your dulcimer and playing from memory. (You'll play easier and have one less thing to carry!)

1. You already know Ex. 2 is a five-note scale. Great start!

2. What position(s) will you play the scale in? Ex. 2 is all in first position (no positions symbols over the music).

3. Park your fingers on all five courses. Note where step #5 is (see page 12). Just as in Chapter 2, you'll look mostly at steps 1 and 5 while you're playing.

4. To play any music from memory, you've got to know how the melody sounds. ★ Sing Ex. 2 twice.

5. With what *syllable* did you sing the exercise? (Believe it or not, the syllables you sing affect how musically you'll play!) Was it "dah-dah-dah-dah-dah" or "la-la-la-la-la"? Sing it with either syllable once more and listen. Then sing it with these syllables: "DUH-kuh-duh-kuh..." on the first three measures and a bouncy "DUM" for each note of the last measure. (This is a wind-instrument technique called *double tonguing*.) Hear how short the notes sound? ★ If you *hear* short notes, you'll *play* short notes, a must for dance music. Save "la" and "dah" for a waltz.

6. Set your distance from the first scale step (G), and *now* play Ex. 2 from memory. Scissor, then bounce your strong hand on each note in the last measure as shown.

Now that you know what you're doing (you do, don't you?), loosen up. ★ Play Ex. 2 at least four times nonstop. As soon as possible, let go of your shoulders and elbows. ★ A loose feeling lets gravity help you play easily and produce a full, rich sound.

If you missed a lot, play it again and catch a side view of yourself in a mirror. (Oops: You'll miss *more* by looking away from the strings, but seeing your actions can help you improve.) If your elbows shuttle forward and back between strikes, your hammers will continually lose their place and you won't be able to aim squarely. ★ Let your upper arms *guide* your forearms. To help them, ★ "sway" (lean) forward and back on your feet slowly (with your heels on the floor) so you can strike from directly above, not from behind. Both will improve your aim—and your sound!

Ex. 3 is a longer scale. How many tones does it have?

Nine. You can look at the music to play, but remember all those scales you found in Chapter 3? What numbers would you use to describe the scale pattern here: 4/4, 5/3, something else? ★ Count up the tones in each position, using the position symbols over the music as a guide. Once you know the pattern, you won't have to look at the music to play it.

Righties play a 5/4 pattern (remember, it's nine tones); the left-handed pattern is 4/5. How many times will you play the scale (with repeats)? Four. Sing the scale up and down at least twice ("DUH-kuh-duh-kuh" plus a final "DUM"). Set your playing distance from step #1 of the D-major scale (south of G major; take a small step away to maintain your upper-arm slant) and scissor away. ★ Play the scale *at least* four times to let go and loosen up.

Fig. 4-2 shows scales from two tunes. The scale in m. B4* of *Soldier's Joy* is all in second position (Fig. 4-2a). To play one-position scales, ★ let your arms and body flow backwards ★ very slowly so your upper arms can continue slanting as your hammers descend. Do that now.

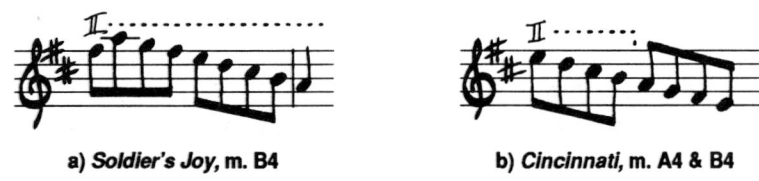

a) *Soldier's Joy*, m. B4   b) *Cincinnati*, m. A4 & B4

Fig. 4-2 Two examples of scales in tunes

Fig. 4-2b shows a scale in m. A4 and B4 of *Cincinnati*, a tune you'll play in Lesson 2. What scale pattern do the position symbols outline? This is a 4/4 scale (LH: 5/3) beginning one course above a bridge mark! Play it once. ★ When you know what scales in tunes look like on the dulcimer, you'll strike them right every time.

---

* m.=measure. For an explanation of measure numbers, see *How to count measures*, page 171.

Striking Out and Winning!

How to learn a tune

As you may have figured out, looking at music and playing the dulcimer is difficult (worse if you don't read music!), but that doesn't mean written music is useless. If you use it to get a tune in your head and hands *before* you strike it out, you'll get to the business of playing sooner.

I used to learn tunes in ten minutes or less with this method. (Now I can sight-read on the spot!) While I can't and won't promise the same time frame for you, if you could play a new tune from memory in two *hours* instead of two weeks, wouldn't you be happy?

Ex. 4 will show you the process in 10-20 minutes. (If you need aural assistance, get the companion cassettes to this book.) It may seem like a detour, but it's really a shortcut, as many of my students attest after trying to learn tunes other ways.

1. Sit in a chair and *look* at Ex. 4. What do you see?

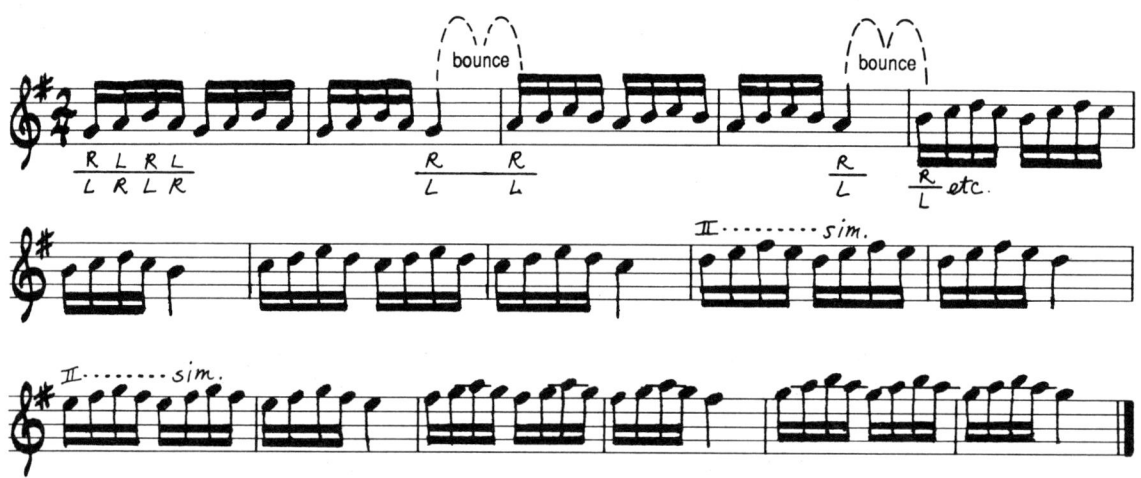

4 (positions shifts are the same for all players)

It's an up-and-down pattern rising one step each time it repeats. This is called a *sequence*. ★ Look for sequences to learn tunes fast. Tunes in this book having sequences include *Soldier's Joy*, page 126, m. B7; *Cincinnati*, page 127, m. B5-6; and *On the Road to Boston*, page 133, m. B1-6.

The pattern in Ex. 4 is two measures and 13 notes long. How many *tones* does it have? You guessed it: three.

2. Look at the music and:
   listen to it on the companion cassettes to this book (at least twice) *or*
   play it on another instrument (at least twice) *or*
   go on to Step 3 if you can already tell what it sounds like!

3. Look at the music and:
   ★★ *sing* the melody (alone *or* with the companion cassette) until you can sing it well *without* the cassette (at least three times).

Batter Up!

Singing ("DUH-kuh" and "DUM") lets you hear *and* memorize the tune. It's also proof that you know the melody inside and out. I sing Ex. 4 an octave lower to keep my voice out of the stratosphere at the end; feel free to do the same unless you're a lyric soprano.

If you play the melody on another instrument, ★ sing it anyway! Knowing a tune in your fingers isn't the same as knowing it between your ears.

4. Look at the music, sing the melody and:
   pat the rhythm (not the beat) on your lap until it's solid (2-4 times).

   You need the same upper-arm slant and loose (not limp) wrists for patting as for playing. Sit in a chair (see pp. 9-11), hold your forearms about four inches above your lap and relax your shoulders and elbows. Don't let your hands droop; they should be horizontal in the air. Finally, hold your fingers together gently, not tightly.

   Begin with your strong hand and scissor (only the first note of a scissoring passage gets a mark), then ★ bounce both hands lightly in the air on the "silent" second half of each quarter note (♩) as shown. ★ Both hands must be in *constant* motion from start to finish; if either one sits on your lap or stops in mid-air—even once—tension will take over and make playing unnecessarily difficult. ★ Bouncing helps your arms stay loose and keep moving.

   Patting is a great way to teach your hands where to play without the hassle of "right notes." It also teaches your arms to be active. (You can't sing through your dulcimer if you expect your hammers to do the work. They can't.) ★ If you've been playing for a while and need to redo strokes, this is an excellent way to make changes, because the dulcimer can't influence your moves.

5. Look at the music, sing the melody and:
   pat the rhythm *in position* on your lap (at least twice)

   Hold *both* hands over your right thigh. This is "first position;" start patting there and shift to your left thigh at "II."

   If you can't remember when to shift: How many sequence patterns do you play in each position?*

6. Look at the music,
   sing the melody and:
   pat the rhythm *up and down* in position on your lap, ★ like you're
   playing the dulcimer (at least twice).

   ★ Pat a little slower this time so you can think ahead. This is the hardest step, but it's the best way to teach your hands where to strike. (No mistakes!) Start by patting on your right thigh close to your hip, progressing toward your knee; return to your hip to shift.

   As you get better at recognizing patterns in melodies, or if part of a tune is especially simple (played all in one position, for example), you may be able to skip steps 4 and 5 and do this step right away.

   Now turn the page for the moment you've been waiting for!

---

* Four. The first note of each pattern outlines a 4/4 major scale.

Striking Out and Winning!

    7. Play the tune on the dulcimer *by ear!*

        Your eyes, ears and hands must know Ex. 4 by now. Close this book(!), ★ visualize the music and sing along in your head while you play ★ *by ear!* If you need aural support, ★ sing aloud.

        ★ Set your playing distance by resting your hammers on step #1 of the G major scale (first-position G). Scissor your forearms and take your time. Finally, ★ bounce your strong hand up and over and back in an arc (shaped like the Gateway Arch in St. Louis, Missouri) to strike squarely:

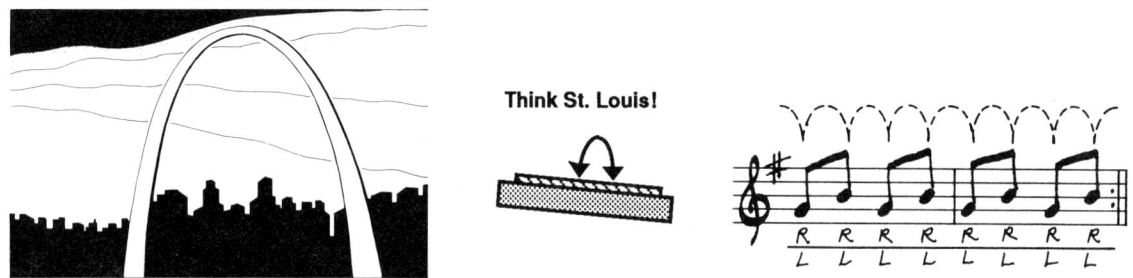

Fig. 4-3   Arching your strong hand in one position

    As you shifted to second position, did you feel your body "shift" back to its "starting place"? You leaned forward as you played up first position. ★ Leaning is a natural part of playing and helps make all the strings more accessible to your hammers. (♪ Play the first half of Ex. 4 without leaning and you'll understand what I mean.) This, along with other moves, improves your aim and enhances the danceable/musical qualities of your playing.

Should you think about note names while you play?

    Players often ask me what I think about while I'm playing. Certainly not about washing dishes! But to answer the question: I don't think about the names of the notes at all, even though I read music well.* I use the written music to find out how the tune goes, then I consider its larger intervals and such. I then take a mental picture of the music to the dulcimer. As I play from memory, the melodic patterns I "see" in my head change into visual patterns on the strings. After I've played the tune once or twice, I no longer think about the written music; I've linked it to those visual patterns. So when someone says, "Let's play *Swinging on a Gate,*" I think of how the tune goes and its first pattern.

    Sing Ex. 4 (don't peek at the music) and imagine yourself playing it. Don't look at the dulcimer. Can you see each pattern and the position shift? Now play Ex. 4 with that picture in mind. When you can do this, you'll learn tunes faster and play with confidence.

---

*   Which reminds me: Don't write the note names on the music; that's simply another crutch which doesn't give you any useful information.

A mini-lesson on shifting positions

You may have questioned staying in first position in m. 5-8 of Ex. 4. What would happen to the stroking if you played m. 5-8 in two positions?

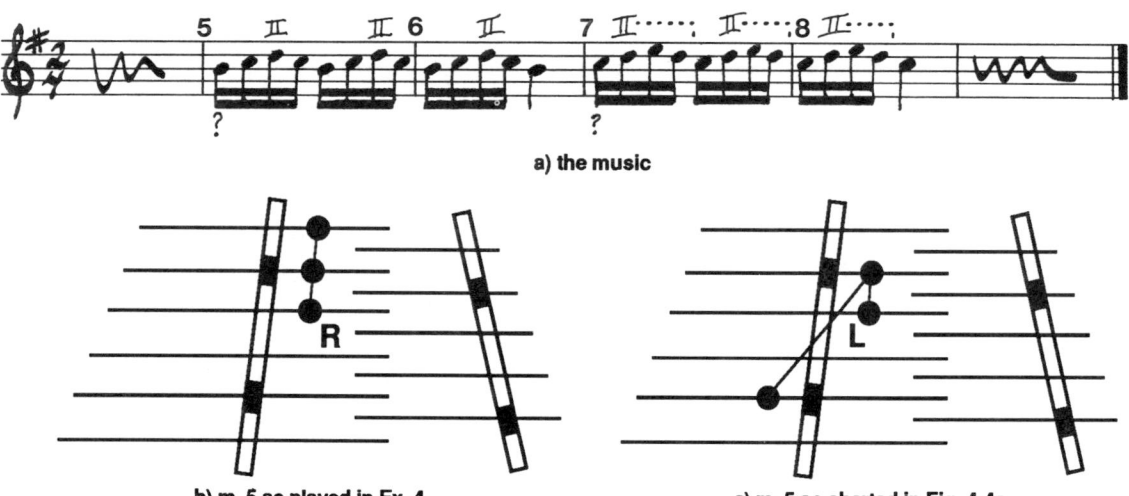

Fig. 4-4 Playing Ex. 4, m. 5-8 in one vs. two positions

Be you right- or left-handed, you'd work overtime. Righties would have to lead with the weak hand to play, weakening the sound. Also, the pattern in Fig. 4-4c would be the *only* one that doesn't look like any of the other two-measure patterns. ★ Consistency when possible gives you less to think about. If you're thinking about shifting, ask yourself if it's practical. If it smooths your playing ★ without changing the strokes, great!

Other one-position passages: 1) Ex. 2 (same reason as above); and 2) the A section of *Galopede*. When a stepwise melody spans five or six tones, it's probably better to play in one position. What about when the notes jump around? That's for the next section to explain!

Your first reel

Your first reel is *Soldier's Joy*, page 126. To play it with a loose, dancey feeling, know what its melodic patterns look *and* feel like by playing each one individually. It's a fast way to teach your eyes, hands and ears what to expect. And it'll help mistake-proof your playing.

When you play a tune's patterns is up to you. If you think you'll fare better by knowing how the tune goes, sing and pat the rhythm as described earlier. Or dive into the patterns and sing and pat the tune later (singing is still necessary so you'll know the tune in your head to play it by ear).

Before you begin, set your playing distance from ★ step #1 of the tune's treble scale (in this case, it's D major, so set it from first-position D). ★★ Do this for any tune, no matter what the key, how high or low it goes, or what its first note is. Lean forward to strike further away, and lean or step back the closer they become to your body. As you play more, you'll set your playing distance automatically.

Striking Out and Winning!

M. A1, 3 and 5—This pattern is a chord. How many tones does it have and what position(s) are they in?

5a (all in I)

Only three (of the first four notes, the second and fourth are the same), all in first position. This chord is called a *triad*, made up of steps 1, 3 and 5 of the five-note scale on page 12.* Its jumping notes may look hard, but such patterns are easier than the other patterns you've struck out so far.

Park your fingers on all three tones and look at them. They fall in a line on every other course (steps 1, 3 and 5 of a five-note scale). ★ Where is each course in relation to a bridge mark? Once you know, you'll always remember where to strike. Scissor and ★ think St. Louis to play Ex. 5a.

The one-position pattern works fine for *Soldier's Joy*, but you can make it easier by substituting one of the courses with its unison. Look at Ex. 5b (RH) or Ex. 5c (LH). Refer to the positions to finger the pattern. Both form a triangle (check it on page 54). Look at its relationship to the bridge marks. Finally, which way will your strong hand travel in this pattern? *Horizontally!* Relax your strong elbow, think St. Louis and bounce and ★ pivot your forearm. ★ Focus your eyes in the middle of both positions so you can see all three courses without turning your head.

5b (RH only)

5c (LH only)

Use this pattern instead of the vertical one to play m. A1, 3 and 5 of *Soldier's Joy*. If you're right-handed, don't use the left-handed pattern in Ex. 5c just because the reach is smaller. The horizontal right-hand route is still easy. Your first concern is making music, and that comes from always

---

* For more about chords, see *The Hammered Dulcimer A-Chording to Lucille Reilly*.

having the downbeat in your strong hand. You can't stay loose and play freely if your lead switches hands all the time.

Make sure your strong hand bounces in an arc, not an "M" (Fig. 4-5c). The "M" makes your hand stop at the peaks, causing tension. To release it, relax your shoulders and elbows and ★ keep your arm moving and the "M" will become an arc.

a) Ex. 5b   b) Ex. 5c   c) the "M;" a sign of tension

Fig. 4-5 Bouncing the strong hand in an arc across positions

Isn't it safer to play close to the strings instead of arching? ♪ Try it. Your forearm action may transfer to your wrists. This freezes your arms so they can't move. When your arms can't move, you goof! And did you notice how lackluster your dulcimer sounded? The arc's height adds depth to "that sound" while improving your ease and accuracy of playing.

M. A7—A lot of players do fine with *Soldier's Joy* until they reach this measure, where they slow down and fumble.

6 (first pattern for RH and LH: 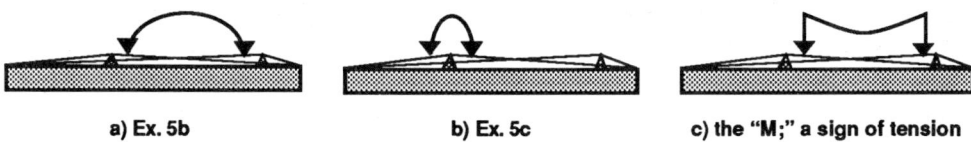)

You can avoid fumbling by knowing *where* to look first. Here's how:

1. *Look* at m. A7 on page 126. It's simply two triad patterns!
2. *Finger* the first triad and hold that pose. (LH: Stay in second position.)
3. The second triad is one step lower on the staff than the first. *Move* your fingers ★ *simultaneously* down one course to this triad (doing so ensures that you can see the whole pattern *before* you play it), then back and forth a few times.
4. *Play* it 8-4-2-1 to sharpen your vision gradually. ★ While you play the first pattern, look for the next so you can change smoothly. This will take ±60 seconds. (Repeat part or all of an exercise until your hands are on "automatic pilot" wherever you see what I call a "secondary" repeat sign [:‖].)

By the way, both patterns appear again in m. B1-3 and 5-6.

If you're right-handed, why not play the first triad of Ex. 6 in a triangle for a smaller reach? Looking at both a triangle and a line is harder than

Striking Out and Winning!

two lines and a larger reach. ★ When you stay in one position, you can refocus on new courses for the *same* visual pattern, not two separate ones. ♪ Plus, the strong-hand reach is vertical, instead of vertical and horizontal. ★ When one of two musically similar patterns must be linear, stay in one position for both to ease your vision and mind.

M. B4—This scale pattern appeared in Fig. 4-2a. Play it at least four times and draw your scissoring forearms back slowly with your elbows (see page 46). It may take a little while to find the elbow pace, but you'll enhance it by ★ scissoring so your hammers have the height they need to strike squarely. A forearm action is absolutely essential.

M. B7—A sequence. This one isn't usually a problem unless your elbows shuttle. Again, draw them back slowly and scissor your forearms.

Ex. 7 is a "bottomless" exercise based on the sequence in the tune. It goes all the way down the dulcimer (shown by the line at the end). Sing Sing what's shown so your ear knows what to expect, then play it by ear. (It'll go out of key toward the end, but you're after feel more than melody; you can hear what it will sound like on Companion Cassette #1.) As your hammers descend, ★ lean back slowly, then step back a little to keep your upper arms slanting forward for a full sound. (If you're sitting, lean back or scoot your rear end back.) Stop when you run out of courses at the bottom of second position.

7

Whenever you hit a rut in a sequence or any pattern, ★ stop playing the whole tune (seems obvious but many players don't do it) and play only the trouble spot several times. You'll succeed sooner and save time besides.

When will you know you've found a pattern deserving individual attention? You may see large-ish leaps in the music. Or you'll goof a lot!

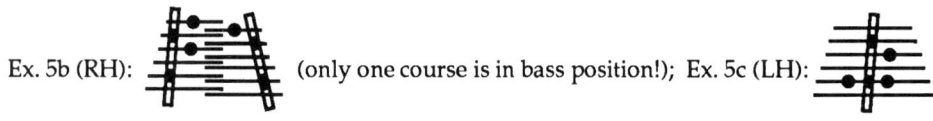

It's play time!

Now teach yourself *Soldier's Joy* with the steps in *How to learn a tune*, page 48. ★ Here are some tips to help you learn this and every tune:

1. Sing the tune and envision yourself playing all the patterns you just reviewed. You'll learn tunes faster with this picture in your mind.

2. Commas over the music (') mark off phrases, generally but not always four measures long (an exception: *Black Joke*, page 154). Phrases can be *identical, similar* (starting the same but ending differently or vice versa) or *different*. Compare both phrases in the A section as you ★ sing them. They're similar phrases. Whatever parts of these phrases sound the same you'll strike out the same. Compare the phrases of the B section; they're similar, too.

   In other tunes, you may find one phrase from each section matching up. Sometimes knowing only two measures of a tune can mean you instantly know how to play half of the tune!

3. The rhythm of the first two measures (or half-phrase) repeats for the rest of the A section (four times in all); the stroking is identical each time, even though the notes change at times.

   If you're right-handed, pat the bass notes off to your right on a table or in the air alongside your right lap.

4. Play all slashed notes ($\sharp, \sharp$) with single strong-hand strokes, like this:

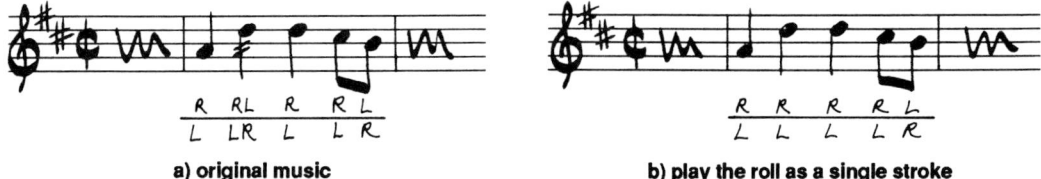

a) original music   b) play the roll as a single stroke

Fig. 4-6 M. A2 of *Soldier's Joy* showing the roll played as a single stroke

The slashes represent *rolls*, the subject of Lesson 9. Notice in Fig. 4-6b that you'll strike several notes in a row with your strong hand. Playing single strokes now will make adding rolls easier later. (You can hear how *Soldier's Joy* and other selected tunes sound without rolls on Companion Cassettes 2 and 3.)

5. ★ The entire B section is in second position. Knowing this, you can focus on patting the ups and downs in that position right away.

6. Watch the stroking in the B section! In m. B1-3 and 5-6, I do *not* alternate strokes on the quarter notes (♩). Three strong-hand strokes in a row give a brighter sound befitting dance music (see page 87 at "➤").

Expect to goof more now—and be thankful! (You'd be in more trouble if you *couldn't* tell!) ★ Give each step more repetition (you have more notes now). Don't skimp. When the first step is solid, the second will be easier. Above all, ★ keep singing! Every time a student can't get the notes from brain to hands, singing aloud while playing works wonders.

Striking Out and Winning!

Tune to play:

(See page 125 before you begin.)

Soldier's Joy, page 126

Lesson 2: Building your pattern vocabulary

Soldier's Joy was a good start towards playing by ear via patterns. This lesson presents more melodic patterns in tunes. The more you recognize, the easier you'll play. In addition to what's here, you can be sure to see them in different keys or raised or lowered a course so the bridge-mark relationships change.

Ex. 8 is the same pattern in *Soldier's Joy,* but with its tones juggled:

(LH: The temptation may be strong to play Ex. 8 right-handed, but again, if you switch your lead, you'll lose the music and court stroking confusion.)

Here is another familiar pattern with a different feel:

Your *weak* hand is the travelling hand! (Again, don't switch your lead; it'll weaken the sound of the tune.) If Ex. 9 is tough to play, ★ bounce your weak hand in an arc (a look in a mirror helps).

If you're left-handed, you may also play the lowest tone in first position; however, considering the rest of the B section of *St. Anne's Reel,* you might be better off staying in second position. The choice is up to you.

Batter Up!

Now for an entirely different pattern. Play each part 8-4-2-1:

10 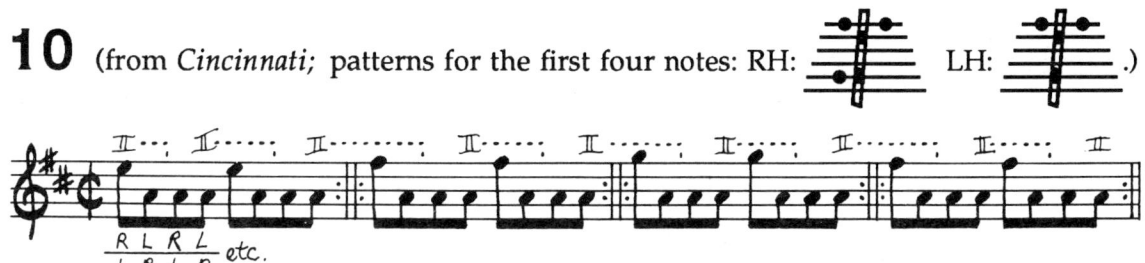 (from *Cincinnati*; patterns for the first four notes: RH: LH: .)

If you're right-handed, you may be puzzled about a *three*-course pattern for two tones. That's not an error; this pattern is easier to play with two unison courses! Why not shrink the distance and play the left-handed pattern instead? Again, you'll transfer the lead to your weak hand and weaken the sound. (A smaller pattern doesn't always produce a musical result.) Then why not play it all in second position? That works; however, when you strike both unisons, your strong hand can arc horizontally like the lefty's and improve accuracy. Whatever your lead, play Ex. 10 and think St. Louis in your strong hand.

Ex. 11 and 12 outline chords having more than three tones. Count up the tones—the number is different in each one—and refer to the position symbols to finger them. (RH: You may play notes marked "(B)" in either bass or first position.) ★ Set your playing distance from the lowest tone in *first* position, even if you have a choice of unisons.

11 (from *MacIlmoyle Reel*; LH: upper 3 tones in II *or* top note only in II)

12 (from *Swinging on a Gate*; LH: highest 3 tones in II, all others in I)

Now that you know where the notes are, ★ sway a little from side to side as your arms sweep across the dulcimer to connect the notes into a *flowing* musical phrase!

See how easy playing the dulcimer can be when you look for patterns? Now for one more "bottomless" sequence on the next page:

Striking Out and Winning!

13 (from *Arkansas Traveller*)

If this was difficult, did you scissor *both* arms? Students often miss the fourth note of the pattern only because they don't scissor and arc the weak hammer up after the *second* note! ★ Get thee to a mirror and watch thy scissoring. (★ Bounce thy hands!) Expect mistakes; your hammers *will* wander. ★ Singing along always helps.

Tunes to Play:

Cincinnati, page 127
Golden Slippers, page 128

Optional:

Optional tunes are for more playing pleasure, just in case you prefer to build your tune list before going on to the next lesson or section.

On the Road to Boston, page 133   *The Devil's Dream,* page 143
Pretty Little Dog, page 142   *Hull's Victory,* page 143
MacIlmoyle Reel, page 144 (this one is challenging!)

Postscript: The comedy of errors

It's a rare student who doesn't slow down to play the unavoidably vertical pattern in m. B7b of *Cincinnati* correctly (Ex. 14 at "*"). Obviously that's not a good idea. No one at a jam session is going to wait for you to catch up, but worse, if you do it enough, you'll teach yourself to hear the tune lag at that point, something you can do without.

Even if you've fingered the pattern and observed nearby bridge marks, you still may be missing notes. Why not live with the mistakes for a while? Here is how to make them less jarring to your ears:

1. Sing Ex. 14 ★ up to tempo, then sing only the part from the "*":

14 (all in II)

Batter Up!

2. Get the feel of this pattern away from the dulcimer so "right notes" won't frustrate you. Sing and pat from "*" only. ★ Bounce your hands about four inches high. Do this four times ★ up to tempo.

3. Sing and scissor that much again *in position* down your left lap. ★ Let your upper arms guide your hands down the dulcimer (see page 46). Again, play four times ★ up to tempo.

4. Play from "*" down the dulcimer, but *don't* aim for the notes. Start high, go low, make sounds and miss *on purpose!* (Go ahead! Relive the fun you had as a child banging on piano keys or pots and pans!) Feel that downward scissoring swoop—and keep your arms moving! Don't stop and search; you'll slow down. Repeat this four times ★ up to tempo.

5. Repeat the mess in step 4, but play the last three D's correctly.

6. Now try for the notes from "*." (If you miss, ★ try to miss *on purpose*, and you'll probably strike it right! Funny, but it really works!) Do this—oh, you know how many times by now—up to tempo!

7. Play the *entire* exercise at least four times.

8. Sing the B section twice (you need to hear what the whole thing sounds like), then play it at least twice. If you miss: Thankfully, dance tunes let you make good on the repeat! ★ Keep playing to keep your momentum going.

Playing the right notes may still take some time, but ★ relax and remember: They fly by so fast, no one will notice—unless you slow down!

Another vertical pattern appears in *St. Anne's Reel*, m. B3b-4. It feels easier because you ★ "scoop" the notes up (more on scooping in Lesson 3).

Just in case you goofed a bit too much, or your playing sounded uneven, check for relaxed elbows and shoulders, loose thumbs, firm yet loose wrists, swinging hammers and scissoring, piston-like forearms.

Striking Out and Winning!

Lesson 3: The basic rhythm in reels

★ The stroke order for any rhythm *always* comes from the alternating strokes for notes of equal duration. Here is the stroke order for the most common rhythm in reels:

Fig. 4-7 The stroke order for the most common rhythm in reels

Whenever two notes are combined with a tie (⁀) to form a longer note (♩ or ♪), the stroke of the second note is dropped. ★ In this rhythm, your strong hand strikes two notes in a row. Because both notes are accented notes, ★ your strong hand leads in this rhythm and is *constant*, no matter where the notes in a tune may wander on the dulcimer.

This rhythm appears in many reels in this book and beyond. I've underlined some of the more memorable spots below:

Fig. 4-8 Examples of the most common rhythm in reels

The notes jump around a lot in *Petronella*, but its rhythm and stroke order are the same as in *Galopede*, despite their differing note values.

Say the word "blackberry" several times nonstop to hear this rhythm (Ex. 15), then pat it on your lap to get your arms moving (don't play from your wrists). Then play it on any course in first position using the stroke order shown; *do not alternate strokes or play it RLL (LRR)*:

15 (shown in both note-value combinations)

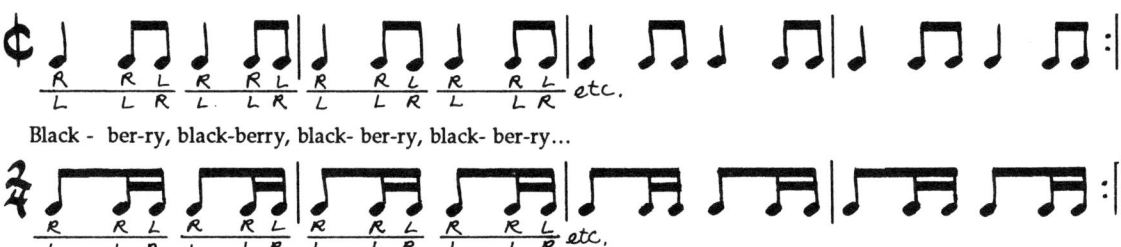

Black - ber-ry, black-ber-ry, black- ber-ry, black- ber-ry...

(Four "blackberries" played in front of a reel are called *four potatoes*. They set the tempo and signal both dancers and musicians to begin the fun.)

If you remove the syllable "-ry," from this rhythm,...

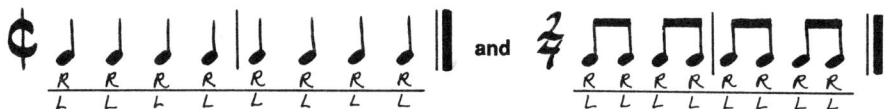

Fig. 4-9 "Blackberry" without "-ry"

...you hear a steady beat struck by your strong hand!

Musicians usually read the "blackberry" rhythm a beat at a time. I've underlined the notes that way (grouped R-RL or L-LR).

Playing by beats is fine; however, the stroking has boggled the hands and minds of many a dulcimer player. (You, too? Welcome to the club!) In response to all the boggling, I invite you to try this approach:

Say the words "going up" several times nonstop (Ex. 16), emphasizing the word "up," then pat it, too. It's the same rhythm and stroke order as Ex. 15, but it begins with a *two-note pick-up*:

16 (shown in both note-value combinations)

pick-up

Going up, going up, going up, going up...

Striking Out and Winning!

I ignored note beams and bar lines and underlined the notes to form groups of three from the pick-up. What is the stroking of each group now? RL<u>R</u> RL<u>R</u> (LR<u>L</u> LR<u>L</u>) or *alternating* strokes! It's the same stroke order as in Fig. 4-7 and Ex. 15; all I did was change the way you look at it. Playing by pick-ups (or *upbeats*) is not only easier, it helps contra dancers step the downbeat with the music. (Fact: The foot must go up before it can go down!) It's a very danceable way to play reels.

Speak and play Ex. 16 at a moderate tempo on any first-position course, bouncing your hands six inches high. ★ Before you begin, set your weak hand about two inches higher in space. This sets it up to strike second. ★ *Always* play "go-" with your *strong* hand, and ★ always return your weak hand to its higher position to avoid confusing your hands.

When you've got the stroking, play Ex. 16 on any course in second and then in bass position. ★ The stroke order is the same regardless of the position; don't reverse your lead to play in the far east or west.

After all that, were your hands *still* confused? I can *smell* what you're doing! ★ Play in front of a mirror and watch your hands: Do they keep moving between "going ups" or do they stop in mid-air? Or does your strong hand move and your weak hand stop? If either or both hands stop, your playing is laced with tension! (It's like driving a car by pumping the brakes; how far will you get?) All that stop-and-go is wasted energy and gives your dulcimer an acute case of *overtonitis* (a tinny sound)!

To avoid tension, tin and tangles, ★★ keep your arms moving through the "spaces" of this (and any) rhythm. In "going up," your weak hand strikes less often and will find trouble if it isn't kept busy.

The motion you need to play "going up" is a scoop, like you're ★ bailing water out of a boat with your hands. Feel this motion in space:

1. Step away from your dulcimer and stand sideways to a mirror with your weak arm in view. Position your hands in front of you at waist height, palms up, fingers cupped and forearms pigeon-toed.

2. Say "going up" eight times in rhythm (Ex. 17). At the same time, ★ scoop the air in backwards circles with both hands together as if to bail water (Fig. 4-10a), ★ *without stopping in between*. Your forearms will remain pigeon-toed. Bend your knees a little and ★ lean forward as you scoop on "up." Don't shrug your shoulders.

17

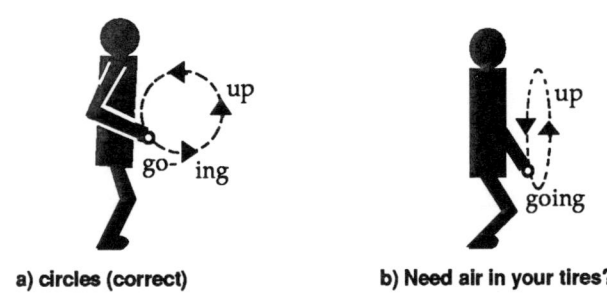

a) circles (correct)   **b) Need air in your tires?**

Fig. 4-10 A side view of the scooping motion for Ex. 17

Circle your hands ★ straight ahead, not towards each other. If your knees bend a lot and only your forearms are active, your hands will go up and down in ovals instead of circles (Fig. 4-10b; you're bailing a boat, not pumping air into tires!). ★ Watch your moves in the mirror.

The pattern in Ex. 18a will let you scoop while playing "going up" on the dulcimer. Finger the pattern (A-B-D). Sing and scissor "going up" several times in this pattern until your hands know the stroking:

18a (RH and LH pattern:)

Great! Now make those notes *sing*. Play "going up" just once (Ex. 18b). To do it, hold your hammers about an inch above the strings. ★ *Lift* them together about six inches so they "breathe" first (dashed arrow), scissor the notes, then lift again about ★ *12 inches* (solid arrow—and yes, that high!). Don't stop first to think about lifting afterwards; loop them up immediately. Not sure how to make your hands breathe to start? ★ Sing along (your lungs are your hands' best teachers). Oh, one more thing: Of the two dots over the arrows, one is higher. That means ★ lift your weak hand a little higher. When you do, you ensure that it'll strike second.

18b (no positions shown; lift *both* hands before and after playing)

RH: LH:

Striking Out and Winning!

Play that again. ★ You want to feel as if you scissored all three strokes in *one* motion. ★ Breathe with *both* hands to start, not just your strong hand alone. It's just like singing; you have to breathe first with both lungs(!), and so do your hammers if you want your *dulcimer* to sing.*

Now scissor "going up" *twice* nonstop (Ex. 18c). Breathe with both hands and ★ lift your weak hand a little higher after each three-note chunk (follow the arrows and dots):

18c

RH:    LH:

Did you feel both hands circle back together into the second "going up?" That's the motion of effortless dulcimer playing! If you missed it, play it again and ★ lift *both* hands after the first three notes. (Nudge your weak hand up and over if it needs it!)

Now play "going up" *ad infinitum* (Ex. 18d) until your arms fall into a natural momentum. ★ Let go of your shoulders and elbows so your hands can breathe freely. ★ Feel the spaces in the rhythm. Your strong hand *always* strikes "go-;" it'll remember its place as long as your weak hand lifts a little higher. ★ Finally, focus on your strong hand's steady beat. Make sure it bounces to the same height between strikes. (Pretend you're ★ hammering a nail into a board—gently!)

18d

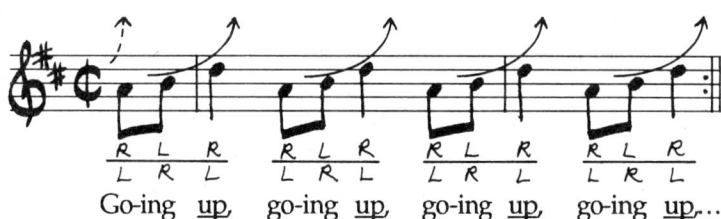

When you've got the feel of the scoop, gradually increase speed. Notice that you'll lift less and less as you play faster. That's all right. I started you out with a 12-inch lift to make sure your arms were in the act.

Start Ex. 18d again and when your arms are on automatic pilot, go nonstop into Ex. 18e (the lift will feel vertical instead of circular), and play four "going ups" on each tone of a five-note scale. (Change courses on "up.")

---

* I know I'm asking you to do a lot of things at once, but breathing with your hands needs to be as natural as the breathing you do to survive. Make it automatic now and you'll barely have to think about it in the future.

Batter Up!

18e

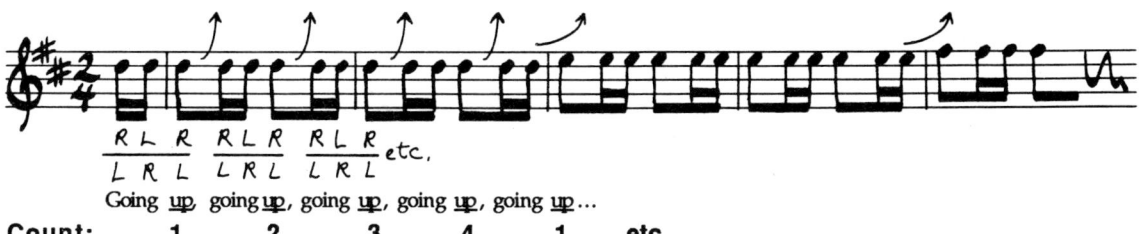

R L R R L R R L R etc.
L R L L R L L R L

Going up, going up, going up, going up, going up...

Count: 1   2   3   4   1   etc.

♪ Every now and then, stop your hands between chunks or play from your wrists and listen. The difference in sound is amazing when you keep your arms moving.

Just in case it took a while to establish a momentum, ★ be sure *both* hands breathe to begin this and *any* exercise or tune beginning with a two-note pick-up. ★ That first breath really does help your hands get in motion and *stay* in motion. A dashed arrow in front of an exercise will remind you to breathe. (By the way, all the exercises in Lessons 1 and 2 begin more solidly with a two-hand breath. Try it now with any exercise or tune. And do you remember when you bounced your hands between sequence patterns in Ex. 4? Each bounce was a breath for the next two measures.)

Lift, as I call it, is what makes rhythm played on the dulcimer flow. While its motion may feel large (but it isn't), ★ *that's* where the music is, not when the hammers strike the strings! Lift prepares your hammers to strike again. Without it, or if you lift but stop your hands, you play notes instead of music, and your hands have to "restart from zero" every few strikes, increasing your difficulty to play. And remember what I said about the weak hand's strength being on the weak part of the beat (page 44)? Lift is more of a weak-hand activity (remember, your strong hand strikes a steady beat and "lifts" anyway). When your weak hand keeps moving, it controls the tempo of any tune, fast or slow *and*, as you'll see later, it makes the dulcimer's sound float in a magical way and is an integral part of playing rolls (Lesson 9).

If you can sing a tune in your sleep, the only thing that will prevent you from playing with your arms and lifting in a rhythm is unfamiliarity with its patterns. You can't play freely if you don't know where your hammers are headed beforehand. ★ That's why playing short patterns within tunes is such a good way to learn them. Knowing what the patterns look and feel like will help you play any kind of music easily.

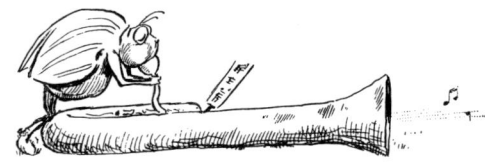

Striking Out and Winning!

Lesson 4: Easy rhythmic sequences

Your strong hand pumps a steady beat (★ "hammers a nail") on the lower tone in Ex. 19a. ★ Keep your weak hand rising higher (at arrows).

19a (all in I)

➤ You say getting started was tricky? Good for you! ★ To begin on the downbeat, *do not breathe with both hands to start!* ★ Strike the first note with your strong hand, *then* lift your weak hand (arrow). If your weak hand won't budge, talk to it nicely, ★ then teach it to lift by striking the first note only with *both* hammers. You could say "blackberry" for this and the remaining exercises, but "up, going up" helps your hands stay in motion so the notes connect into music. (Note: I sing reels with the syllables "DUM duh-kuh DUM duh-kuh" to make this rhythm dance.)

Ex. 19b is a "bottomless" version of Ex. 19a. Again, lift the weak hand.

19b (from *Galopede*, all in I)

Now play the first two measures of *Galopede* several times with lift. It begins with a pickup; ★ breathe with both hands to start.

20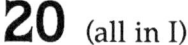

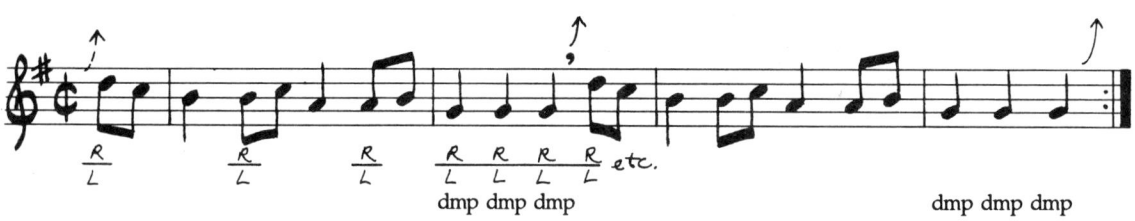

Your strong hand played "dump, dump, dump" alone, giving your weak hand a chance to sit still and be lazy. To put it back in motion, let it breathe with your strong hand after the third "dump." If it doesn't, your wrists will take over and you'll have to work harder to play. (★ My weak

Batter Up!

arm "rocks" up and down gently while my strong hand strikes, giving it the breath automatically.)

Why not alternate strokes on the "dumps"? Doing so won't switch your lead, but ♪ it makes the tune sound *legato* (smooth) when dancers need a *staccato* (short) sound. ★ Go for a bright, danceable sound!

In Ex. 21, lift and shift positions simultaneously. ★ Think St. Louis with both hands, and feel your arms sway from side to side as you shift.

21 (from *Galopede*, too! LH: shifts are the same as RH)

Now for one more "bottomless" sequence:

22 (from *My Love Is But a Lassie Yet*; all in II)

Tunes to Play:

Galopede, page 129

My Love Is But a Lassie Yet, page 129

A position-shift puzzle

Ex. 23 is Ex. 22 inverted and in a different key. Sing it twice, then sing it four more times while patting the rhythm with lift:

23 (from *Successful Campaign*)

Now for the puzzle: Starting in first position, play Ex. 23 and find a place to shift to second position *without* changing strokes or crossing

Striking Out and Winning!

hammers. ★ Take your time, look at your dulcimer and sing along. (If you're right-handed, don't shift at "><;" you *will* cross hammers there.)

When you've found a route, play it four times with lift. Bounce your weak hand in an arc ★ toward the next course between strikes. Don't withdraw it toward your body, a common, erroneous move.

Now find another shift point in Ex. 23 (righties have four spots, lefties have two), then see how you did in the *Appendix* (page 173).

Tune to play:

Successful Campaign, page 130

Lesson 5: "Aerobic" sequences

Now for a workout! Ex. 24 involves a large jump.

★ Don't play Ex. 24 left-handed if you're a righty! True, it *is* a shorter reach, but ♪ you'll reverse the stroke order and weaken the tune's sound. ★ Compromising sound for convenience won't work to your advantage musically and is likely to confuse your hands.

If you're right-handed, the large reach can slant your weak upper arm backwards. ★ Turn your body to the left and that arm will slant forward.

Let's try that again with scissor strokes in between. The scissored notes below aren't in *Liberty,* but they'll give you practice schlepping in time during a jam session. (The actual notes can be tricky, so I'd rather you have a strong feel for the rhythm right away. The notes will come!)

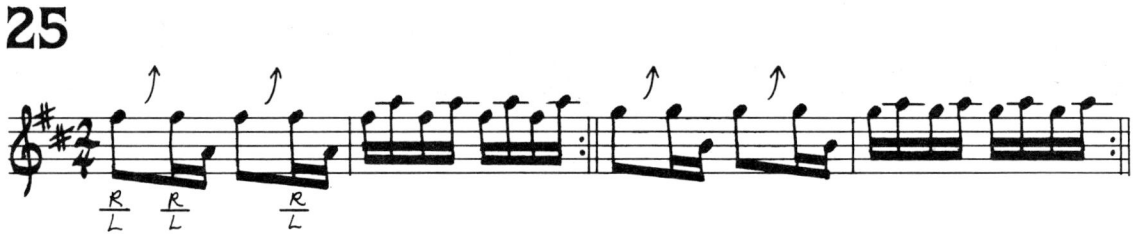

Batter Up!

There's one more pattern from *Liberty* that's good to review before you play the tune. Feel your weak arm swing as it lifts in Ex. 26, and ★ let your arms and body sway with it, too.

26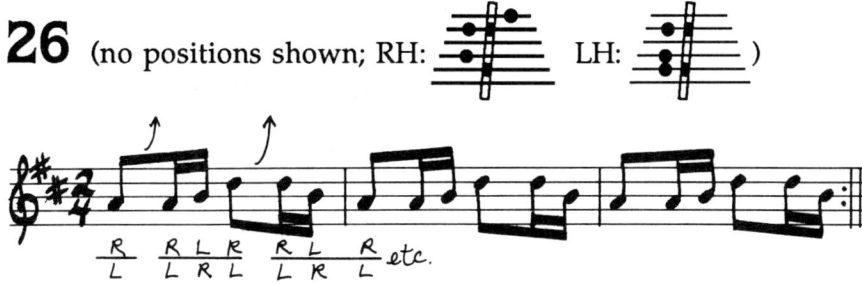

Tune to play:

Liberty, page 131

• • • • • • • •

Your strong hand will jump more vigorously in the next two sequences. Lift your weak hand after your strong hand strikes the first note.

27 (from *Staten Island*; all in II)

28 (from *Whiskey Before Breakfast*; all in II)

Wouldn't it be less work to alternate strokes in the above exercises? ♪ Try it and notice how you feel and how the dulcimer sounds:

a) Ex. 27   b) Ex. 28

Fig. 4-11 "Going-up" played with alternating strokes

69

Striking Out and Winning!

You may have felt like a waddling penguin, but did you hear how "flat" the rhythm sounded? That happens because your weak hand *can't* lift! Why play notes when you can make music? ★ Always let the rhythm set the stroking. All that strong-hand jumping may seem excessive, but ★ that's where your dulcimer's "voice" is.

There's another reason why you don't want to alternate strokes in rhythm: You have to memorize which hand plays *every* note. When you goof, you've blown it. ★ A strong-hand lead lets "automatic pilot" take over; if you goof, you can jump back in on the next beat. And when it comes to variations of tunes (a subject for another book), rock-solid stroke order will rudder you easily through swirling streams of running notes.

Tune to play:

Staten Island, page 131

• • • • • • • •

I close this lesson with some scoopy and not-so-scoopy three-note patterns. The stroking remains the same regardless of the courses played (remember, the rhythm determines the strokes), and so does the lift!

I call the pattern in Ex. 29 "the *Petronella* pattern" because it appears often in that tune (it appears in others, too). Finger the pattern and play it. (★ Your strong hand always strikes, "go-.") As soon as your hands know where they're going, feel the scoop and lift.

29 (from *Petronella*; no positions shown; pattern: RH: LH:)

Now play the same pattern in reverse. You won't feel the scoop this time, but lift just the same.

30a

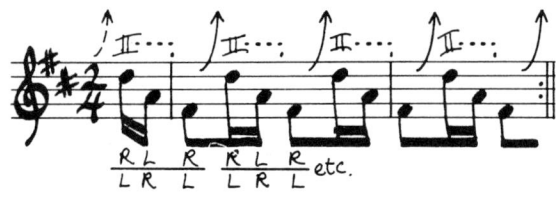

Going down...

Batter Up!

Ex. 30a was the first three notes of *Petronella*. It's followed by two more patterns in the tune, shown below. Finger and play each with lift:

30b (all in I; note: strike the highest note with your *strong* hand!)

30c (a triad all in I; again, strike the highest note with your *strong* hand)

Now play Ex. 30a, b and c nonstop 8-4-2, going to Ex. 30d for 1. (★ As you play one pattern, look for the next.) ★ Lift *both* hands after the third "dump" to set your weak hand in motion. Watch the stroke order!

30d

What comes after the "dumps"? The pattern in Ex. 29! After that there isn't much more to know to play the A section to *Petronella*. To find out what's left, sing the A section at least twice nonstop, sing and pat it twice (can you pat it in position right away?) then follow your inner voice and play it at least four times nonstop with lift.

The *Petronella* pattern opens the B section, too, but is followed by other patterns (see the tune). Handle them the same way.

My pre-second-edition students always shuddered at the sight of *Petronella's* jumping notes, but once they knew its patterns, it became a favorite tune. "Tough" tunes often center around one or two key patterns. Handle them the same way and you'll learn tunes in no time.

Tune to play:

Petronella, page 132

Lesson 6: Hiccups and the art of dulcimer playing

As you may have noticed in the reels you've played so far, lifting isn't as constant as it is in the exercises. It's easy to forget to lift after you've scissored for a while. Think of the space in each measure of Ex. 31a as a "hiccup" performed by both hands together after each eighth note (♪).

31a (LH: upper tone in II, lower tone in I)

I've added one more tone to this exercise to form the two visual patterns comprising most of the A section of *St. Anne's Reel*. Finger and play each pattern alone, then combine them and play 4-2-1. (Take the paper bag off your head; this is one case of hiccups you don't want to cure!)

Here is the same rhythm in a four-note chord pattern. Finger it (it's easier to play than it looks on the music staff), then play with hiccups:

Hopefully by now you're beginning to look less at the stroke marks under the music and relying more on how to play the rhythm by what each beat looks like. The more you can do this, the sooner you'll be able to "choreograph" strokes and positions for tunes beyond this book.

Tune to play:

St. Anne's Reel, page 132

A true confession

Now that you've had an uplifting experience (ahem!), I can tell you: When I first learned *Staten Island*, I alternated strokes all the way through (I let the melody tell me how to play m. A3 and B1-2). One day, I realized *Galopede* had the "going up" rhythm, too (m. A1-2), but I played it with a strong-hand lead. I wondered: What would happen if I played "going up" in *Staten Island* with a strong-hand lead? I still remember how I loosened up and *danced* with my playing. I knew *that* was the way to play! Lifting may still feel clumsy even now, but keep it going (up!) and one day you'll exclaim, "This feels great!" *Then* you'll understand what I've been driving at for the last four lessons.

Ducka, Ducka and Dum!

Keeping the magic

When I first got my dulcimer, I already owned a few tune books with scads of reels and jigs, but didn't want to waste time learning tunes no one else knew. This led to another problem: I didn't know anyone who played this music! I eventually found a contra dance group with a live band (infinitely better than a dead one), and soon I not only found out what was hot or not, but I also found plenty of musicians to play with. The tunes in this book reflect just a smattering of the tunes played for those dances.

Now that you've got a few tunes under your belt, keep the excitement alive: Play with other people. Don't be shy; it's good incentive, and you'll get lots of good tunes and tips. Contra dances often feature pick-up bands where anyone can join in. (Why not get the feel of dancing in your bones, too?) Folk clubs host regular jam sessions. Dulcimer clubs set time aside at their meetings to play and exchange ideas. If none of these is immediately available, start your own monthly jam or go to the nearest folk festival to meet other musicians. (Bring your dulcimer; you don't want to kick yourself for leaving it home.) Or grow your own musicians! One student's husband learned to play guitar after she took up the dulcimer, and now they play together every evening before dinner.

Striking Out and Winning!

Lesson 7: "Blackberry" in reverse

When you play "blackberry" in "reverse," the stroking looks like this:

Fig. 4-12 Stroke order of the "reversed" rhythm

This is a *downbeat* rhythm which sounds like "waterfall." Sing and pat it, then play it, putting a little more emphasis on "wa-":

33 (play on any course)

Wa- ter-fall, wa- ter-fall,...

This rhythm will try to confuse your hands; you'll feel like playing the *next* downbeat with your weak hand, but don't! Instead, ★ lift your weak hand higher and the confusion will disappear. One place where this rhythm occurs is at the end of the A section of *Cincinnati*. (It ends on the "and" of beat 2; all the other tunes in this book end *on* beat 2.)

Tune to play:

Over the Waterfall, page 133 (What other tune *is* there?!)

Tune to Review:

Cincinnati, page 127

Batter Up!

Optional:

The White Cockade, page 145
Reel de Montréal, page 145

Lesson 8: "3D" sound

There's one more aspect of lift I want you to have. To me, it's the most exciting part of playing, for it makes the dulcimer sound "three-dimensional" (similar to a graphic equalizer on your stereo system) and makes it float in a magical way.

Play "going up" in Ex. 18d again and watch a side view of your weak arm in a mirror. If you play by bending only your elbow, your forearm, hand and hammer angle sharply upwards:

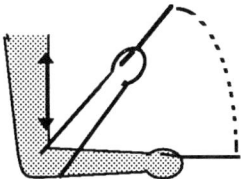

Fig. 4-13 **Lifting the weak arm with a stiff wrist**

As I said in Chapter 2 (page 18), angling increases your chances of missing because it takes the hammer out of the "line of fire" (not helpful when striking one course repeatedly). Loosening your wrists a little lets your hands remain level as they go up and down to scissor, but how do you keep your weak hand level in the "going up" rhythm when it needs to lift even higher? ★ Lift that *entire* arm from the *shoulder*. Your elbow won't have to bend as much, leaving your forearm, hand and hammer fairly level. And when that happens, you'll find the graphic equalizer and a wonderful 3D sound!

Let's take a close look at how your weak arm lifts before you play "going up" with both hands:

1. Sit down wherever you have plenty of elbow room (literally!). Rest your weak hand atop your weak shoulder with fingers "pointing" behind you. Your arm is now in a "chicken-wing" position and slants your upper arm forward automatically, something you definitely need for this technique.

2. Explore the space with your elbow in the following ways:
   a. Raise your elbow up and out sideways s-l-o-w-l-y to shoulder height (90°), then let it fall to your side quickly on its own. (See "a" in Fig. 4-14a or b and Fig. 4-14c). Notice that your shoulder doesn't shrug; it "rolls" in the socket as your upper arm rises.
   b. Raise your elbow directly forward to shoulder height, then let it fall to your side (at "b"). Again, slow rise, quick fall.

c. Raise it "northwest" (LH: "northeast") slowly at 45° to shoulder height, then let it fall to your side (at "c").

d. ★ Repeat "c" but lift your upper arm half as much, to 45° (Fig. 4-14c). Notice that your upper arm ★ slants forward as it rises.

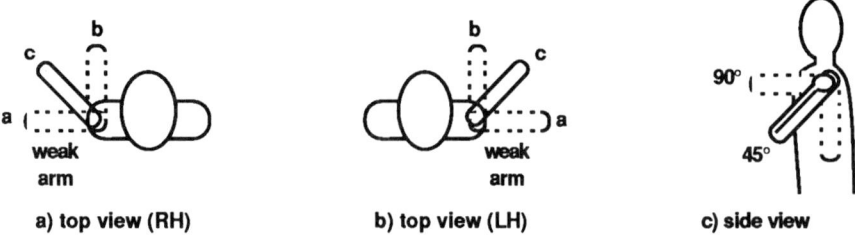

Fig. 4-14 Exploring space with the weak arm folded up in a "chicken wing"

3. Part 2d is how your upper arm needs to move to produce 3D sound. Hold the chicken-wing pose (hope you're alone!) and lift and drop your elbow over a continuous, *steady* count of four (at least eight times). ★ Think about what to do before you try: Raise your elbow slowly to 45° on "1-2-3" and let it fall to your side on "4." (Pretend there's a balloon inflating under your arm on "1-2-3" which "pops" on "4" so your elbow falls naturally; don't force it down.) ★ Your arm will rise slower than it falls.

1 2 3 4 1 2 3 4 1 2 3 4 1 2 3 4...

Fig. 4-15 Lifting and dropping the weak elbow over a steady count of four

★ Your elbow *must* rise for three *full* counts. It goes up only about four inches, so raise it *very* slowly! If your upper arm stops ahead of time, playing will become more difficult. ★ Slow down.

4. ★ Think about how to do this before you try: Say "going up" several times ★ in rhythm slowly and "pat" your weak elbow on the side of your body on "-ing." (This is the syllable your weak hammer strikes; "-ing" is still count #4 if #1 falls on "up." Don't count, though; just say the words). This *will* feel odd! No matter what your arm does, *don't* change the rhythm of the words!

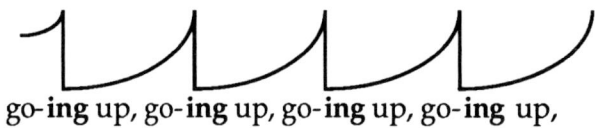

go-**ing** up, go-**ing** up, go-**ing** up, go-**ing** up,

Fig. 4-16 Lifting and dropping the elbow on "-ing"

If you've done this 16 or more times and still feel uncoordinated, go on to the next step; you've got enough of an idea!

5. Say and pat "going up" with your weak elbow and your strong *hand* (scissor your strong forearm; ★ slant your upper arm forward). Your weak elbow will "thud" against your body silently, and you'll hear your strong hand pat a steady beat. Start slowly, then increase to a moderate speed when your arm catches on.

6. Now open the chicken wing to an arm. Speak and pat "going up" with both hands. ★ Your weak elbow will rise out and up diagonally, taking forearm, hand and hammer up with it. Your elbow will need to bend *a little;* let it happen. (A possibly helpful hint: Think of your elbow doing the patting as if your arm ended there.) Your strong forearm still *scissors* from the elbow; *don't make it mirror the weak arm!* Don't shrug your weak shoulder (it'll try to scrunch up without a hand on top of it), but ★ watch it "roll" in the mirror. Also, don't rock your body and shoulders from side to side.

7. Now play Ex. 18d. Keep that weak elbow rising, and ★ let it bend a little so the hammer goes straight up and down. (If it doesn't bend, the hammer will rise up and *forward*, instead of straight up.) At the same time, feel your *strong* elbow rise up and out just a pinch with your weak elbow. If you ★ bend your knees in rhythm as you did to scoop Ex. 17, your whole body will lift (★ like you're posting on a horse), and your weak elbow won't need to bend as much.

8. The finishing touch: As you lift, release both wrists so your hands ★ droop straight down naturally; don't force them. (If they flop sideways, rotate your forearms in or out a little). Now ★ "pull" the sound out of the dulcimer by imagining that you're pulling wads of bubble gum off the strings with the mallets! Both hammers will droop a little if your dulcimer is angled at about 10° (Fig. 4-17), or they'll be level with the floor if the dulcimer is closer to 30°.

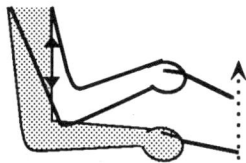

Fig. 4-17 Pulling the sound out!

Some of my students say my weak arm moves in a "wave."

9. ♪ In contrast, play Ex. 18d from your elbows so the hammers angle up. Even though the rhythm is accurate, you'll hear a "two-dimensional" or "flat" sound quality. Stiff wrists are the cause, and you may feel like you're not as relaxed as you could be, even though your arms are moving. Activate your whole weak arm (and your body!), relax your wrists on the rise and listen again: The hammers strike a little more softly, producing a lustrous, floating sound! Relaxing your wrists also gives you more energy to play longer.

10. Once you've got the idea of whole-arm lift in Ex. 18d, gradually increase speed to dance tempo. ★ Your weak forearm, etc. should still lift (though not as high), even when you play faster.

Striking Out and Winning!

Apply whole-arm lift to other exercises as a warm-up to the tunes they come from, starting with Ex. 18d. In the case of 31a-b and 32 where you lift occasionally, ★ always *scissor* from hanging elbows and "hiccup" your weak arm a lot and your strong arm a little in the spaces.

Just in case part or none of this made sense (I never said it was going to be easy), catch the action on the companion video!

Lift your whole weak arm *every* time there's a space in the rhythm and *only* when there's a space in the rhythm. (In other rhythms, your entire *strong* arm lifts, and in jig rhythm, your arms take turns.) Whenever you scissor, ★ let *both* elbows hang quietly; don't lift them.

Tunes to Review:

All exercises and tunes from Lessons 3-7! You may forget how to play some tunes because of this new way of lifting, but hang in there; it's *worth* it! The exercises will help this lift become second nature. Let your entire body follow its somewhat circular feel and you'll pick it up quickly.

Lesson 9: Multiple-bounce strokes and rolls

Make sure you're comfortable with Lessons 3-7 before you begin.

The slashed notes in the tunes in this book are *rolls*. Rolls make reels *zing* on the dulcimer in a way that can't be duplicated on any other danceband instrument.

The roll consists of two of what I call *multiple-bounce strokes*. A multiple-bounce stroke is three to five bounces of the mallet on the strings within *one* forearm stroke.

How to play multiple-bounce strokes

1. Hold one hammer ★ *loosely* in your strong hand about an inch above any course.

2. *Lift* the hammer (with your *forearm*), then strike the course. Let your forearm sit at the bottom of the stroke so the hammer bounces eight-plus times on the course (don't let it rebound as for single strokes). It'll bounce faster as it loses force. Don't control the hammer or its bouncing. Do this a few times with each hand separately.

3. You want to control the quicker bounces to play multiple-bounce strokes. ★ Point your thumb tips towards the *mallets* (not the handles). It'll feel a little like you're turning on a flashlight. Your hold will firm up, and only the top half of the thumb pad (see Fig. 2-6, page 15) will sit on the handle. ★ Don't hook your thumbs over; they'll actually become *straighter*. (A hooked thumb slows the bounces and may pigeon-toe the hammer too much; see page 18.) Point and relax your thumbs a few times.

4. Now play a multiple-bounce stroke with your strong hand. ★ Lift and ★ let your forearm sit at the bottom of the stroke so it bounces four to six times. (It's a "soft" stroke; like a brush stroke in painting.) ★ If only one bounce occurs, let go of your shoulder, soften your strike and/or point your thumb more. If the hammer lands dead on the string and buzzes, either the entire thumb pad is on the handle or you may be bending your wrists from quiet forearms to strike the strings.

Practice each hand separately at least four times. Both hands should produce the same number of bounces equally well.

May we have a drum roll, please?

We'll start with a long roll (it'll come in handy for any beauty pageants or door-prize drawings you play for). Start with eight counts of single strokes (16 strikes; let go of your shoulders and elbows), then ★ keep scissoring and point your thumbs to play a long roll for eight counts (Ex. 34). When you point your thumbs, ★ *do not slow the scissor pace of your arms* (rolls fall apart if played too slowly). Listen for a "blur" of sound. Switch from single strokes to the roll at least four times nonstop.

34

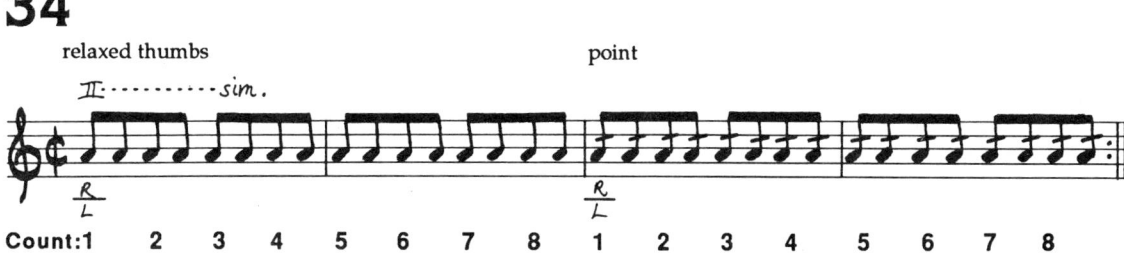

If you hear each bounce distinctly, your hammers are bouncing too slowly. ★ Relax your arms, ★ scissor smaller and softer, and/or point your thumbs more. You'll have to experiment to determine what you need. (Most of my students need more thumb point.) If none of the above works, a differently balanced pair of hammers may do the trick.

♩ Now scissor the roll from your wrists only and listen. The dulcimer sounds "nasal." Roll with scissoring forearms again, and the roll's sound becomes rounder and fuller.

Striking Out and Winning!

Two-stroke rolls: The *reel* reason for this lesson!

Most rolls are *two-stroke rolls*. Play two multiple-bounce strokes on "going" of "going up" and you've got it!

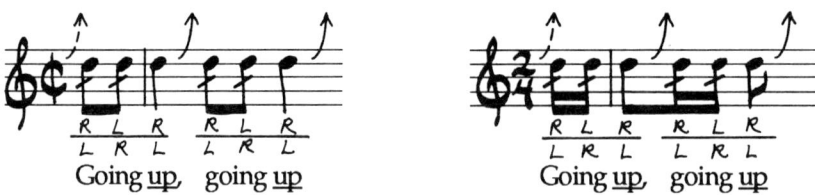

Fig. 4-18   Where to play the two-stroke roll

As you can see from the arrows over both examples, ★ lift is essential for rolls. I've seen too many times that rolls without lift don't roll!

Play "going up" several times, first with single strokes and then with two-stroke rolls. ★ Feel each group of three scissor strokes as a unit. ★ The lift is *the same* for both; the only change is your thumb pressure. Oh, and you won't hear three distinct notes, either; they'll merge into one long "blurred" sound. ★ A roll *always* connects into the single stroke following it. Don't let bar lines or the beams joining eighth notes tell you to break the sound between the roll and the next single stroke:

35 (no positions shown; all in II)

Just in case that didn't work, approach the roll from the three-note scoop:

36 (optional; no positions shown; all in II)

Did you play the same rhythm as you did for single strokes? All too often, a student cheats the weak hand by pushing it through its multiple-bounce stroke too fast. (My guess is they think the weak hand can't hold its own. It can!) ★ Saying "going up" aloud encourages your hands to follow your mouth and straighten the mess out.

Now you're on a roll! (If you think you can do better, ♪ lift higher, keep your arms moving, "hammer" a nail with your strong hand, point your thumbs more and ★ check your roll-playing in a mirror. But please, no orations from *Julius Caesar*.) ★ I find rolls easier to play and fuller sounding when my whole weak arm lifts.

The two-stroke roll is really written as one note with two slashes in the stem and two stroke marks underneath:

Fig. 4-19 Writing the two-stroke roll

Here is Ex. 35 with rolls the way they appear in tunes:

35 (revised; no positions shown)

Could you roll with a single multiple-bounce stroke? After all, it doesn't switch the lead to your weak hand. You could, but I wouldn't. One-stroke "rolls" sound flat and uninteresting (Fig. 4-20), *except* in a jig, as you'll see later on. The second stroke packs in twice as many bounces, enabling you to *crescendo* (make the volume gradually louder) into the single stroke following the roll. That translates into *zing*. (Comparing is worthwhile *only* if you played a one-stroke roll.) Rolls fill in time space not to be dead weight, but to make a tune exciting! And you'll need two-stroke rolls for other techniques in this book. ★ Make absolutely sure you're playing two-stroke rolls before you go on!

Fig. 4-20 How *not* to play rolls

Striking Out and Winning!

Adding rolls to reels

Now put your hammers down and sing the A section of *Soldier's Joy* two or three times nonstop with the nonsense word "berUMP" for every roll/single-stroke unit (Fig. 4-21; "ber-" represents the two-stroke roll). ★ Singing the rolls will help you remember where they are and what they sound like when you play the tune from memory. ★ Scoop your hands in the air every time you sing "berUMP" to feel the lift going in and out of each roll. Don't roll your tongue or flap it vigorously ("badaladalump!?") or you may teach yourself to hear and play a bunch of impossibly fast single strokes. "BerUMP" will do.

Fig. 4-21 Singing *Soldier's Joy* (A section) with "berUMP"
(no positions shown)

Play the A section four times nonstop, lifting before and after each roll (at arrows above). Your first roll may be a surprise, but try to continue playing the tune. *Then* break out the champagne!

If you need an intermediate step, sing and play "going up" with single strokes in place of "berUMP," then try again.

★ Sing any tune with "berUMP" first so your hammers will be able to follow your ear. That way, you won't have to look at the music to figure out where to put them in. (Always sing "ber-" on the roll.)

Tunes to Review:

Add rolls to these tunes:
Soldier's Joy, page 126
Cincinnati, page 127

Batter Up!

Lesson 10: Rolls within the "going up" rhythm

Rolling within a long passage of "going up" single strokes is easy! Lift nonstop and point your thumbs to roll. Sing and play:

37a (RH & LH: play in either I or II)

1. play in I; then go to 37b

2. play in II; then go to 37c or 37d

Ex. 37a has the same rhythm as parts of some tunes in this book. Play it at least twice until you let go and lift, then go nonstop into:

37b (from *Galopede*; all in I)

37c (from *Petronella*)

37d (from *My Love Is But a Lassie Yet*; all in II)

Turn the page for another excerpt with more frequent rolls:

Striking Out and Winning!

38 (last half from *My Love Is But a Lassie Yet* and *College Hornpipe*)

Going up, going up, going up, going up Going up, berUMP, going up, ber-UMP

Tunes to review with rolls:

Galopede, page 129* *Staten Island,* page 131
My Love Is But a Lassie Yet, page 129 *Petronella,* page 132

  * Roll the middle note anywhere you play three quarter notes (♩ ♩ ♩) on the same course.

Optional:

Red-Haired Boy, page 146
College Hornpipe, page 146

Lesson 11: Ginger snaps

"Ginger snaps" is my name for a bouncy alternating-stroke technique. It's different from scissor strokes, producing *staccato* (short) sounds within the dulcimer's sustain. My students are always amazed at how the dulcimer talks with ginger snaps. I think you'll like what you hear, too.

1. Set your playing distance. Your elbows need breathing room for ginger snaps to occur. Play a steady beat on first-position G with both hands together ("LR" under each note). Let go of your shoulders and elbows, then★ pump your forearms (not wrists) as if you were filling a tire with a hand pump.

39

2. Now play 8 strong-hand strokes followed by 8 weak ones and ★ *bounce the inactive arm* in the air (R^L and L^R) at the same time. (watch this in a mirror.) Then reduce to 4-2-1.

Batter Up!

40 (in I; play 8-4-2-1)

One stroke is ginger snaps!

How did you do? Most people snap fine on 8, 4 and 2, but then scissor on 1. Chances are good you did this, too, so double-check your moves. Go back to 2 strikes per hammer, feel the inactive arm bounce, then alternate strokes while bouncing *both* forearms. Listen for a bright, "detached" sound (shown by the dots over or under the notes); this is *you* talking through your dulcimer!

4. Ginger snap Ex. 40 again, then go nonstop into a five-note scale:

41 (all in I)

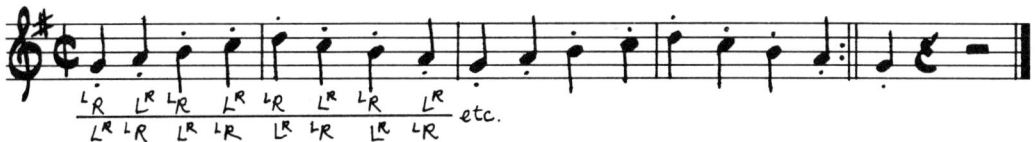

3. ♪ In contrast, *scissor* the five-note scale (hanging elbows, quiet upper arms). The dulcimer sings *legato* (smooth) instead of staccato. Which is preferable? It depends on the effect you're after. More about this later. Meanwhile, ginger-snap these tune excerpts:

42 (the *Petronella* pattern in *On the Road to Boston*; no positions shown)

Now play *On the Road to Boston* on the next page with ginger snaps.

1. Stand up and pretend you've got a bass fiddle. (I mean, put your arms around the thing!)
2. "Plunk" the melody on your imaginary bass fiddle while singing the tune with the syllables "dump, dump, dump" (not "dum, dum, dum;" see Fig. 4-22). This will help you hear, feel and play staccato. (Ginger snaps are shown by a dot either above or below the note.)

Striking Out and Winning!

dmp dmp ber–UMP d k dmp dmp dmp dmp dmp dmp dmp dmp dmp dmp dmp dmp, etc.

**Fig. 4-22 Singing and playing *On the Road to Boston*
(no positions shown)**

3. ♪ Now sing the A section with "dah." It's fine for a waltz, but this tune needs more brightness. Sing it again with "dump" (and occasional "DUH-kuhs"), then ginger snap it to match the short notes you hear in your head and listen to your dulcimer talk. Wow!

4. Play *On the Road to Boston* with ginger snaps—and rolls! Play the first two notes with your strong hand; ★ lift your weak hand after the second note so it breathes, and lift again afterwards.

Ex. 43 is another great ginger-snap exercise which will also prepare you for the next part of this lesson. Right-handers will cross hammers slightly between the first and second notes; ★ hold that stroke order for a bright sound!

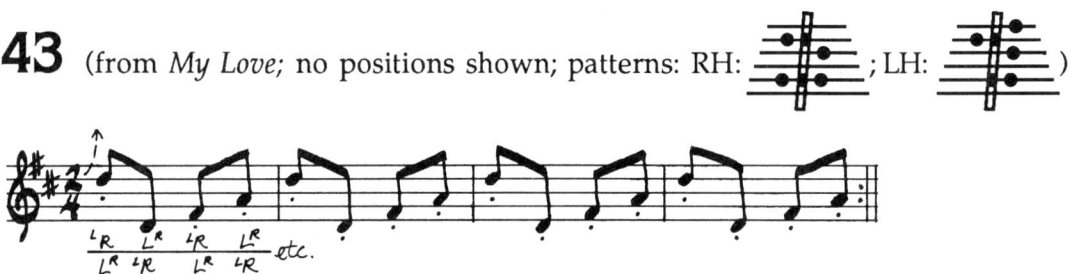

When to ginger snap

Ginger snap wherever you play two or more notes of the *long* note value. Look at Fig. 4-22 again: The long notes in *On the Road to Boston* are the eighth notes (♫). If you learned this tune in Lesson 2, you may have scissored and played it too fast! ★ Ginger snaps steady your tempo.

In *Successful Campaign*, the quarter note (♩) is the long note and the eighth note is the *short* note. Ginger snaps on the *quarter* notes:

**Fig. 4-23 Where to play ginger snaps in *Successful Campaign*
(no positions shown)**

Finally, strings of *short* notes always require *scissor* strokes, as in *Cincinnati, Fisher's Hornpipe* and *The Devil's Dream.*

➤ How about ginger snapping the quarter notes in *Soldier's Joy, Galopede* and *Pretty Little Dog?* You could, but I don't because they sound unequal in volume. (Your weak hand can't strike as loud *because* it's weaker!). ★ Strong-hand strokes give more punch in these tunes. The technique I use is often based on a gut feeling; you'll have to experiment. I hope this lesson and the tunes will help you decide.

Ginger snaps with rolls

A most unusual lunch. ★ When you bounce both arms to snap, you automatically lift and are ready to play a roll when the time comes.

This rhythmic chunk appears a lot in *Golden Slippers:*

44 (LH: all in II)

Dump berUMP bmp, dmp, berUMP bmp
(going up)   (going up)

Ex. 45 is the beginning of *My Love Is But a Lassie Yet* (a combination of Ex. 38 and 42).

45 (from *My Love Is But a Lassie Yet*)

Going up, up, up, up, up, ber-UMP
(going up)

Tunes to play/review:

Sing these tunes and plunk your "bass fiddle" before playing:

On the Road to Boston, page 133   *Golden Slippers,* page 128
My Love Is But a Lassie Yet, page 129   *Over the Waterfall,* page 133

Striking Out and Winning!

Lesson 12: Rolls 201

All the roll/single-stroke "sets" you've played have occurred on one course and on the "and" of beat 1 in a measure. Now for some deviations.

Rolls passing the bar (line, that is!)

Rolls may fall on the "and" of beat 2. When they do, they have a nice way of thrusting the melody (and any dancing feet) forward. All the rolls in *Successful Campaign* fall on the "and" of beat 2:

Fig. 4-24 M. A7—A1-3a of *Successful Campaign* showing rolls on the "and" of beat 2

I took out the repeat sign (:|) at the end of m. 8 because it looks like a stop sign (see the tune on page 130). ★ Continue to connect a roll into the single stroke following it, regardless of bar lines or repeat signs.

The single stroke following the first roll above (at "*") is on a different course. ★ Treat it as if you were playing all the notes on one course. Warm up to it with single strokes and lift below.

46 (LH: all in I; RH: the right hand will "circle" counterclockwise)

Going down, going down...

★ Any time you're unsure of how a roll should sound, play two single strokes in its place first. Sing "going up" instead of "berUMP."

To begin the repeat of the B section, reverse the tones and scoop:

47 (RH: all in I; LH: high note in II; the left hand will "circle" clockwise)

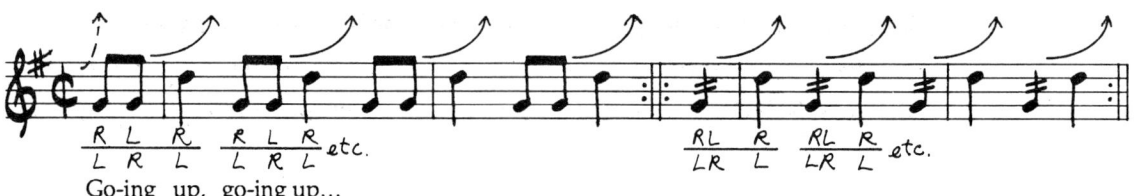

Go-ing up, go-ing up...

88

Batter Up!

The second "and"-of-beat-2 roll (at "†" in Fig. 4-24) is on one course. Speak and pat the words to this rhythm, then play it with single strokes before adding rolls:

48 (LH also in II)

Going up in a bal-loon, going up in a bal-loon...

Now sing, pat and play the A section of *Successful Campaign*. Turn to page 130 if you need help with stroke order.

Tunes to review:

Successful Campaign, page 130   *St. Anne's Reel*, page 132
Liberty, page 131

Optional:

Swinging on a Gate, page 147   *Gaspé Reel*, page 148
La Bastrangue, page 147

"Rapid-fire" rolls

Some tunes include a *series* of roll/single-stroke combinations. I call them "rapid-fire" rolls (underlined in both examples below):

d k dmp berUMP ber -uh k d k dmp d k dmp dmp dmp dmp dmp berUMP d k

a) from *Over the Waterfall*

dum d k d k dmp ber-UMP berUMP berUMP berUMP ber - uh k d k dmp dmp

b) from *Arkansas Traveller*

Fig. 4-25 "Rapid-fire" rolls shown with syllables for singing

You played rapid-fire rolls earlier in Ex. 35 and 36.

Striking Out and Winning!

Play single strokes before the actual rolls in *Over the Waterfall* first:

49

Going up, going up, going up, going up...

Now sing the B section, then play it (Fig. 4-25a; note ginger snaps in m. B3).

In *Arkansas Traveller*, some rapid-fire rolls require a larger reach:

50 (LH & RH: no positions shown; play in I on 15-14, or all in B on 12-11)

Up, going up, going up, going up...

Sing, then play the A section of *Arkansas Traveller*. What a handful!

If you're ever unsure of how to play a roll in this or similar situations,
★ warm up with single strokes in its place first.

Tune to play:

Arkansas Traveller, page 134

Tune to review:

Over the Waterfall, page 133

Lift?

Batter Up!

Downbeat rolls

Downbeat rolls, underlined in Fig. 4-26, usually occur on dotted notes (but I often play single strokes instead; see page 173):

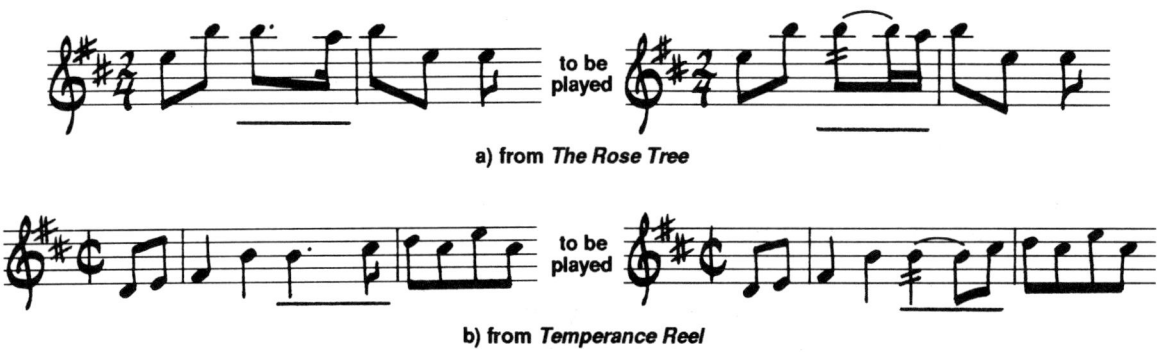

a) from *The Rose Tree*

b) from *Temperance Reel*

Fig. 4-26 Downbeat rolls in tunes

This sounds and feels more like a *three*-stroke roll.

Warm up with single strokes for feel before you try the rolls in Ex. 51.

★ Breathe to start. When your inactive arm bounces in the air for the first eighth notes in each measure, it automatically lifts to play the roll.

51 (from *The Rose Tree*; no positions shown; all in II for RH and LH)

Wa-ter-mel-on pits—yuck! Wa-ter-mel-on pits—yuck!...

(I know. Watermelons have *seeds*, but that word doesn't sound as good!)

Now play that portion of *The Rose Tree* as shown above to play the downbeat roll in its actual setting, then play the whole B section. *Voilà!*

Finish this lesson by single-stroking your way into a *four*-stroke roll. (Hint: Lift both hands in an arc to play the higher tone.)

52 (from *Old Grey Cat*)

Run! Run! Al - li - ga - tors!...   Run! Run! Alligators!...

Tune to play:

The Rose Tree, page 134

Striking Out and Winning!

Optional:

Temperance Reel, page 149
Old Grey Cat, page 148

Lesson 13: Syncopation

Syncopation places an accent on a normally unaccented part of the beat. In music, it looks like this:

Fig. 4-27 The syncopated rhythm

The stroke order for syncopation also comes from alternating strokes:

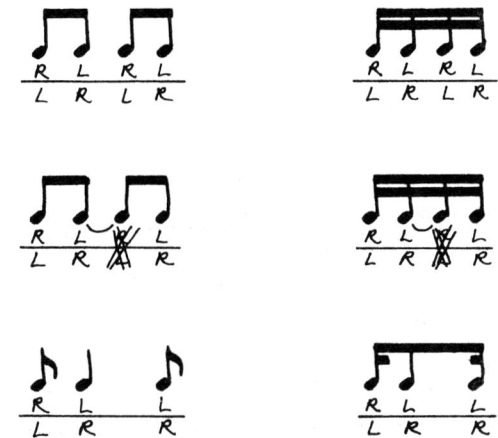

Fig. 4-28 The stroke order for syncopation

To play syncopation, you'll strike two *weak*-hand strokes in a row.
Play this rhythm on any course ★ with the stroke order shown:

53

92

Batter Up!

Was the stroking uncomfortable? It won't be if you ★ keep your arms moving in its spaces and lift your entire *strong* arm higher (shown by the dots over Ex. 54). Slant your upper arms forward and pat Ex. 54 with a ★ large, slow motion (à la football instant replay). ★ Swing your strong elbow up to lift that entire arm. Then your arms will be able to "sneeze" on the last two notes of each measure!

54

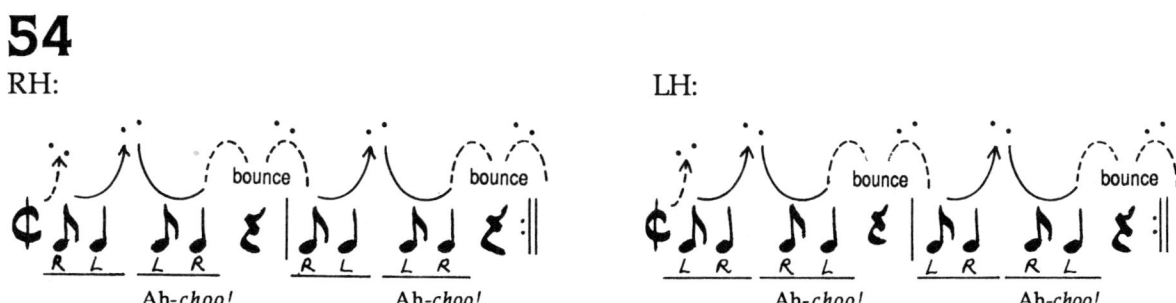

Gesundheit! Play it again and note the following:

1. Syncopation is made up of ★ two pairs of alternating strokes: RL, then LR (LH: LR, then RL).

2. Your *strong* hand rises higher between pairs of notes, but your weak hand lifts higher after both hands bounce together on the rest (𝄽). So both hands take turns lifting.

3. Feel each pair of strokes in two swoops, up then down (Fig. 4-29). Your hands will *seem* to rise and fall along the shape of a "J" *without actually doing it* (they'll go straight up). Righties "draw" it from the hook up; lefties "draw" it backwards:

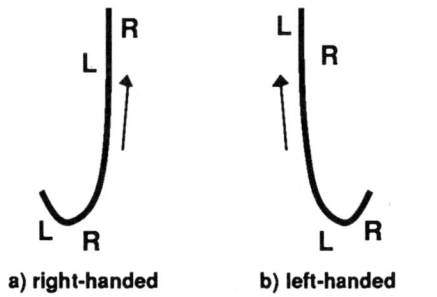

Fig. 4-29 The "J" motion in syncopation

Watch for the "J" in a mirror. (Right-handers will see a backwards reflection and left-handers will see a normal "J.")

Now play Ex. 54 slowly on any course to feel the arm motion, then gradually increase speed. To avoid angling the strong hammer up sharply as it lifts, ★ slant your upper arms forward so your strong elbow lifts your forearm and the hammer almost horizontally ★ without shrugging your shoulder (see *3D Sound,* page 75). Also, don't let your weak hammer sit at the bottom of the stroke path after its first strike or bend your wrist to lift it; the rhythm will be less solid. Nudge it up to follow your strong hand.

Striking Out and Winning!

No matter where the hammers fly in syncopation, ★ the stroke order is the same. That certainly goes for Ex. 55, whose syncopation occurs on two tones. Feel your hands travel in a ★ forward circle (instead of a "J") in each measure. Start slowly until your hands know what to do, then increase speed. Swing your arms a bit; go ahead and dance!

55 (from *Turkey in the Straw*)

Once you have a better feel for syncopation, substitute the sixteenth-note pairs (♫) above with rolls where shown.

Give the second measure some extra time alone. In it, you lift twice, first with your strong hand rising higher ("s" over arrow), then with your *weak* hand higher ("w" over arrow). Your hands will seem to travel along a "U!"

Another mini-lesson on stroke order

Wouldn't it be easier to *alternate* strokes in Ex. 55? ♪ Yes, but play it and listen to the results. Two different ways are shown below:

Fig. 4-30 Playing syncopation with alternating strokes
(LH: Reverse the strokes shown)

In the second stroke pattern, the lead transfers to the weak hand, trying hard to confuse you. In both cases, you hear a flat, dull sound. Give your dulcimer some life by lifting after the second note; alternating strokes won't allow lift to happen. That's another reason why I'm so insistent about stroke order. Never deprive your dulcimer of the chance to sing.*

Ex. 55 was the opening of the B section to *Turkey in the Straw*. But wait! The last two measures at the end of the A and B sections are identical and contain syncopation. Let's take this passage a few notes at a time:

---

* Still not convinced about organizing your stroke order? See page 175.

Batter Up!

1. Sing, finger and play Ex. 56a. ★ Breathe first to feel all four notes as *one* motion, then lift. ★ Lean into the *third* note of each pattern (at "—"). Your strong hand lifts first, and higher than your weak hand:

56a (all in I)

2. Add two more notes and ★ sneeze! ★ Begin each six-note chunk with your *strong* hand! (Your hands will seem to move in a "U.")

56b (all in I)

Ah-*choo!*   Ah-*choo!*...

3. Finish it off!

56c (the last two measures of each section to *Turkey in the Straw*; all in I)

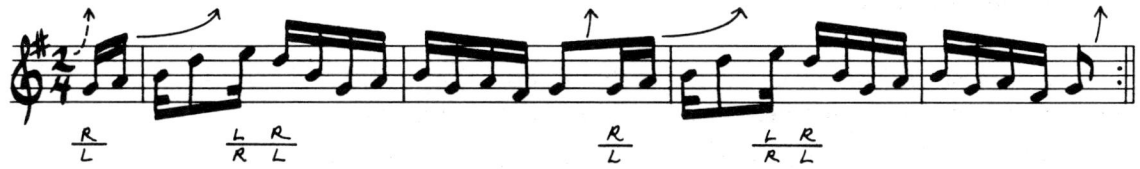

The stroke order may feel strange for a while and seem to be more effort than necessary, but if you want to make music that also makes a difference, it's worth the trouble.

Tune to play:

Turkey in the Straw, page 135

Optional:

Whiskey Before Breakfast, page 150

Striking Out and Winning!

JIGS

If reels run, then jigs jump! But my first jigs *didn't*. For a long time, I thought they were unpredictable stroke-wise, so I memorized which hand hit what where, exactly what I told you not to do for reels.

I finally got the hang of jigs while learning a lot of them for a big contra dance. (I hadda do *something!*) Now they're fun to play.

The next four lessons will introduce you to an array of tunes which tend to be a no-man's land in hammered dulcimerdom. I'm told the exercises make great warm-ups to the jigs you're bound to enjoy!

Lesson 14: Alternating strokes

Whenever you play a steady stream of eighth notes (♪) in a jig, alternate strokes. But note a difference here: With each beat divided into *three* eighth notes instead of the two or four you see in reels, *both* hands share the downbeat in a jig (Ex. 57). The hand striking the first note of each *measure* has the lead, so in a jig, the lead can be in either hand and still feel comfortable. (Two jigs in this book are "choreographed" left-handed. They seem to play easier that way.)

Say *tentacle* several times (think octopus!) and you'll hear what a jig sounds like. To play, breathe with both hands to begin, and speak and scissor in jig time at a moderate (not slow) tempo to prevent your hands from faltering or stopping between strikes:

57 (pronounce both "t's" in *tentacle*)

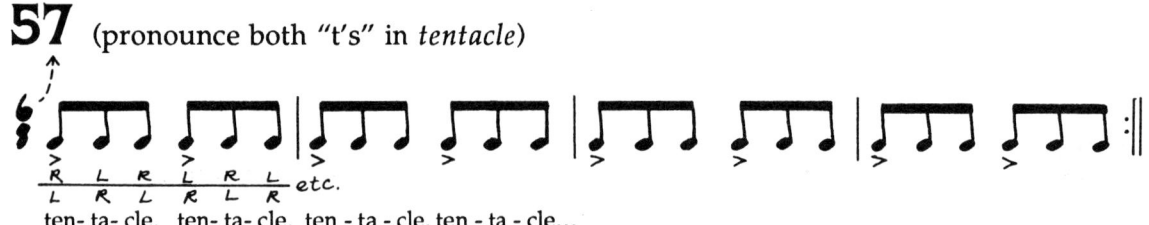

ten-ta-cle, ten-ta-cle, ten-ta-cle, ten-ta-cle...

Did that sound like a jig or a bunch of repeating notes? To make it jiggy, ★ accent each downbeat (on "ten-," at ">"). Here's how:

1. Play Ex. 57 *without* accents to get your arms moving. ★ Scissor your forearms and ★ relax *everything*. (Are your wrists loose enough to keep your hands level as described on page 18?)

2. Now ★ pretend to swat flies with one hammer then the other on each downbeat *or* ★ imagine your *wrists* are striking the strings instead of your hammers. You want to ★ loosen your wrists a little more to play an accent. ★ Don't stop to think about it; let it happen.

Why are accents important? They organize the notes to make sense; otherwise, jigs sound like a sea of unrelated tones. My students usually accent fine with the strong hand but hardly at all with the weak. (★ Relax that weak shoulder and arm!) ★ It'll take time to accent equally well with both hands (it certainly didn't happen for me overnight), so keep at it and one day you'll suddenly realize you've got it.

To sing alternating strokes in jigs use the syllables "DUH-kuh-duh DUH-kuh-duh" (*triple tonguing*). They're a tongue twister, but they'll help you hear short notes and accents clearly.

Now play a two-tone jig. The accents will shift from one tone to the other. (If you accent the low tones only, you'll play a waltz.)

58

When the accented notes are strong enough, they'll ring almost as if they were the *only* notes you played.

The following "topless" and "bottomless" sequences will give you practice with accents in jigs. (If you have a 15-14 dulcimer, you may start on low A at the lowest bridge mark of Ex. 59a and 60a to stretch it out.) Accent each downbeat and you'll hear a kind of *Mixolydian* scale ring out.

59a (all in I)

59b (all in I)

60a (all in I)

Striking Out and Winning!

60b (all in I; begin at the highest *bridge mark,* not the highest course)

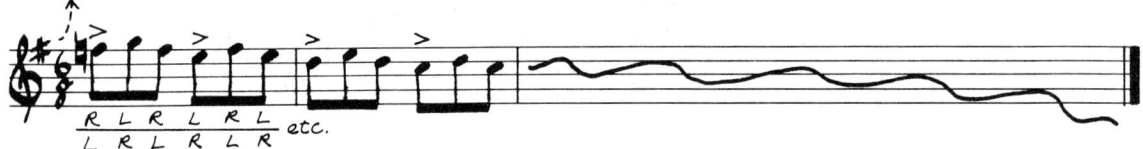

Part of a major scale can be heard in m. A2-4 of *Top of the Cork Road*.

Ex. 61 appears with positions for a right- *and* left-hand lead. ★ Finger the patterns and play both. The visual patterns change with the lead. When you accent each beat, you'll hear the octave tones ring through.

61
RH: LH:

★ Don't worry about accents in the early learning stages when you're struggling for notes, but do it once your hands know where to go. Then keep it up. Accents will become easier and more automatic the more comfortable you become with the jigs you know.

Ex. 62a and b look easy enough, but they will confuse your hands if you're tense or tentative! ★ Start at an easy tempo until your hands know what to do, then increase speed. Accents will seem to occur naturally, but help them along with a little extra oomph from your arms.

62a (all in I)

62b (all in I)

Add Ex. 62a and b together and you get Ex. 62c. Play it 4-2-1. I find Ex. 62c easier than either of its parts and hope you will, too:

62c (from *The Irish Washerwoman*; LH: lowest tones may be played in B)

Why not play Ex. 62c RLLRLL (LRRLRR)? ♩ Try it:

Fig. 4-31 Ex. 62c without alternating strokes

It may sound okay at a slow tempo, but ♩ now play it at *dance* tempo. The notes sound uneven and choppy because your weak arm muscles freeze up to play two notes in a row fast enough. Alternating strokes let you play tension-free. (★ Relax those shoulders and elbows!)

Tunes to Play:

The Irish Washerwoman, page 135
Tobin's Favorite, page 136

Lesson 15: Quick, two-note pick-ups

So those two-note pick-ups at the beginning of each section in *The Irish Washerwoman* were giving you trouble, huh? (I thought they might.) The solution: Play the pickups alone in Ex. 63a and b. ★ Lift both hands before playing, then ★ feel the striking of each three-note chunk in one motion. ★ Bounce both hands on the rest to lift and play again:

63a (RH and LH: all in I)

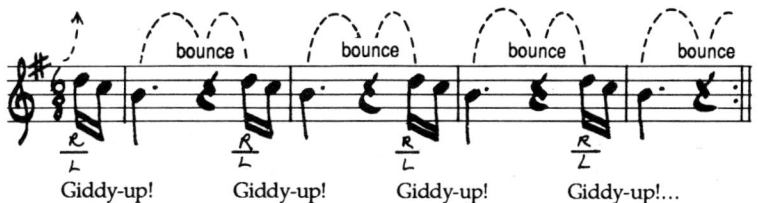

(LH: You could strike the first note in II, but it's trickier and less accurate.)

Striking Out and Winning!

63b (all in II)

If your hands become confused, ★ lift your weak hand a little higher.

Add three more notes to each exercise for two six-note "phrases." Sing the exercises below, then ★ sing and play at a moderate (not slow) speed until your hands know when to breathe and where the notes are ("hiccup" at each arrow). ★ Lift your weak hand a little higher each time it breathes. This may feel awkward at first but it does great things for the music.

64a (all in I; ★ arc both hands as they lift)

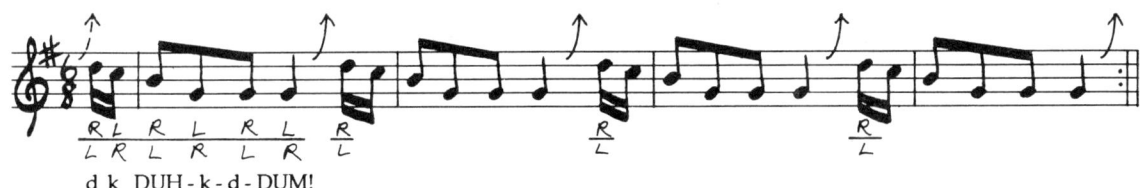

64b (all in II)

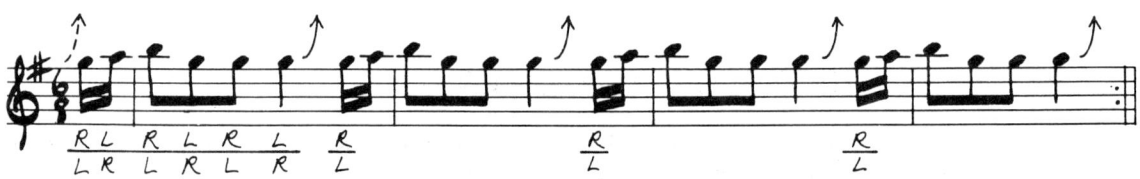

Ex. 64c is a combination of 64a and b inspired by the end of the A section in *The Irish Washerwoman*. ★ Know where your hammers are headed beforehand and arc both hands over the treble bridge.

64c

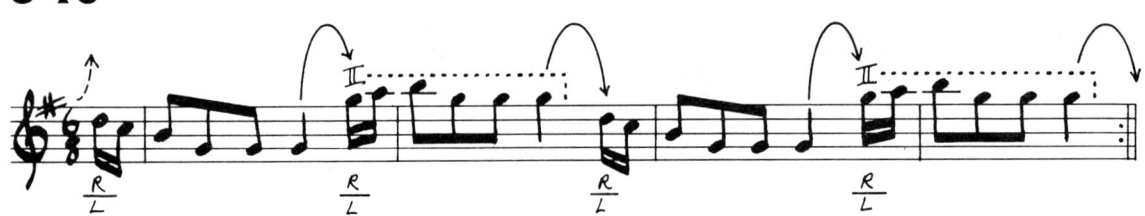

Batter Up!

Tune to review:

The Irish Washerwoman, page 135

Optional:

Top of the Cork Road, page 150   *Shandon Bells,* page 151
Tenpenny Bit, page 151   *Maggie Brown's Favorite Jig,* page 152

Another mini-lesson on shifting positions

Given the stroke order in Ex. 65, in what position(s) would you play it?

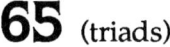

I'd play it all in first position. If you play it in two positions...

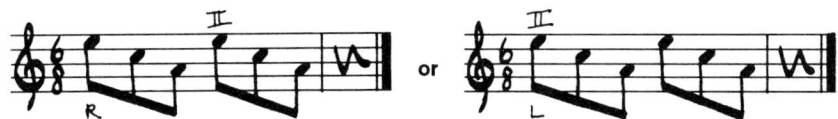

Fig. 4-32 Two not-so-great ways to play Ex. 65

...your hands will have to hunt for two patterns and could lose their sense of direction by shifting positions all the time. ★ Try to play similar melodic patterns with like visual patterns when possible.

Did she say *breathe* or *kiss*?

Striking Out and Winning!

Lesson 16: The most common rhythm in jigs

The stroke order for the most common jig rhythm comes from notes of equal value the same way you determine stroking in reels:

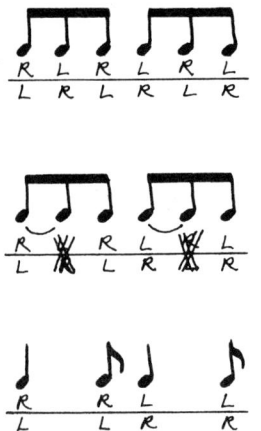

Fig. 4-33 Stroking the most common jig rhythm

This rhythm sounds like you're skipping down the street; in fact, the stroking (two rights and two lefts or vice versa) lets your hands skip on the strings like your feet would.

Speak and pat *Humpty Dumpty* in the rhythm of that poem and you'll know what the jig rhythm sounds like:

66

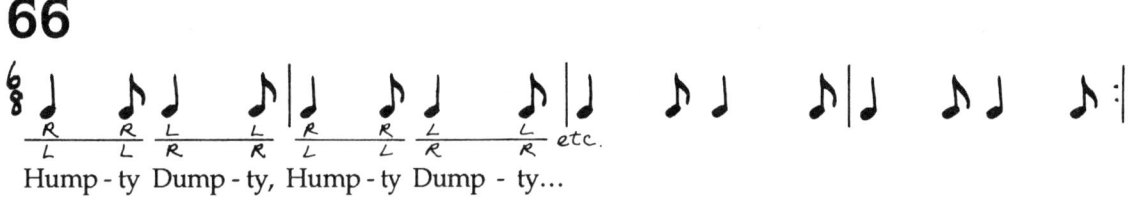

Hump - ty Dump - ty, Hump - ty Dump - ty...

You can look at and play the notes of this rhythm in pairs (R R L L; I call them *double strokes*); however, just like reels, you may have an easier time if you start with a ★ pick-up and group the notes in pairs of alternating strokes: R L L R (L R R L). Say *Tibet* and play the rhythm this way (your *weak* hand plays the pick-up):

67

Ti - bet,   Ti - bet,   Ti - bet,   Ti - bet,...

You're still playing double strokes, but now you're playing from a dancer's point of view. (Remember, the foot must go up!)

Batter Up!

What makes this rhythm talk as well as easy to play is—you guessed it—★ lift. Without lift, single jigs sound stiff and unrhythmic.

Refer to that part of Ex. 68 corresponding to your lead and pat *Tibet* eight times (★ slant your upper arms forward) in slow motion to see and feel lift in action. The dots over the arrows show which hand lifts higher. ★ Lift the higher hand almost as high as your shoulder and the lower hand ★ an inch or two below it. Feel the spaces in this rhythm!

68 (Note: Strike the pick-up with the *weak* hand)

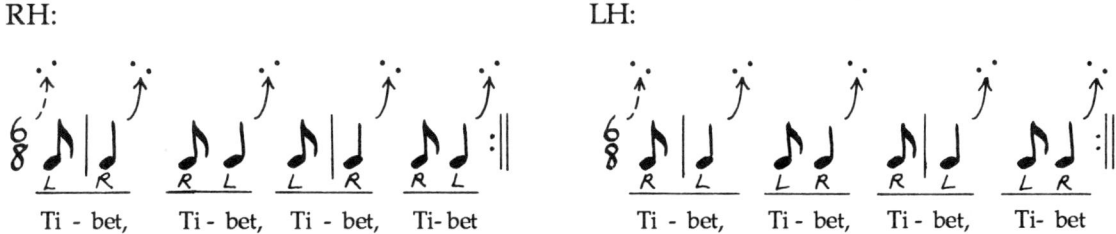

Note that ★ your hands took turns alternately as the higher hand. If you did it right, your hands would have seemed to travel along a ★ "U" (Fig. 4-34a), without actually doing it, similar to the "J" in syncopation:

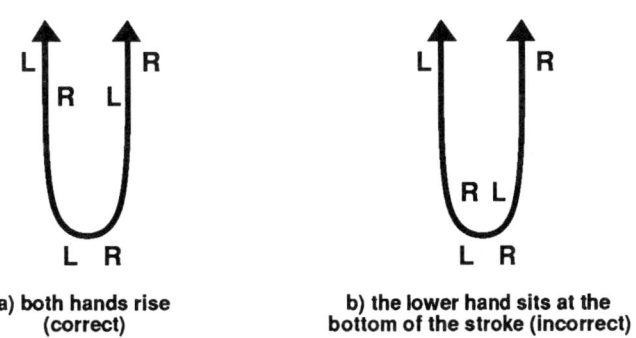

a) both hands rise (correct)

b) the lower hand sits at the bottom of the stroke (incorrect)

Fig. 4-34 The "U" motion of the jig rhythm

This rhythm takes ★ whole-arm lift in *both* arms for an easy motion to keep your hammers level so your dulcimer can sing 3D (see *3D Sound*, page 75). It'll happen easily as long as your upper arms slant forward. Don't lift the lower hand by bending your wrist; it'll sit at the bottom of the stroke path and make all the eighth notes (♪) sound less distinct and rhythmic (Fig. 4-34b).

Speak and pat *Tibet* in Ex. 68 *ad infinitum* in slow motion with whole-arm lift, and then increase speed gradually to dance tempo. ★ Feel your elbows "rock" from side to side (don't shrug your shoulders). You'll lift less as you pat faster, but ★ both elbows must continue lifting.

Now play Ex. 68 up to tempo on any course on your dulcimer. Don't cheat on your arm motion; ★ your hammers can't dance without it!

It's time to skip your hammers all over first position on your dulcimer. Skip on first-position D in Ex. 69 for eight beats, then skip all the way up and down first position. (Note: For any jig exercise or tune beginning

Striking Out and Winning!

on the downbeat with a quarter note— ♩ —★ let your strong hand breathe alone; *do not breathe with both hammers first.* Lift your weak hand after the downbeat is struck.)

69 (play m. 1 at least four times)

Hump-ty Dump-ty, Hump- ty Dump-ty...

To sing a jig, I use the syllables "dah-DUMP dah-DUMP dah-DUMP."
Your hands will ★ travel in forward circles in Ex. 70. ★ Play only the first measure several times slowly until your hands know what to do and can increase speed, then take this two-note "jig" up and down the dulcimer as far as you can. It'll feel like you're climbing up and down a ladder:

70 (all in I; up: from *Smash the Windows*; down: from *Kitty McGee*)

When you reverse the tone order, your hands circle backwards:

71 (all in I; up: who knows?! down: from *Smash the Windows*)

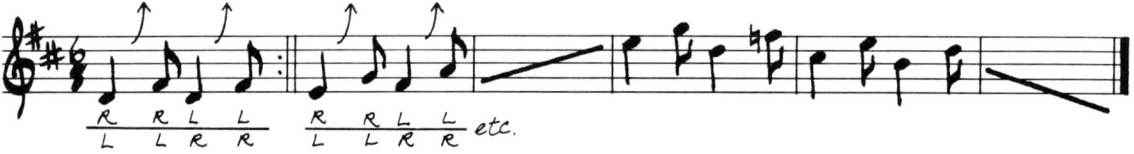

Last of all, jig up and down a five-note scale. Rock those arms!

72 (all in I; end on the first note)

104

Batter Up!

I can guess what you're thinking: "Isn't it easier to alternate strokes in the last three exercises?" ♩ Play Ex. 72 that way (your hands will gallop rather than skip), and listen to the *spirit* of your playing. Flat and blah! As I said for reels, ★ the stroke order comes from the rhythm, and the *music* comes from movement in the spaces of the rhythm (*lift!*). ★ Double strokes *do* feel strange at first, but they are exactly what give jigs their lilt and joy. Remember, you're not playing notes; ★ you're making music!

I close this lesson with some "real-life" exercises combining single and double-jig rhythms. ★ Feel the motion of each exercise.

73 (from *Kitty McGee*; no positions shown; play 4-2-1; 1st half=*Petronella* pattern; 2nd half all in II)

dah- DUMP duh-DUH- k - d-DUMP duh-DUH- k- d...

74 (from *Tenpenny Bit;* same stroke order as Ex. 73; lift and arc as you shift!)

dah- DUMP-duh-DUH- k - d DUMP duh-DUH- k - d...

Notice that the same hand struck the first note of each measure. That's the beauty of double strokes. (Just like reels, if you goof, you can jump back into the tune in the next beat or measure.) If your lead switches hands, you may be alternating the first two notes of a measure somewhere.

75 (from *The Quaker's Wife;* all in II; LH: low tone in I)

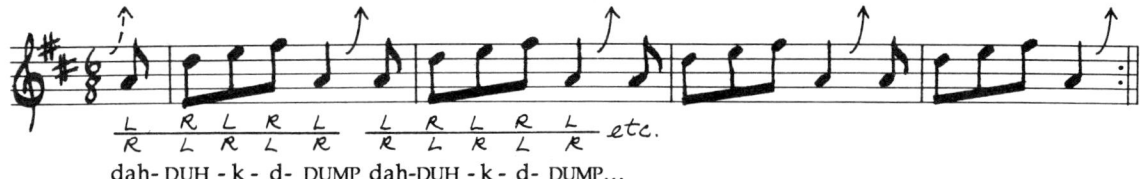

dah- DUH - k - d- DUMP dah-DUH - k - d- DUMP...

Play Ex. 75 with your weak hand in the lead, too.

Striking Out and Winning!

Watch the stroking on this next one!

76 (from *Swallowtail Jig*; all in II; scissors to a backwards-circle motion)

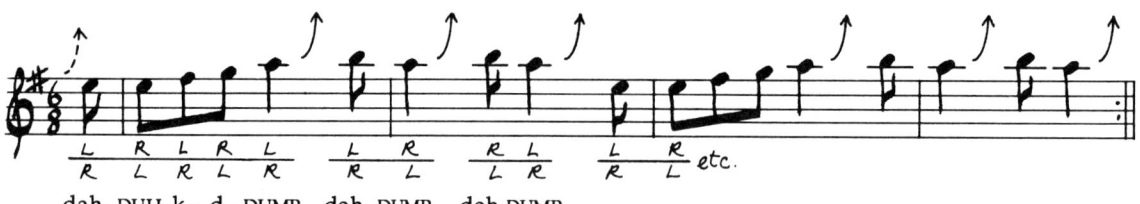

dah- DUH-k - d- DUMP   dah-DUMP   dah-DUMP...

If you're unsure about the backwards circles, start again and tack more eighth/quarter pairs on the end of the first phrase.

Ex. 77 isn't from a tune, but it'll prepare you for just about anything jiggy! Before you play it, sing and pat the rhythm with lift so your ears and hands know what to expect, then finger the pattern of each measure (there are two) to teach your eyes what to look for.

77 (RH: up on 5/3, down on 4/4; LH: up on 4/4, down on 5/3)

Tunes to play:

Kitty McGee, page 136   *Swallowtail Jig,* page 138
Smash the Windows, page 137

Optional:

The Quaker's Wife, page 153   *When Daylight Shines,* page 154
Old Rosin the Beau, page 153   *Black Joke,* page 154

Play any rolls as single strokes with the hand shown.

Lift at last!

Lesson 17: Rolls

Rolls in jigs usually fall on the last eighth note (♪) of a measure. ★ Sing and play them as you did for reels (two strokes, "berUMP," and connect into the next note).

★ Two-stroke rolls usually fall at the end of an A or B section. ★ Pat Ex. 78 before playing it, and watch the stroke order! ★ The weak hand normally lifts higher after a roll, but here your *strong* hand lifts higher to play the downbeat ("-bet") of the next *Tibet*; (dots over arrows). You'll alternate strokes for a moment. If your weak hand lifts higher, the stroke order may reverse and cause position-shift confusion in a tune.

78 (play on any course)

Before you go on, play the other part of Ex. 78 with your weak hand leading in each measure, but ★ do not reverse the rolls' strokes. ★ Lift your weak hand higher as preparation and you'll do fine.

Now try this tune excerpt. ★ I recommend singing and patting it first.

79 (from *Kitty McGee*)

As I said in Lesson 9, *one*-stroke rolls (or multiple-bounce strokes) are possible and effective in jigs. That's because eighth notes take up less time space in jigs than in reels. I play them mostly on one-note pick-ups. When my strong hand leads, my weak hand rolls, and vice versa. One-

Striking Out and Winning!

stroke rolls have more of a knack for helping the dancer's foot go up with a new phrase or section in the dance-step pattern.

Ex. 80 will give you the feel of one-stroke rolls in jigs. ★ Play the first four notes (two *Tibets*) at least four times to get your lift going, then add a one-stroke roll every fourth, then every second *Tibet*. ★ Point your weak thumb (see page 78) and ★ lean into each roll for vigorous bounces.

80 (play on any course)

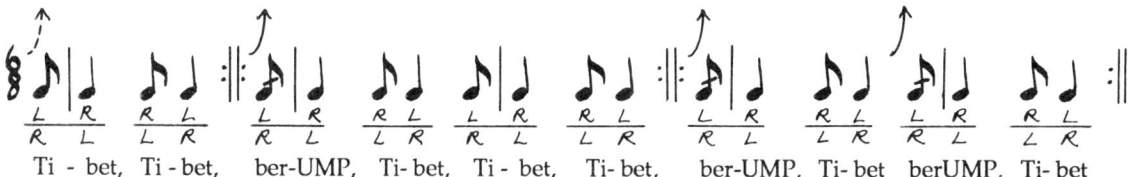

You just played the same rhythm as Ex. 78. Was it easier to play? I hope so! That's because the one-stroke roll lets your elbows continue rocking. (If you missed this, play it again and check your lift in a mirror.)

Play Ex. 80 again with the opposite stroke order so your strong hand rolls this time. (Your weak hand takes the lead.) To me, this feels awkward; my weak hand does it with more zing! (Don't be surprised if yours does, too!) When your strong hand leads in a tune, your weak hand plays any one-stroke rolls occuring on pick-ups.

★ Play Ex. 81 without rolls first for patterns and strokes. ★ Breathe with both hands to start so the roll connects into the downbeat smoothly.

81 (from *Kitty McGee*; no positions shown; pattern=*Petronella*)

Now go back to Ex. 79 and play it with one-stroke rolls wherever two-stroke rolls occur (roll with your strong hand). ♪ How does it feel to you?

All rolls in the jigs in this book appear as one-stroke rolls. (You *can* play one-stroke rolls anywhere, but my own rule of thumb is to play one-stroke rolls on pick-ups and two-stroke rolls at the end of a section or tune. As you will....) Only the most obvious places are shown. See the *Patterns, etc.* paragraphs with each jig for other possibilities. For jigs beyond this book, ★ roll with discretion. (When in doubt, leave it out!)

Tune to review:

Kitty McGee, page 136

HORNPIPES

If reels run and jigs jump, then may we assume hornpipes hop?!

The hornpipe was a primitive European instrument. During the 16th to 19th centuries, the word became associated with a type of dance and its accompanying music.

While the hornpipe's chief characteristic is a *dotted rhythm*,* many hornpipes are written and played as reels. Why? They can be written faster without the dots. And as hornpipes increase in tempo, dotted rhythms become impossible to play.

Lesson 18: The dotted rhythm

Here is the stroke order for the dotted rhythm:

Fig. 4-35 Stroking the dotted rhythm

It's scissor strokes, but with a twist: ★ Your weak hand "limps" to dot the rhythm. To make the "dot" happen, ★ know what this rhythm sounds like (it's a little more regimented than the skipping rhythm in a jig), then ★ bounce your strong hand higher than your weak hand (don't let your weak wrist take over the playing action).

You can turn any reel into a hornpipe by playing it slower to dot the rhythm. Play a "dotted" version of Ex. 4, begun in Ex. 82:

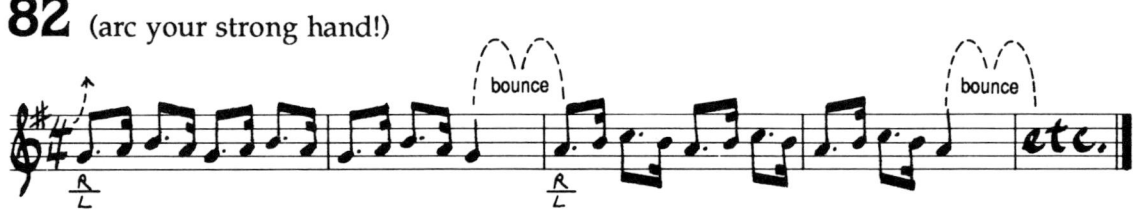

---

* Dulcimer players often call the dotted rhythm *syncopation*, but that's not what this is! (See Lesson 13, page 92.) Prevent language barriers and choose your words carefully!

Striking Out and Winning!

➤ Don't dot a reel's rhythm during the learning stage if you intend to play it up to tempo *as a reel*. This is another form of the "stop-and-search" method (page 13). Scissor strokes may be difficult to smooth out once you've taught yourself to dot the rhythm. Knowing where you're going ahead of time will help you scissor smoothly.

The singing syllables for a hornpipe are ★ "DUCK-uh-duck-uh-DUM," rather than "DUH-kuh-duh-kuh-DUM." "DUCK" dots the rhythm naturally, while its short sound brightens the rhythm. (My friends on page 73 must really be playing a hornpipe!) In addition, ★ everything I've said about lifting and breathing in reels applies to hornpipes, too.

In Ex. 83, ★ arc your strong hand up to strike the highest course:

83 (from *Keel Row*; the *weak* hand strikes the highest note; LH: all in I)

(Lefties: You could play the first note in II *if* you didn't have to worry about where the rest of the tune would wander on the strings!)

Watch the stroking of Ex. 84. (Playing Ex. 27 with a dotted rhythm first is a good warmup.) Because it begins on the downbeat, ★ lift both hands after the first note is struck (see page 66 at "➤").

84 (a dotted "going up" from *Keel Row*)

85 (from *The Boys of Bluehill*; finger the pattern first; "hiccup" at arrows; LH: highest note in II)

Tune to play:

Keel Row, page 138

Lesson: 19: Triplets

Some hornpipes include an occasional beat of triplets. This poses a problem: One beat of triplets switches the lead to your weak hand on the next beat. To hold the lead in your strong hand, ★ double-stroke (R-R or L-L) the preceding *or* following dotted beat, as if you were playing a jig. (Sing hornpipes with the same syllables as jigs.)

Double-stroke *before* the triplet in Ex. 86. ★ Pat its rhythm before playing. ★ Feel the space between the double strokes by lifting both hands after each dotted note (at arrow). ★ Your weak hand will rise higher.

86 (from *The Boys of Bluehill*; no positions shown; LH: 1st 3 notes in I; arc both hands to shift; RH: lowest note only in I)

In Ex. 87, double-stroke the dotted rhythm *after* the triplet. ★ Pat the rhythm with lift on your lap, then play it down your dulcimer as far as you can. Feel ★ your *strong* hand rise higher and arc backwards prior to playing each triplet. (Note: This exercise consists of five-note chunks of alternating strokes, except for the first chunk, which has four.)

87 (from *The Boys of Bluehill;* all in II)

♪ Now *alternate* strokes all the way through Ex. 87. What do you hear? (I hear a "flat" sound.) How do you feel? (I feel frozen!)

Tune to play:

The Boys of Bluehill, page 139

Reels you can play as hornpipes (very optional!):

(Note: I have yet to hear anyone play these tunes as hornpipes.)

Cincinnati, page 127   *The Breakdown,* page 141
Fisher's Hornpipe, page 140   *College Hornpipe,* page 146

Learn each tune as a reel with scissor strokes first.

Striking Out and Winning!

SPECIAL EFFECTS WITH MULTIPLE-BOUNCE STROKES

At various points in this chapter, you discovered how rolls can add zing to dance tunes. The multiple-bounce stroke need not be limited to rolls only. I use them to play ascending and descending triplets, which serve as ornaments in Irish jigs and reels, although I also play them in French-Canadian and Southern dance tunes for a little extra zing.

a) descending (on the downbeat)   b) ascending (on a pick-up)*

Fig. 4-36 Two examples of triplets

❥ If you play a triplet with three single strokes, you'll shift the lead to your weak hand, tense up, and possibly lag behind at your local jam session or dance band. Throwing in a multiple-bounce stroke or two keeps the lead in your strong hand and adds a fun kind of frenzy to the music. And beyond triplets, I've found other ways to fit multiple-bounce strokes into tunes that drive listeners wild! So while these last two lessons will teach you an exciting technique, they should also open doors to many more useful possibilities limited only by your imagination.

Lesson 20: Descending triplets

The descending triplet occurs on a downbeat. To play it, slide your strong hammer down the first two courses with a multiple-bounce stroke, then strike a single stroke on the last note with your weak hand. (If you have the companion cassettes to this book, listen to the descending triplets in *Swallowtail Reel* now so you know what you'll be shooting for.)

First, your strong hand alone. Play single strokes on first-position C at a somewhat fast tempo (Ex. 88a). ★ Bounce the hammer with your forearm, not your wrist; hand height is essential. At the same time, ★ let go of your shoulder and elbow; a relaxed arm makes this technique easier. Now point your thumb and play multiple-bounce strokes at the same tempo (soften the arm stroke). Then ★ "brush" the multiple-bounce stroke down to include the course below ★ without slowing down. Your strong hand will rise and fall in a ★ vertical hot-dog shape. You'll hear the reverse of a dotted rhythm in a "buzzing" version of a *Scotch snap*† (it sounds like the word "pickles"). Don't try to make both tones sound equal in length; it won't happen.

---

* Fig. 4-36b shows triplets followed by an extra note; I'll explain why in Lesson 21.

† The Scotch snap is usually found in a slow Scottish tune called a *strathspey* and is really played with alternating single strokes (RH: R̲L; LH: L̲R).

88a

Now scissor first-position C and the A below it in Ex. 88b (single strokes). It has twice as many notes as Ex. 88a, so play them twice as fast. Establish hand height, then point your thumb and brush every fourth, then every second pair of notes. ★ Keep scissoring, and don't slow down!

88b

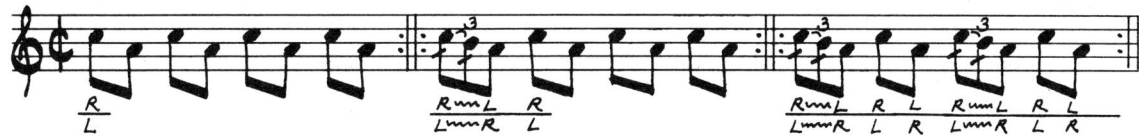

★ Only your strong thumb points during descending triplets. If your weak thumb points, too, it'll bounce more than once, making the triplet muddy. ★ Keep your weak thumb (and shoulder and elbow) loose. It'll be a challenge, but it *can* be done! Play Ex. 88b again with this in mind.

Now add descending triplets to the triads in *Swallowtail Reel*. Scissor single strokes first for a while.

88c (triads; RH and LH: all in I)

★ Omit the middle note in a descending triplet when you're first learning a tune. Include it when you can play the tune well. Its motion feels different enough that it may confuse your hands.

Tunes to play:

Swallowtail Reel, page 140

Optional:

Drowsy Maggie, page 155

Striking Out and Winning!

Lesson 21: Ascending pick-up triplets

Many jigs and reels with pick-ups open with an ascending triplet (see Fig. 4-36b). It's really a four-note figure, including the next downbeat note.

The ascending triplet is a variation of "going up" in Ex. 18d (Lesson 3) and 36 (Lesson 9). Park your fingers on A, B and D in second position. The pattern spans four courses. In this section, you'll understand why I chose those courses: to eventually include the C#!

Say "going up" as you play the A-B-D pattern with single strokes in Ex. 89. Scoop both hands in between, and ★ lift your weak hand a little higher. Then play multiple-bounce strokes on "going" (a two-tone "roll"). To catch the third course, ★ slide your weak hammer up as it scoops:

89 (all in II; no positions shown)

★ As long as both hands breathe and scoop, you should feel no change in lift going from single strokes to ascending triplets. That goes for the sound of the rhythm, too. Many players often prevent the weak hand from bouncing for its full amount of time space, throwing off the rhythm. Also, *do not* slide both hammers up the courses together; ★ your hands must scissor in turn. Starting with single strokes, saying "going up" and scissoring will help balance your strokes out in either case.

Ease your way into ascending triplets for these tune excerpts:

90 (from *Fisher's Hornpipe*; no positions shown; triplet + *Petronella* pattern)

Ex. 91 is similar in feel to quick, two-note pick-ups in jigs (see page 99).

91 (from *Larry O'Gaff*; no positions shown; first three notes only in II)

Batter Up!

By the way, if the triplet proves difficult at first, you can always "fake it" by playing a two-tone "roll." Above all, the most important thing is to ★ play the triplet in rhythm; don't slow down!

Finally, for extra credit: Although *Flowers of Edinburgh* doesn't show it, you could begin each phrase of the A section with a descending *and* ascending triplet back-to-back! In this case, ★ when a downbeat note follows the descending triplet, your weak hammer must slide down the second and third notes, just as for the ascending triplet. ★ Feel your body sway away, then towards the dulcimer as you play this exercise.

92 (all in I)

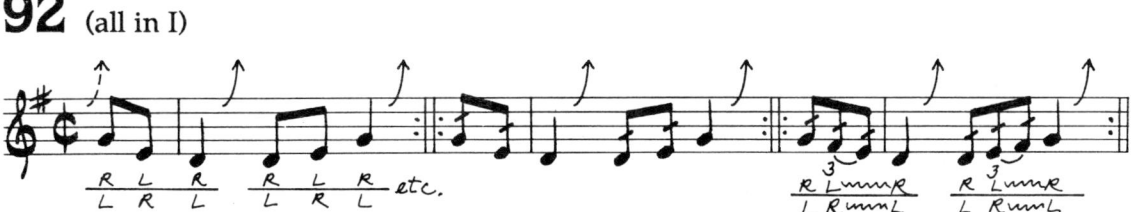

Tunes to play:

Fisher's Hornpipe, page 140
The Breakdown, page 141

Optional:

Flowers of Edinburgh, page 156
Larry O'Gaff, page 156

Other tunes to which you may add ascending triplets

Whenever a tune begins with what I call a "rising fourth" interval...

Fig. 4-37 Some examples of "rising fourth" intervals

...add some zing with triplets. Try it in these tunes:

Arkansas Traveller, page 134   *Reel de Montréal*, page 145
The Devil's Dream, page 143   *Temperance Reel*, page 149
Hull's Victory, page 143 (pick-up to B section, but maybe to A, too!)
Swinging on a Gate, page 147 (add to the pick-up of each section)

And now:

You're on your own! Have fun!

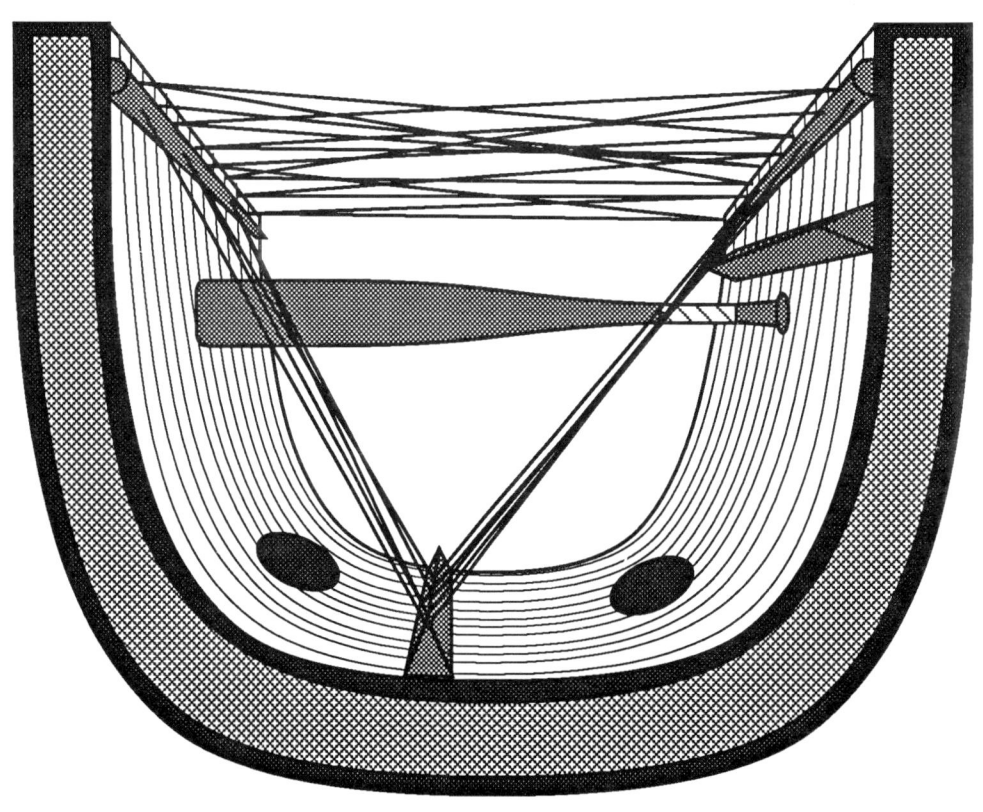

Whoops! Too tight!

Time Out! Tuning and Maintenance

Tuning the dulcimer

The easiest way to tune is with an electronic tuner; however, tuning can be faster *and* sweeter-sounding when done by ear. (I tune 68 strings in 10-15 minutes.) Whatever method you use is fine, as long as you *do* it!

Before you begin, practice plucking the strings in one course s-l-o-w-l-y with your fingernail or a guitar pick (1-2 seconds apart) so you can hear each one separately to tune them. The nail or pick "brakes" against the *next* string before plucking it. Whenever you pluck only the top or middle string of a course, ★ always run the nail or pick into the next string until the ringing string is tuned. Don't remove it, as it may touch the ringing string and stop it. (★ *Never* tune a string you can't hear.)

If you want to tune by ear, here is the method I use:

1. Place your fingers on steps 1, 3, 5 & 8 of the treble D major scale (Fig. 5-1a). These are the *chord tones*. You'll tune these first (in the order 1, 5, 3 & 8; pluck them now) and then fill in the rest of the scale.

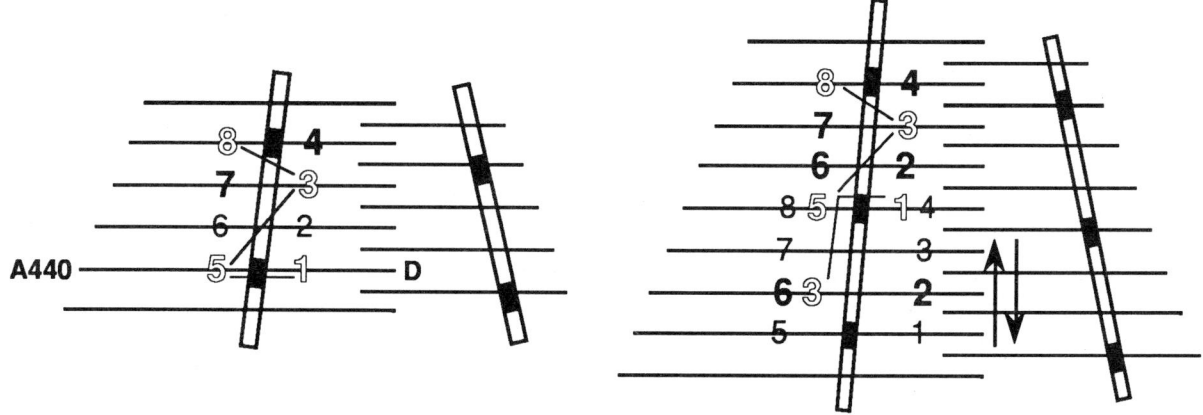

a) chord tones of the major scale b) finishing the first scale and tuning the second

Fig. 5-1 Tuning the treble strings

2. Tune step #5 to A440 with a tuning fork *while the fork vibrates*. (Don't use a pitch pipe; its tones fluctuate with heat and humidity.) Tuning by ear depends on ★ constant comparison to a "reference frequency." Next, pluck the tuned string and its neighboring string and tune the latter *while both vibrate*. For dulcimers with three strings per course, pluck all three strings slowly, then tune the third while they ring; if four strings per course, ditto as for three!

3. You've tuned 5 *and* 1. ➡ Pluck 1, 5 & 3, and tune 3 so it "grins." (Play D, A and F♯ on a tuned piano to see what I mean.)

4. Pluck 1, 5, 3 & 8, and tune 8. Check 8 to 1 (the octave).

5. You've now tuned 1 & 5, 7 & 4 and 3 & 8. To tune 2 & 6 (Fig. 5-1b), go up to the *next* bridge mark (G major; 4 & 8 are now 1 & 5). *In the new key*, pluck 1 & 5, and then go *down* to pluck and tune 3. Check this course by plucking 3-2-1-2-3 (*Mary Had a Little Lamb*) in the *old* key. If 2 sounds fine going both down *and* up, you've finished the D major scale. If not, make adjustments.

Striking Out and Winning!

6. Repeat from "➡" for G and C major.

7. To tune A major on 15-14 dulcimers, pluck second-position A440 again and tune the octave in first position. Then tune from "➡."

8. Tune the first-position side of the top course to its second-position unison, and the bottom course in first position with its octave in second position.

9. The bass strings: You've already tuned the upper half of each bass scale. To tune each lower half, pluck first-position G (12-11) or D (15-14). Tune its bass octave. Pluck 1 & 5, then tune 3 (grin!). Tune 2 by plucking 3-2-1-2-3. Tune 4 to *Here Comes the Bride* or from its first-position octave in the next key above.

A piano technician can show you the finer details of tuning, such as listening for "beats." Tuning by ear takes practice, but the more you do it, the less time it'll take.

Other tuning tips

1. If your dulcimer is a half- to whole-tone flat, tune it a little higher than A440. (In hot weather it may be sharp; tune it a little lower.) If you're lucky, it'll readjust to the correct pitch level by the time you've finished. If not, tune it again. (Sorry!)

2. Very flat dulcimers (an interval of a third or more) will require two or three tunings. Tune one string almost to pitch. How far did you turn the pin? A quarter turn? An eighth of a turn? Turn the remaining pins that much, then tune in earnest.

3. If the strings are very old and flat, turn the pins in small spurts instead of in one sweep. A lot of tension suddenly applied may break a string. (I speak from experience!)

4. Old metal bridge caps may grab the treble strings and stretch them unequally over the bridge, throwing off the fifth interval. To correct the interval, a) lift the string with both index fingers near the treble bridge and tune again, or b) tune both sides separately, starting with the section of string farthest from the tuning pin.

Keeping your dulcimer in tune

The best way to keep any stringed instrument in tune is to *play it!* Not just occasionally, but every day.

Humidity, dampness, sudden temperature changes and draughts can alter the tuning of some strings. I often find that all the strings I tuned during an outdoor summer concert are out of tune the next day at home.

If the tuning pins turn very easily, or slip like violin pegs, check the pins; they may need replacing. If there are cracks in the pinblocks around the pins, the pinblocks may need replacing. (Hope not!)

If the treble bridge needs adjusting

You may never have to do this, but if you do and you're chicken, ask your builder or a knowledgeable dulcimer player to adjust it for you.

As the strings on a new dulcimer stretch, they may pull part or all of the treble bridge along with them, throwing off the fifth interval. (No, the bridge isn't glued to the soundboard.) You'll know the bridge is off if you've tuned until the cows come home and all or part of certain scales or intervals still sound "out."

To move the treble bridge, use an unsharpened pencil with an eraser or a piece of dowel the same length and thickness, and a wider (at least an inch thick), squarish piece of wood for a "whacker."

If the fifth is too large, move the bridge to the right; if it's too small, move it to the left. Set the eraser end of the pencil or dowel against the bridge in the problem area *near the soundboard*. Tap the other end firmly with the whacker to move the bridge *a little*, then check the fifth on that course and its immediate neighbors. Sometimes moving the bridge in one area throws off a fifth interval elsewhere.

Do not loosen the treble strings to move the bridge! This only worsens the problem and takes longer to fix.

Replacing a broken string

Well, it's happened. Now what? (When I break a string at a contra dance, the caller *always* asks if anyone knows any good jokes!)

Here is everything I wished I'd known when I broke my first string.* First, prepare yourself for the unblessed event with the following:

- A tuning wrench (a gooseneck wrench does the job faster *if* you can use it; see page 7)
- One reel of music wire in each gauge on your dulcimer (available from your builder, local piano technician and some music shops)
- Needle-nose pliers with a built-in wire cutter
- A small spring clamp or a hand from a friend
- A pocket-sized chart showing the gauges of the strings
- Micrometer (if you don't know string gauges)

To replace one piece of wire forming two strings:

1. Remove all the old wire (use the pliers for wire on the pins).
2. Unwind both tuning pins counter-clockwise 3½ times (7 half turns). They will stick out more than the others in the pinblock.

---

* I found all of this out by paying a piano technician $12.00 to replace that first broken string. A live demonstration can help build confidence if you're feeling unsure the first time.

Striking Out and Winning!

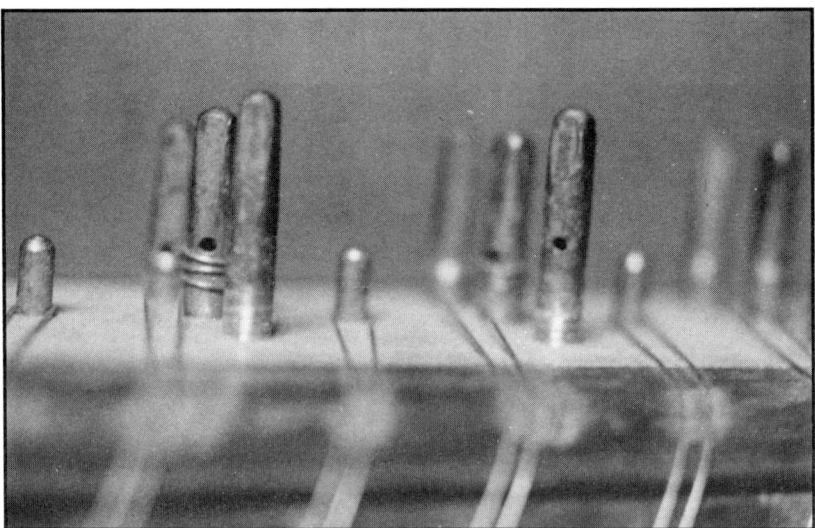

Fig. 5-2 The tuning pins are ready for restringing

3. Unwind a long length of the same gauge wire. Leave it slack.
4. If your bridges are "closed" (see page xii), send the end of the string through the corresponding bridge hole.
5. Insert the end in either pinhole until it *almost* comes out the other side (Fig. 5-3). Hold it near the pin with your thumb and first two fingers. Gently pull the wire toward you *without bending it*. When you feel some resistance, turn the pin clockwise 2½ times (5 half turns). Guide the string toward the pinblock as you turn so it'll sit firmly on the side rail and won't buzz when struck. Don't let the wire overlap; it may cut into itself and break later on. When you're finished, hold the string taut and don't let go!

    (Note: If the string slips out of the pin, cut off the bent end, unscrew the pin and start over.)

Fig. 5-3 Insert the wire almost to the other side of the tuning pin

Time Out! Tuning and Maintenance

6. Pass the wire through the "open" bridge hole to the opposite hitch pin(s). Go around the hitch pin(s) in the same manner as the other strings (Fig. 5-4). Put the spring clamp over the hitch pin (if two pins are involved, clamp the second pin) or ask a friend to hold it for you. Bring the wire back to the second tuning pin. Let the reel dangle off the side of the dulcimer.

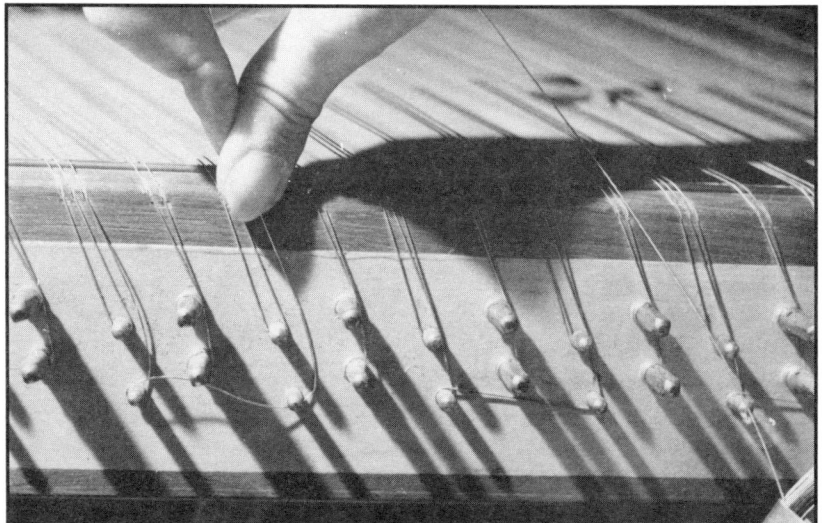

Fig. 5-4 Bringing the wire around two hitch pins

7. Hold the wire as taut as possible and cut it two inches past the tuning pin if it's a zither pin or 2½-3 inches if it's a piano pin. (A string needs at least three wraps around the pin to stabilize its pitch.)

Fig. 5-5 Hold the wire taut and cut it

8. Pass the wire through the same bridge hole (closed or open) and thread and wind the second pin 2½ times or 5 half turns as you did in step #5.

Striking Out and Winning!

9. Now that your hands are free, grab the end of the wire on the reel with the tip of your pliers. Rotate the pliers to curl the wire into a loop so you'll know which end to reel from next time. (*Next* time?)

10. Push the wire against the pinblock with the spring clamp or your pliers (to stabilize string tension). If the wire looks like it may slip out of the pinhole, close your pliers around the pin and over the string's "peak" to push it back into the pinhole.

11. Tune both strings up to pitch. Watch the heads of both pins come back into alignment with the rest.

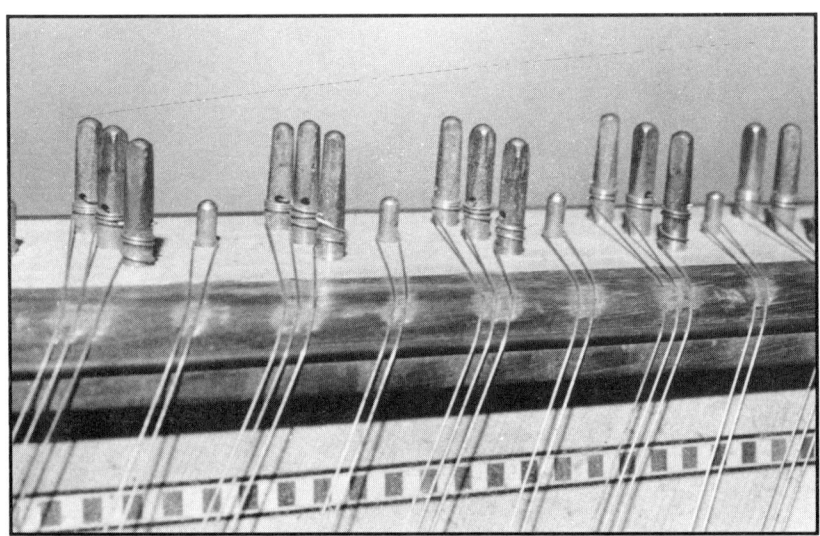

Fig. 5-6 Tuned up and ready to play. The pins are aligned with the rest!

12. *Tah dah!*

How to make loop-end strings

If your dulcimer is strung with loop-end strings, you can make your own when it's time to replace a broken one: Hold the wire in the pliers about 1½ inches from the end. Bring the short end over the pliers and wrap it by hand around the long part several times to make the loop. Slip the loop around the hitch pin, clamp it in place, follow the instructions from step #6 and tune up.

T. L. C.

And finally, to keep your dulcimer in good shape:

1. Light machine oil will keep the strings corrosion-free. Apply it with a soft cloth and wipe off the excess. *Do not* apply oil near the tuning pins or they'll lose their holding ability.

2. You can clean rust off the strings by rubbing them with a block made partially of diamond dust; the block makes them shiny, too!

3. When you transport your dulcimer in very hot or cold weather, leave it in its case for an hour so it can adjust to the indoor temperature gradually.

4. Avoid transporting your dulcimer in the car trunk or storing it in the basement or attic where temperature and humidity can't be controlled. At home, set it up away from air conditioners, heating vents and bright, sunny windows.

5. Last of all, keep playing your dulcimer; it's the best way to keep it healthy and happy!

TEAMS	1	2	3	4	5	6	7	8	9	R	H	E
2/4 TIMERS	0	0	0	0	0	0	0	0	3	3	33	6
ZOIDS	0	0	0	0	1	0	0	1	4	6	17	4

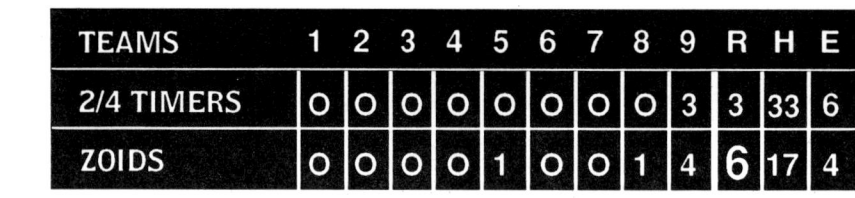

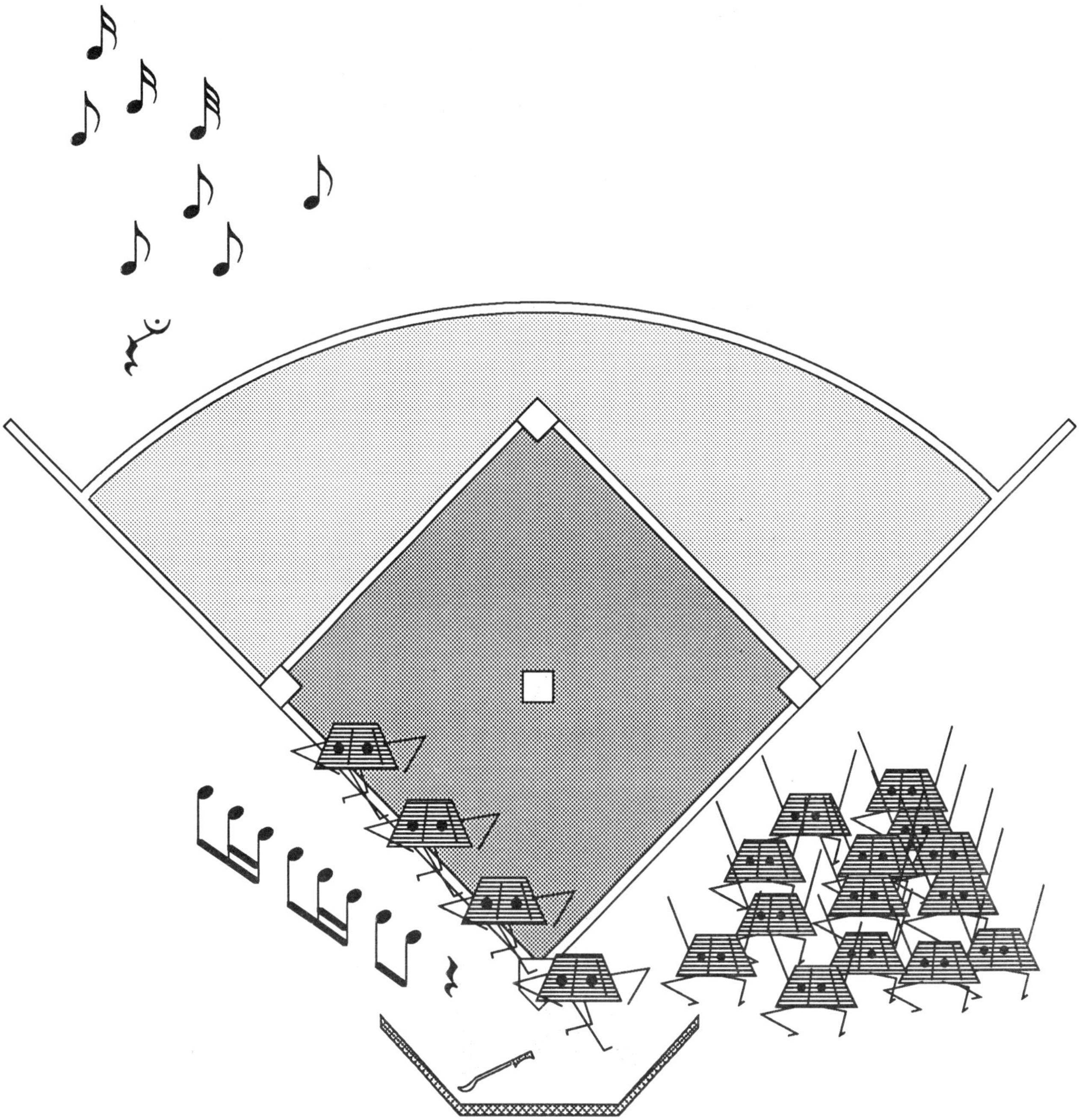

The Grand Slam: Fifty (count 'em, Fifty) Dance Tunes

The Grand Slam: Fifty Dance Tunes

This is what it's all about! These tunes will develop your dance-tune list nicely. While you prepare for your debut (that's de-BUTT), let each one guide you concerning the ways of stroke order and position shifts, too.

A paragraph under each tune labeled *Patterns, etc.* shows patterns you can play first to reduce the learning time. The abbreviations mean:

A/B: A/B section
asc./desc. trp: ascending/ descending triplet
gs: ginger snaps
HD: hammered dulcimer
I/II/B: first/second/bass position
LH/RH: left-/right-hand hints
m.: measure
oct.: octave

pat.: visual patterns(s)
Pet.: the *Petronella* pattern
pos.: position
pu: pick-up
(r), (R): exercises with rolls
scl.: scale
sec.: section
seq.: sequence

How to use the patterns: Listen to the tune or sing it. (Envision where you'll play it on the dulcimer.) Warm up with the patterns listed, then learn the tune as described on pp. 48-50. (Notes: Some pattern references are to exercises you'll play in a later lesson. Play these exercises for notes, but don't worry—yet!—about the techniques they also teach.)

Stick to the strokes and positions shown. They are a rock you can always stand on when you play dance tunes or any other music. I occasionally wrote in the strokes for "questionable" notes (after a large leap, for example); they've tripped up many a student and I want you to avoid these traps. (LH: Mirror the right-hand strokes *exactly*. This will be easy to do if you play the exercises corresponding to the tunes in Chapter 4 or the left-handed patterns listed in *Patterns, etc.* first) If you don't understand the stroking of a particular passage, keep telling yourself that your trusty author put it there for a reason (musical, easy playing!). See Chapter 4 or *Patterns, etc.* for a reference exercise or the *Index* for the answer. And if all else fails, remember this: ★ The first note of *every* measure is always struck by the same hand. Most of the time this will be your strong hand, although a couple of jigs use a left-hand lead.

As to position shifts: What's shown is for right-handed players. If you're left-handed, shift at the same places unless changes are given in *Patterns, etc.* Again, playing the exercises in Chapter 4 and patterns in *Patterns, etc.* can help you shift easily. However, please note that no positions are listed in *Patterns, etc.* where an exercise in Chapter 4 already maps them out. Finally, regardless of your hand dominance, some tunes offer a choice of position shifts. I wrote in the one that seems to work best. If you discover a more comfortable alternate position for a note that keeps the stroking intact without tying your arms in knots, by all means use it.

How to count measures, page 171, explains how to decipher measure numbers, while *How to find the first note of a tune,* also on page 171, offers help for those in need of the ever-important beginning.

Have fun!

Striking Out and Winning!

Striking Out...

These 25 tunes correspond to *Tunes to Play* at the end of each lesson in Chapter 4, *Batter Up*, and may be heard on Companion Cassette 2.

Soldier's Joy   Key: D major   Form: AABB*

This was the first tune I learned to play on the dulcimer—before I even owned one! It's popular amongst dulcimators(?).

    Patterns, etc.: See *Your first reel*, page 51. (R): see page 82.

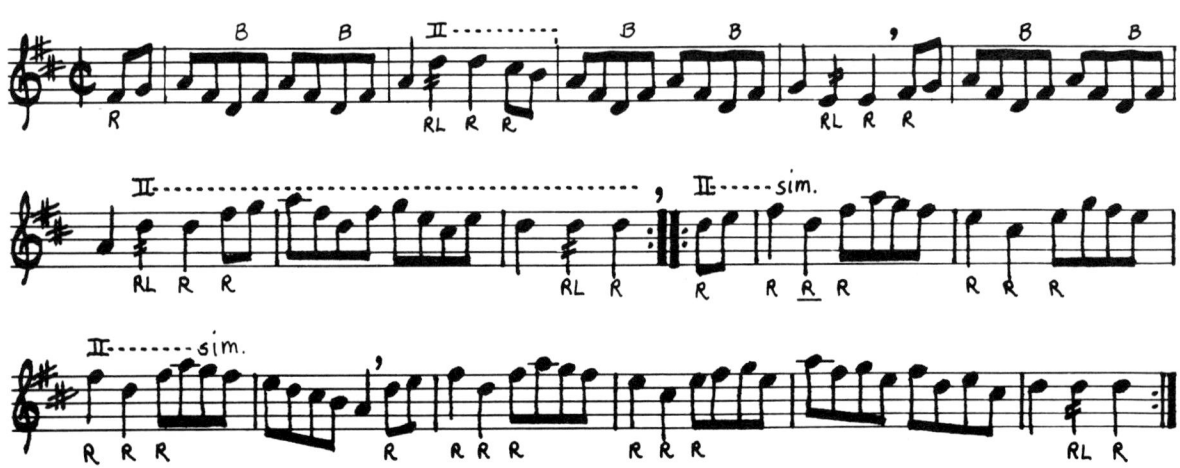

* See *Form* on page 172 for an explanation.

126

The Grand Slam: Fifty Dance Tunes

How to build speed and accuracy

My students usually need to play a tune at least three times before "automatic pilot" kicks in. The first time they goof a lot, the second time they work out the bugs from the first time, and the third time they're off and running. Repetition is the best way to loosen up and have fun.

This method is wonderful for loosening up *and* when you need to learn a tune in a hurry for tomorrow night's dance!

1. Learn the A section by phrases (marked by ').

2. Play the A section slowly ±8 times *nonstop*. Don't stop for small goofs, they often fix themselves the next time around. Turn any persistent mistakes into exercises, then play the entire A section again.

3. Repeat steps 1 and 2 for the B section.

4. Play the entire tune in its proper form (AABB, AAB, etc.) at a s-l-o-w pace. (If you play an AABB tune AB, you'll teach yourself to hear it that way and court disaster playing with a group.) If you have a metronome, set it to sound four clicks per measure. If mistakes abound, slow down so your hands can catch up with your brain.

5. When you can play the tune *perfectly* for at least 2 repetitions, increase the tempo a *little* (one "notch" on the metronome) and play again.

6. Repeat step 5 until desired tempo is reached (about two hours?).

Cincinnati   Key: D major   Form: AABB

There's a similar hornpipe version of this tune called *Harvest Home*.
Patterns, etc.: A1: see Ex. 8. A4: see Fig. 4-2, pg. 47. B1-2: Ex. 10. B5a: oct. B7b: see *The comedy of errors*, pg. 58.*

* The *fermata* (⌢) shows where to end a tune the very last time you play it. (See page 160.)

Striking Out and Winning!

Golden Slippers   Key: D major   Form: AABB´

This is the theme song for the Mummer's Parade on New Year's Day in Philadelphia, PA. (If your father is a Mummer and you can't stand this tune, skip it!) Note: It'll sound blah until you know how to play rolls.

    Patterns, etc.: A sec: in II. B2, 4: gs (Lesson 11, pg. 84). B1, 3: pat; LH: all in II. B1, 3(r): Ex. 44.

* The first three notes of m. A8 & 9 and B1, 3, 9, & 11 are originally ♩. All the notes in m. A9 (the 2nd ending) are one note originally. See *About the footnotes*, page 173.

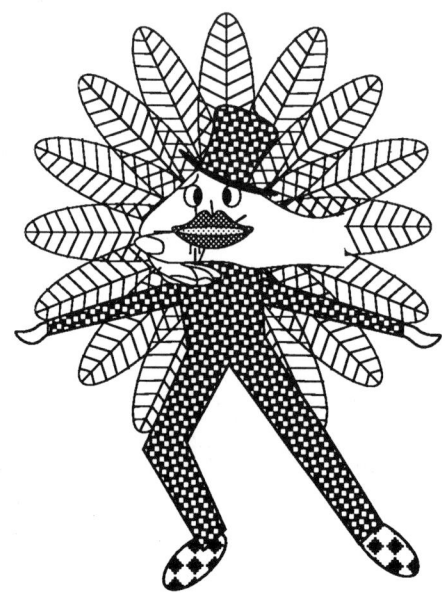

Let your hands do the "Mummer's Strut" with *Golden Slippers!*

The Grand Slam: Fifty Dance Tunes

Galopede Key: G major Form: AABC

Galopede sounds wonderful at an easy tempo. To me, it loses its charm when played fast. The form is AAB<u>C</u> as opposed to AABB.

Patterns, etc.: A sec. in I. pu + A1-2: Ex. 19-20 (r: Ex. 37b). B sec., 1st 6 notes: Ex. 21. B2 & 6: LH shift on 2nd note. C1-2, 5-6: RRRL; LH: LLLL.

My Love Is But a Lassie Yet Key: D major Form: AABB

Ginger snaps, lift, rolls and a chord pattern make this a great tune to sharpen your playing. Give the edited notes in m. B1-4 less weight.

Patterns, etc.: A1: Ex. 43. A1-2: Ex. 45 (r: Ex. 38). All of B sec. in II. B1, 5-6: Ex. 22 (r: Ex. 37d).

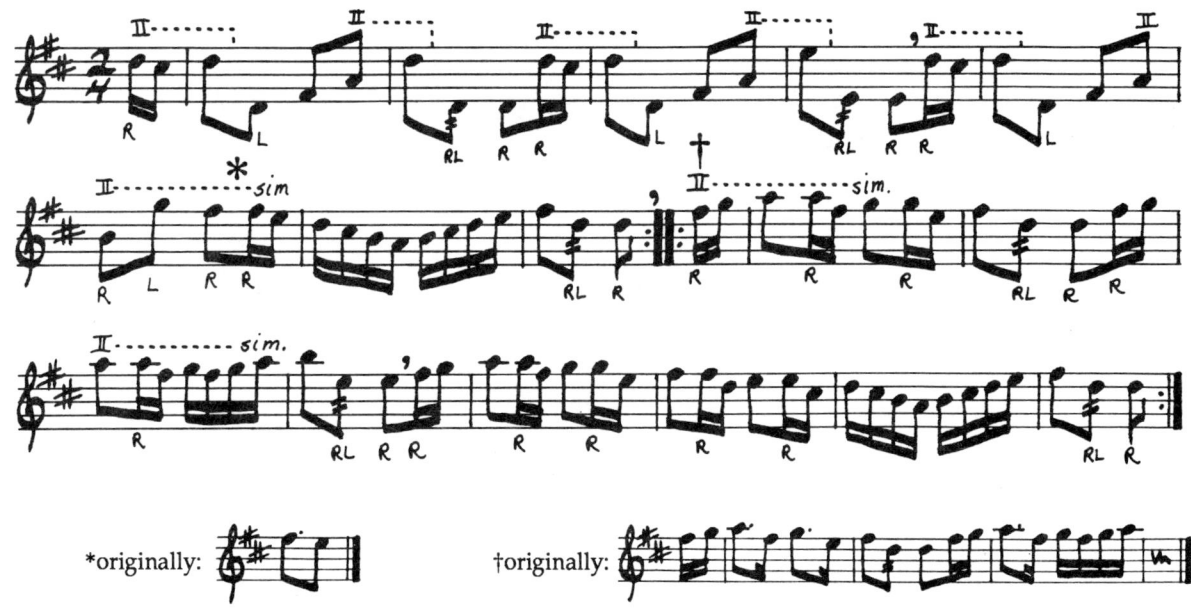

Striking Out and Winning!

Successful Campaign   Key: G major   Form: AABB

This was George Washington's favorite dance tune. It's hard to believe, but back in those days the well-to-do women wore 200+ pounds of clothing to "assemblies" (dance parties). They couldn't turn once around very fast! Think of this when you play this tune at an easy tempo.

Patterns, etc.: A1: Ex. 23. A2: same pat. as Ex. 32. B1-4: gs (Lesson 11). (r): Ex. 46 & 47.

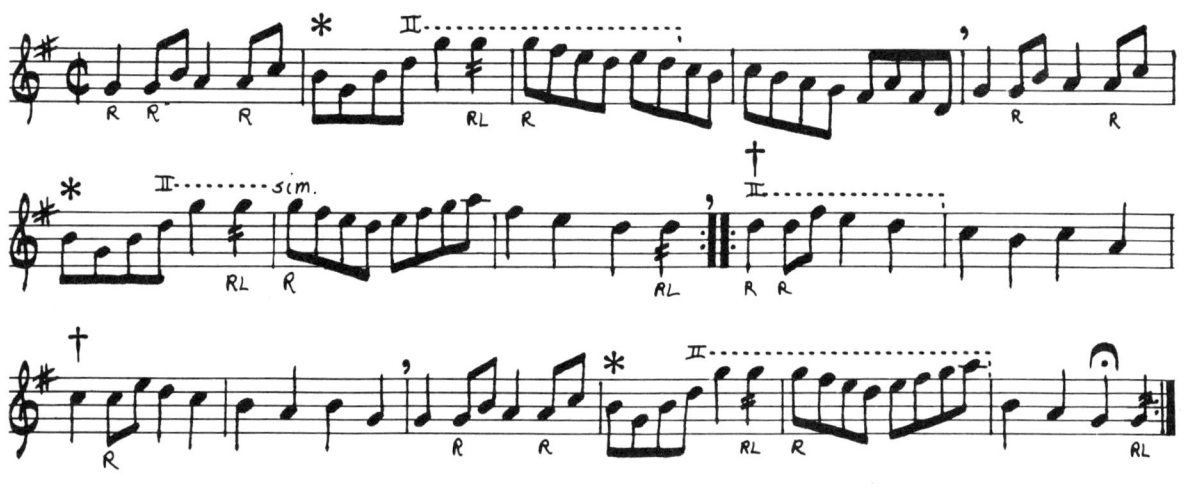

130

The Grand Slam: Fifty Dance Tunes

Liberty Key: D major   Form: AABB

A lively, well-known Southern tune.
Patterns, etc.: A1 & A3: Ex. 24 & 25. B2: see Ex. 26; LH: in I.

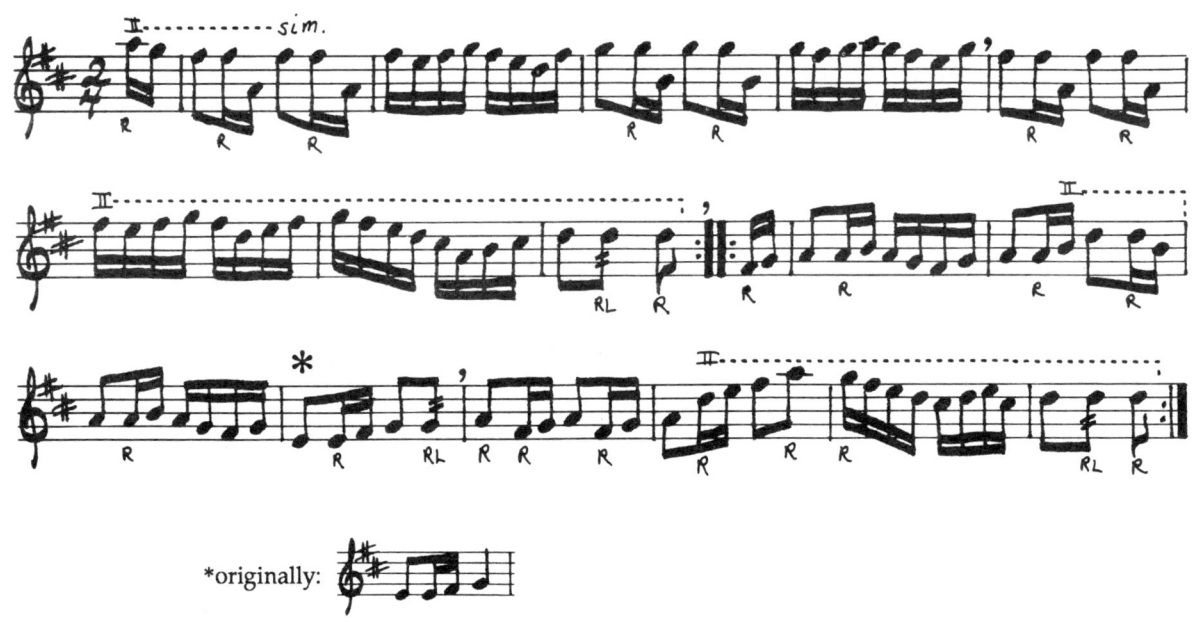

Staten Island Key: D major   Form: AABB

When I performed this tune *on* Staten Island NY, *no one* believed it was called *Staten Island!* The C♮'s in the B section beckon imagination. How about verbal duck quacks or random notes all over the dulcimer?
Patterns, etc.: A3, B1-2, 5-6: Ex. 27. B2b: pat. (LH: all in I).

Striking Out and Winning!

Petronella   Key: D major   Form: AABB

This Scottish tune and its dance steps are a "chestnut" (favorite traditional dance) at contra dances. It's simpler to play than it looks. Don't groan yet; read all about it—and start playing it—on pp. 70-71.

Patterns, etc.: A1-2, 5-6: Ex. 29-30 (r: Ex. 37c). pu + B1-2: 2 pat. pu+B3: pat. B5+1 note: pat; lift after bass note; LH: bass note in I.

*M. A8 & B8 are originally:

St. Anne's Reel   Key: D major   Form: AABB

This is a favorite with dulcimatizers(?) and contra-dance bands.
Patterns, etc.: See Lesson 6, pg. 72. A2-6: Ex. 31b. A7: 2 pats. B1: Ex. 9. B3, 7: see *The comedy of errors*, page 58.

The Grand Slam: Fifty Dance Tunes

Over the Waterfall   Key: D major   Form: AABB

Another popular hammered dulcimer tune.
   Patterns, etc.: See Lesson 7, pg. 74. A2, 4, 6: pat. sim. to Ex. 26; shift to I in A6 to play C♮; LH: in II; 2nd & 3rd notes of A2 & 6 in I. B1(r): Ex. 49.

*originally: ♩.

On the Road to Boston   Key: D major   Form: AABB

Lesson 11, *"Ginger Snaps,"* will show you how to strike out this tune. (It's a country road, not an interstate highway!)
   Patterns, etc.: Entire tune in II except for two notes! A4: *Pet.* & Ex. 42. Lift before playing all 16th notes or rolls.

*original rhythm for m. A1, 5, & B1, 3, 5:   †M. A8 & B8 are originally:

Striking Out and Winning!

Arkansas Traveller   Key: D major   Form: AABB

You probably know this tune. There are lots of rolls (and therefore, lots of lift). Position marks in parentheses are for 12-11 dulcimer players.

Patterns, etc.: pu+A1a: pat; see pp. 89-90. A2a(r): Ex. 41. A7: ouch! B1-2: Ex. 13. B2b: pat; LH: all in I. B3: like Ex. 23.

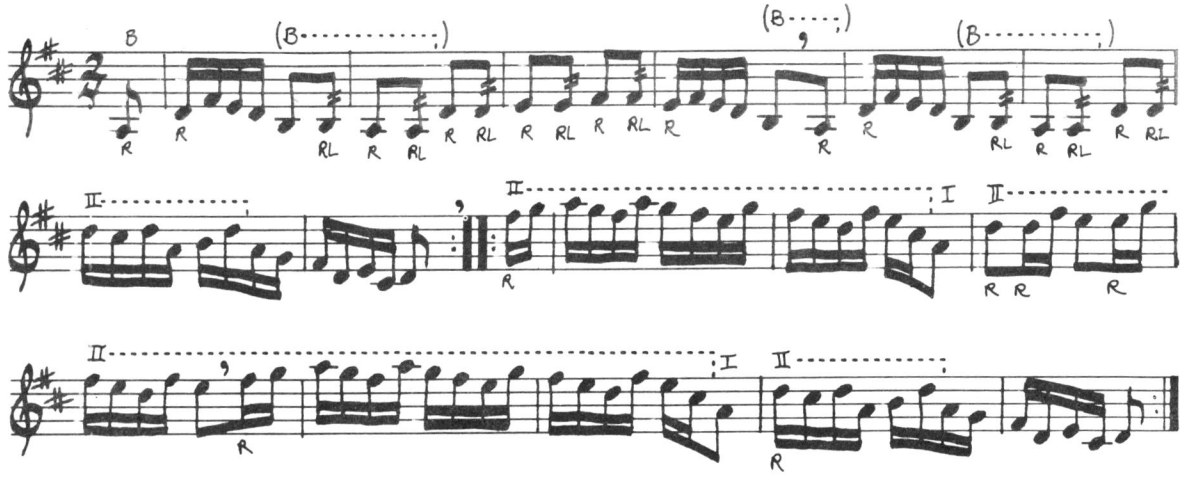

The Rose Tree   Key: D major   Form: AABB

From George Washington's favorite opera, *The Poor Soldier*.

Patterns, etc.: A1: pat. & gs (LH: last note only in I). A2, last 2 notes + 1st note of A3: *Pet*. B3: see pg. 91.

The Grand Slam: Fifty Dance Tunes

Turkey in the Straw Key: G major Form: AABB

This tune plus *Arkansas Traveller* make a nice medley for a square dance. Your dulcimer must have bass strings to play it.

Patterns, etc.: See Lesson 13. A1b: pat; LH: shift to B on 2nd note. A7-8: Ex. 56. B1-4: Ex. 55. B5-6: pat. + lift!

The Irish Washerwoman Key: G major Form: AABB

This is a jig you're bound to strike out fast!

Patterns, etc.: A sec.: all in I. Apu: Lesson 15., pg. 99 A1, 3, 5: Ex. 62. B1, 3: feels like Ex. 62c. Bpu: 63b, 64b & c. B5: LH shift to I on 4th note. B5-6: like Ex. 62b.

Striking Out and Winning!

Tobin's Favorite   Key: D major   Form: AABB

A popular dance-band tune. Play it with accents (see pp. 96-99). Musicians often play the double-stop variation (see footnote) for the repeat of both sections. Play it in medley with *Top of the Cork Road,* page 150.

Patterns, etc.: A1a, 2a, 4a, 7b, B1a, B2: pats. A3, B3: Ex. 60a.

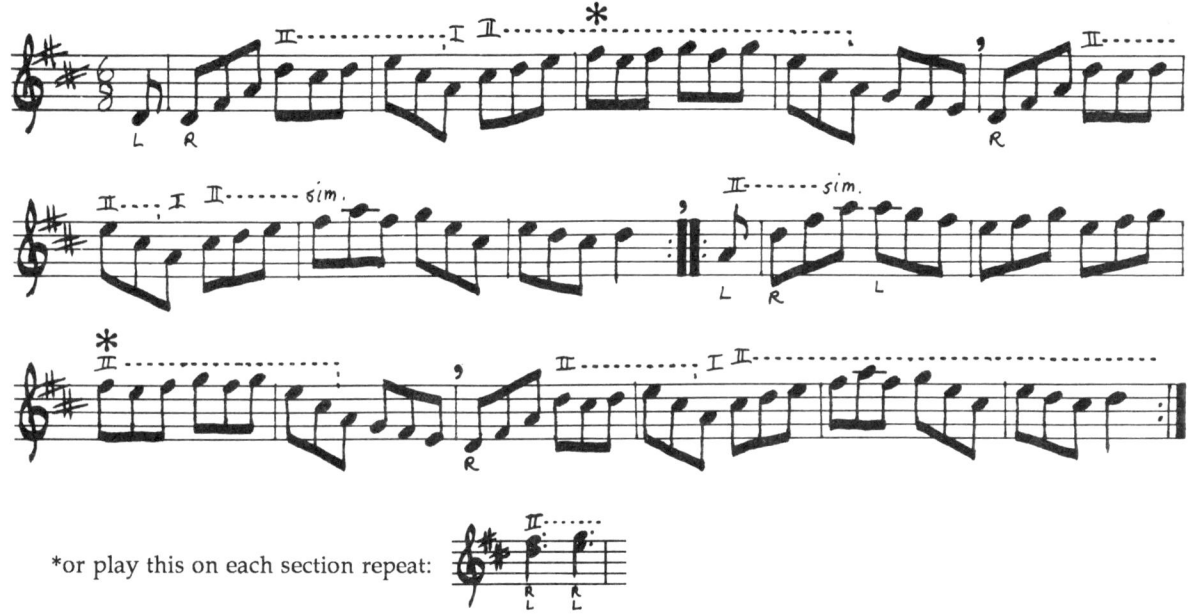

*or play this on each section repeat:

Kitty McGee   Key: D major   Form: AABB

This is one of my favorite tunes. It's guaranteed to make your arms swing with the music.*

Patterns, etc.: A1-2: Ex. 73. A4: pat. B sec.: all in II. B1, 4: pats. (Rolls: see Lesson 17.)

---

* This and *Larry O'Gaff* are performed in medley with variations on my recording *At Last!*

The Grand Slam: Fifty Dance Tunes

Smash the Windows Key: D major Form: AABB

...but if you want your neighbors to like you, please don't!

This tune's alternate title is *Roaring Jelly!* The repeat of the B section (B') is written out in a more notey variation.

Patterns, etc.: pu+A1-2a: pat. A3 & B5: Ex. 71. A6a: pat. Bpu: Lesson 13. B1, 3: pats.; LH: play B sec. in II. B6: Ex. 70. B13: seq.

*Repeat the B section from this point, if you prefer.

Striking Out and Winning!

Swallowtail Jig Key: A Dorian Form: AABB

Also called *Geese on the Bog*. This tune pairs up nicely in a jig-to-reel medley with *Swallowtail Reel*, page 140.

Patterns, etc.: See *The Dorian mode*, pg. 40. A1, 3: vertical pats. (like Ex. 62a). B1-2: Ex. 76. LH: A7b: all in I.

Keel Row Key: G major Form: AB

An old Irishman I once knew sang this song to me in his kitchen. I always think of him when I play it.

This is the only tune in this book that doesn't have section repeats.

Patterns, etc.: Rhythm: see Lesson 18, pg. 109. 1-2a: Ex. 84. A2b: Ex. 83. B1a: pat; LH: all in I *or* shift after 3rd note.

The Grand Slam: Fifty Dance Tunes

Boys of Bluehill Key: D major Form: AABB

Because 32-bar hornpipes take longer to play than reels, it's easy to forget repeats. Be alert! (We need more lerts in the world.)

Patterns, etc.: Triplets: see Lesson 19, pg. 111. 1st 7 notes: Ex. 85. A2: Ex. 86. LH: shift to II on 4th note of A2. A3b-4a: Ex. 87. A8 & B8: optional roll on 2nd note. B1: pat; LH: all in II.

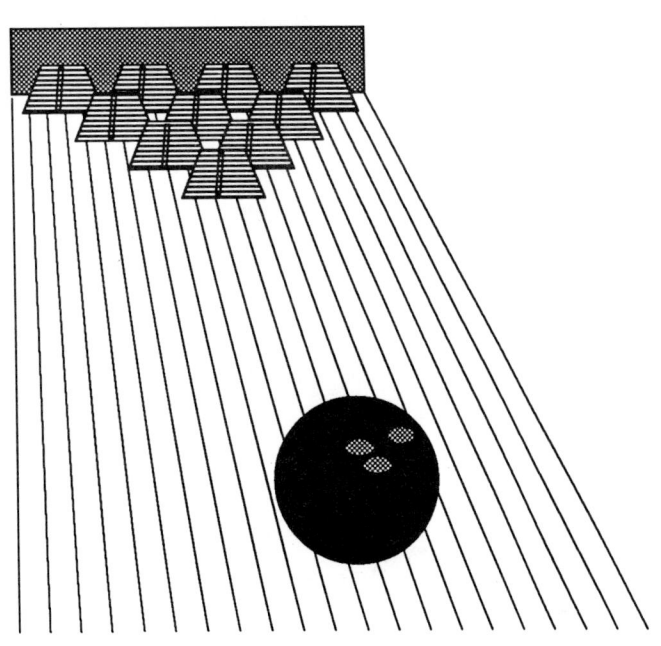

Striking out? No way! I hate bowling!!

Striking Out and Winning!

Swallowtail Reel   Key: A Dorian   Form: AABB

This tune is similar to *Swallowtail Jig*, page 138. Only the meter has been changed to protect the innocent!

Patterns, etc.: Triplets: see Lesson 20, pg. 112. A1, 3, 7b, B3a: Ex. 88. A2b, A7b, B8a: pat. LH: Shift on 3rd note of A2, 4 & 7, and on 1st note of B1.

Fisher's Hornpipe   Key: D major   Form: AABB

I love this tune! At one time it was so popular, over 1,000 versions of it existed. Catch me at a contra dance and I'll play you a few of them!!

Patterns, etc.: Pickup: see Lesson 21, pg. 114. pu + A1a: Ex. 90. A7a: *Pet.*; LH shift on 3rd note. B1a, 2a: pats; LH: B1-4 in II. B5-6: pats; LH: 2nd, 3rd & 4th notes in I; all others in II. B7-8: 5/3 scl; LH: 4/4.

The Grand Slam: Fifty Dance Tunes

How to play the hornpipe

The Breakdown   Key: A major   Form: AABB

This hornpipe-turned-reel is only playable on 15-14 dulcimers one octave lower than written. (Got a 12-11? Play it in D major; see page 174).

If you're left-handed, don't reverse the strokes of the double stops or you'll cross your arms to play them!

Patterns, etc.: Pickup: see Lesson 21, pg. 114. A1a: oct. LH: A1, 2 & 3: shift to B on last note. A7-8+: 5/4 scl; LH: 6/3). A8: see Ex. 32 for pat. B3: double stops may be played in I only; LH: play single notes with rh.

Striking Out and Winning!

...and WINNING!

These 25 tunes may be heard on Companion Cassette 3. Some start out simply but offer challenging B sections. ★ Look for patterns!

Pretty Little Dog   Key: A minor?   Form: AABB

Is this Southern tune in A minor or A Dorian? The sixth step of the scale is missing. It's easy to lose track where you are. Keep singing!

Patterns, etc.: 1st 3 notes: pat; LH: all in II; see pg. 87 at "➤". A1: 1st 3 notes w/ strong hand. A2: scl; LH: top note in II. A7b-pat. B4: LH all in II.

*The first three notes of m. A4 & 8 and B4 & 8 are originally: ♩·

The Grand Slam: Fifty Dance Tunes

The Devil's Dream Key: A major Form: AABB

Also called *The Devil Among the Tailors*. What a tune! Play it one octave lower than written. (12-11: Play it in D major? See page 174.)

Patterns, etc.: A1, 3: pat; LH: low tone in I. A2b: scl; LH: top note in II. A3: pat; LH: all in I. A7b: scl. B1 & 3: similar pats; LH: all in I. B2 &4: 4/2 scl; LH: B2=3/3, B4=5/1.

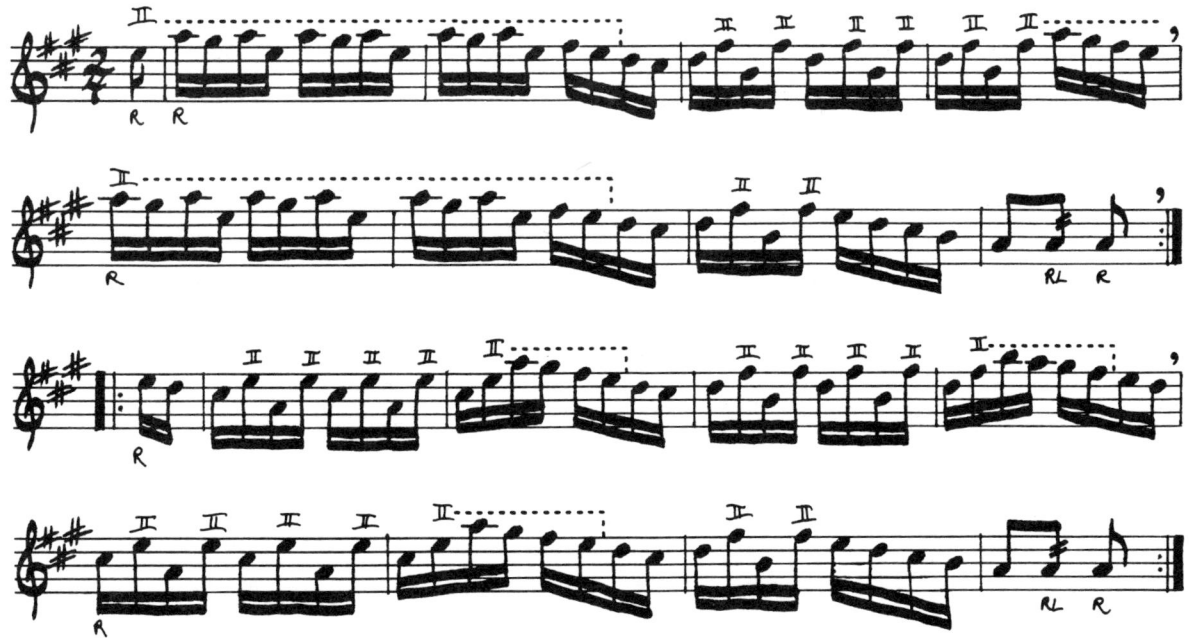

Hull's Victory Key: D major Form: AABB

Attributed to Captain Isaac Hull, who defeated the frigate *Geurer* while commanding the *Constitution* on August 19, 1812, this tune and its dance steps are another contra chestnut. *Hull's* is also played in F major.

Patterns, etc.: A1 & 5: Ex. 9. B6: pat. LH: B2: 1st & 4th notes in II.

Striking Out and Winning!

MacIlmoyle Reel   Key: D major   Form: AABB

French-Canadians start this tune on the downbeat, but in New England it's played with the four-note pickup shown here. Play the first note strongly to feel the pick-up.

Patterns: etc.: 1st 5 notes: Ex. 11. A2a: Ex. 12. A2b: pat. A7a: pat; LH: shift to II on 3rd note. pu+B1a: pat. B7: pat. Accents: see pp. 96-97.

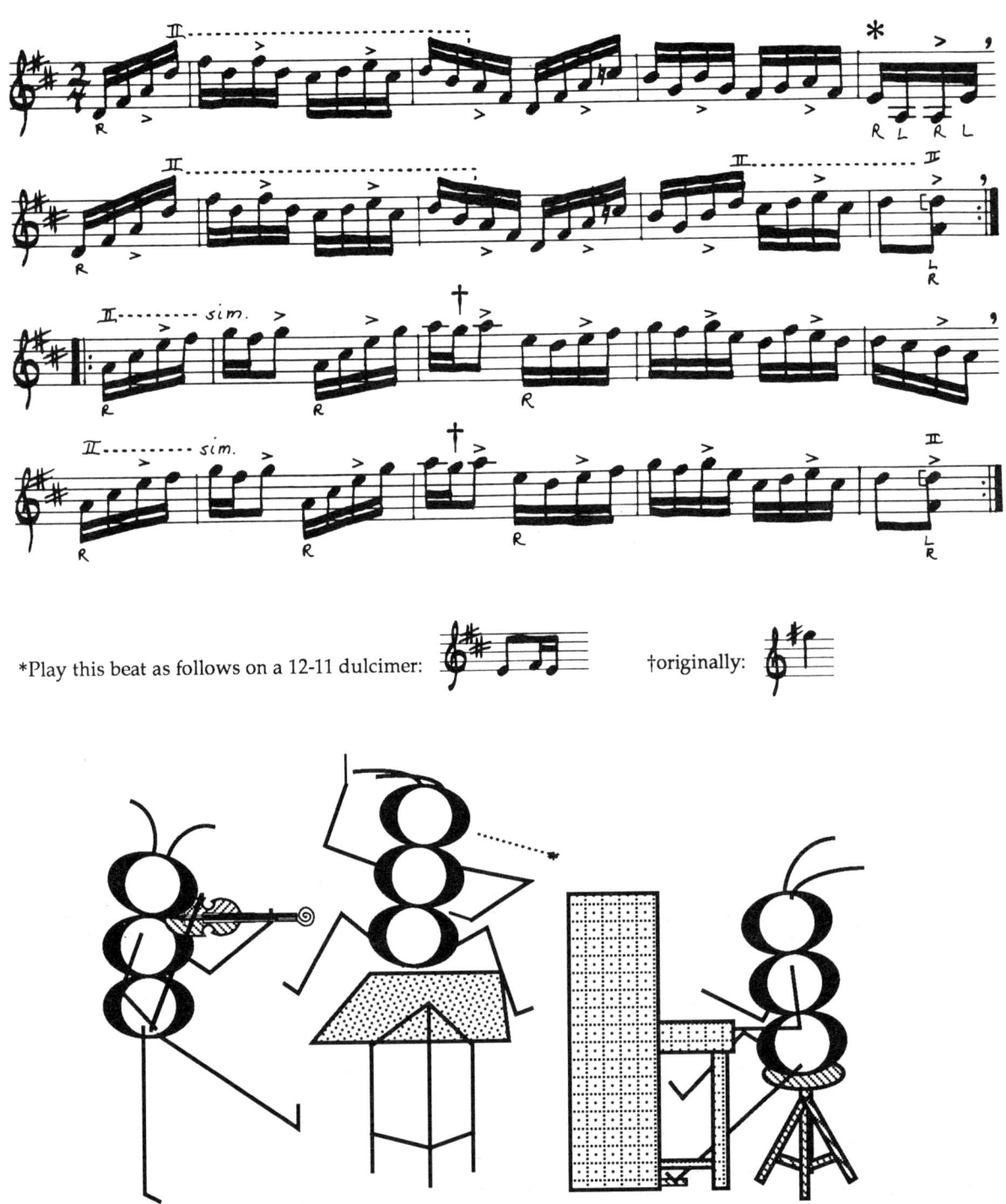

Imagine the fun you can have playing in a group!

144

The Grand Slam: Fifty Dance Tunes

The White Cockade   Key: G major   Form: AABB

This was the opening tune of the first contra dance I ever played for, and one of four tunes familiar to me out of about 25. What a night!
Patterns, etc.: A6, B2, 4, 6: *Pet.* (Ex. 29).

Reel de Montréal   Key: G & D major   Form: AABB

This, like other French-Canadian tunes, is composed in two keys. The A section is in G major and the B section is in D. A dance-band favorite.
Patterns, etc.: A1: 5/3 scl. (LH 4/4). A2a, 3a: pats; LH all in I. A7-8: 5/4 scl; LH: 6/3. Bpu: may be rolled. B1-2: practice like Ex. 30. B3-4: gs; LH: shift to I on last note.

Striking Out and Winning!

Red-Haired Boy   Key: A Mixolydian   Form: AABB

Don't let the key fool you. You *can* play this tune on 12-11 dulcimers!
   Patterns, etc.: See *The Mixolydian mode,* pg. 38. A1-3 scls. A4a: pat; LH: 1st note in II.

College Hornpipe   Key: G major   Form: AABB

This tune is also known as *Sailor's Hornpipe* and may be familiar to you. The B section will send your hammers all over the place!
   Patterns, etc.: A1 & 3: Ex. 38. A2a, 4a, B1: *Pet.* A6 & B6: watch repeated notes. B3: pat. all in II.

The Grand Slam: Fifty Dance Tunes

Swinging on a Gate   Key: G major   Form: AABB

Dance bands often play this tune in medley with *St. Anne's Reel*. Occasional bass notes make for some nice horizontal playing.

Patterns, etc.: A1: Ex. 12. A3: pat; LH: 1st 2 notes in I. A6b-8: pats; LH: all in I. B2: LH shift to I on 3rd note. B3: pat; LH in I. B4: 5/2 scl; LH: 4/3. B6b pat; LH: last 3 notes in I.

La Bastrangue   Key: D major   Form: AABB

A French-Canadian tune our local musicians call *Let's Be Strange!*

Patterns, etc.: A2: see pg. 87 & Lesson 12, Ex. 46-48. B1-2: pats. LH: B1, 3: last note in B. B4: see *The comedy of errors*, page 58.

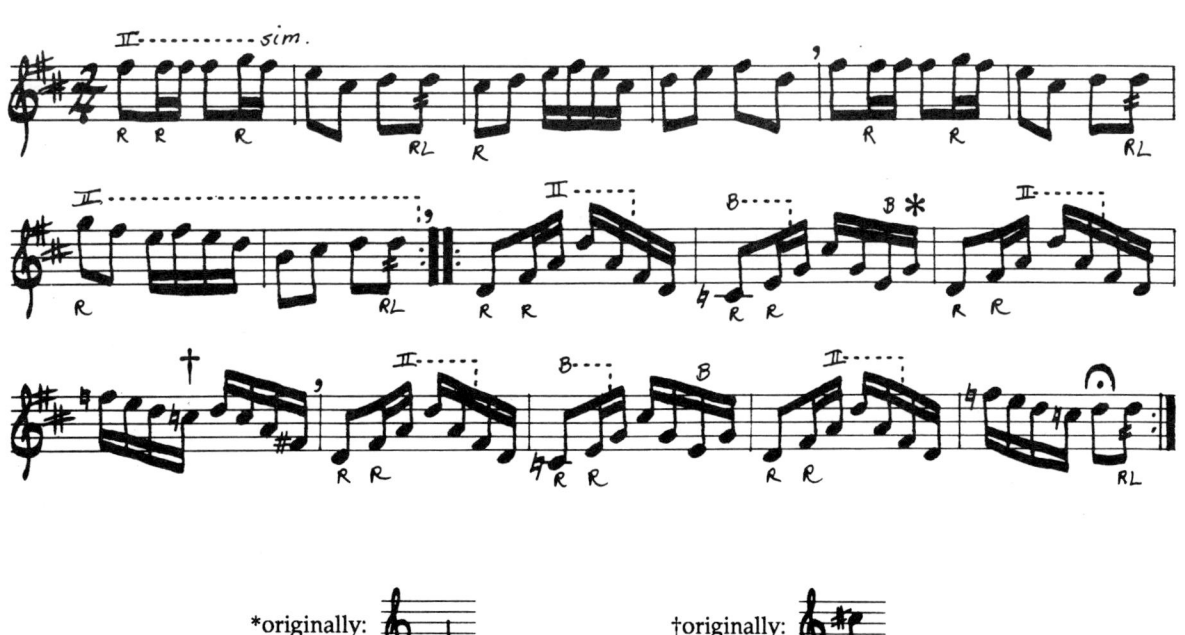

Striking Out and Winning!

Gaspé Reel Key: D major   Form: AABB

The theme music for Public Television's *Crockett's Victory Garden*, *Gaspé* is a well-known tune named for the French-Canadian peninsula.

Patterns, etc.: A2: roll to next note has slight hammer cross (turn left to play easily); LH: shift to I on last note of A1. A7b: pat. A8: Lesson 12, Ex. 46-48. B sec.: all in II.

Old Grey Cat Key: E Dorian   Form: AABB

Hear him (her?) walk all over the dulcimer on my recording, *At Last!*

Patterns, etc.: A1 & 8: Ex. 52. LH: A2 & 6, shift to II on 5th note. A4: 3rd note only in II. A7: shift to I on 5th note. B1-4: in II. B5-6a: low tone in I. Remainder of tune in II; LH: B sec. all in II.

*Play the first two notes like "waterfall" (page 74) with a two-stroke roll on "water-."

The Grand Slam: Fifty Dance Tunes

Temperance Reel   Key: D major   Form: AABB

Also known as *Teetotalers' Reel*. This tune looks impressive to spectators. Its original key is G major, but to me, it has more depth on the dulcimer in D major (see pg. 174). My students love the minor B section. Dig into all the bass notes and let 'em ring.

Because of all the low notes, three *Patterns, etc.* paragraphs appear for this tune. Refer to the one that suits your lead and instrument size best. (If you're left-handed, playing a 12-11 dulcimer and looking for an excuse to purchase a larger instrument, this is it!)

Patterns, etc. (RH): All bass notes may be played in I on 15-14 HDs. A2a & b: pats. A4b: pat. B1a, 3a & 5a: see page 91. B4a: pat.

Patterns, etc. (LH, 12-11): A3, 7 & B7: omit 4th note (C♯; playing it involves a severe hammer cross). A4: omit 6th note. B1a, 3a & 5a: see page 91. B2, 4 & 6: shift to I on last note.

Patterns, etc. (LH, 15-14): Play all bass notes in I. B1a, 3a & 5a: see page 91. B2, 4 & 6: shift to I on last note.

Striking Out and Winning!

Whiskey Before Breakfast   Key: D major   Form: AABB

Yuck, but this is a great Southern tune!

Patterns, etc.: A1: 1st 5 notes: pat; LH: 1st 2 notes in B (LH 12-11: see footnote below); r: Ex. 46-48. A3, 7: (lift!). A4: see footnote for 12-11 HDs; LH: play as written; last note in B. B1: see Lesson 8; LH: all in II. B5-8: Ex. 28. B6: LH last 3 notes in I.

Top of the Cork Road   Key: D major   Form: AABB

Local contra-dance musicians often play this tune in medley with *Tobin's Favorite*. As with that tune, play this one with accents.

Patterns, etc.: pu + A1: pat; LH pat. like Ex. 61. B6: careful!

The Grand Slam: Fifty Dance Tunes

Tenpenny Bit Key: A Dorian Form: AABB

This Dorian tune is popular on the dance scene. Enjoy!
Patterns, etc.: A1, 3, 5: pat. A2b &6b: pat. B2a & b, 4a, 6a: pats. B1, 3: Ex. 74; LH: turn left. LH: A4: 1st note in II. A5: 1st note in II. A7 & B7: 4th note in I. B2, 4, 6: 3rd note in II.

Shandon Bells Key: D major Form: AABB

Named for the bells in Shandon, Ireland, you'll really hear them here! I prefer to play this tune left-handed, but it works right-handed, too.
Patterns, etc.: A1: pats. A3a: pat. A7b: pat. B2b & 6b: pat. B3: pat. RH: pu in I. A1: last note in II. A3: 1st note in I. A4: shift to I after 1st note. A7: last note in II. B sec.: all in II.

Striking Out and Winning!

Maggie Brown's Favorite Jig   Key: G major   Form: AABC

This jig goes all over the place! You must play this tune right-handed unless you have a diatonic 16-15 HD (sorry, I really tried!).

Patterns, etc.: 1st 5 notes: pat; repeats in new chord in A3. pu + A3a: pat. A4: oct. Bpu: lift into it; also Ex. 64b. B3: pat. B10: ouch! B15: 2 pats.

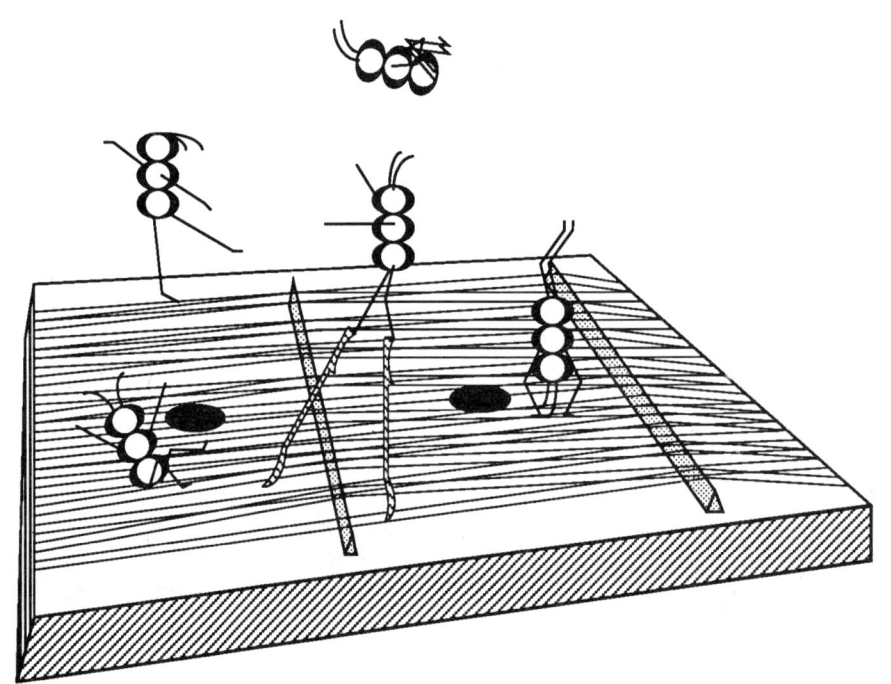

The triants (*Formica silliosa*) invite you to join them for bigger and better things (see page 157 and 173)

The Grand Slam: Fifty Dance Tunes

The Quaker's Wife   Key: D major   Form: AABB

I knew this tune originally as a song. (*The Irish Washerwoman, Tobin's Favorite* and *Top of the Cork Road* are songs, too, with mouthfuls of words!) I choreographed this one left-handed.

Patterns, etc.: A1: Ex. 75. A5-6: pat. (feels good!). B5 & 6: pats. B1: pat. B1-2: Ex. 70. B5a, B6a: pats. RH: A sec.: all but 5th note of A3 & 7 in II. B sec.: all in II *except* 5th note of B7.

Old Rosin the Beau   Key: G major   Form: AABB

I have to question anyone with a sweetheart named Rosin. I might think that person was giving me the rub.

This makes a good medley with *The Quaker's Wife*.

Patterns, etc.: A3a & 7a, B3a & 7a: pat; LH: 1st note in II. Bpu: lift into it; also Ex. 64b. B2: shift to unison on 4th note. LH: A2, 6 B6: all in II. A3 & 7, B3 & 7: 1st note in II. B1: 4th note in I.

Striking Out and Winning!

When Daylight Shines   Key: G major   Form: AABC

I found this gem while looking for new tunes. It's very expressive and sounds a little pianistic. Watch the form!

Patterns, etc.: A1: 4/2 scl (LH: 3/3). A4b + next note: pat; LH: 3rd note in I. Bpu: LH in B. B1 + next note: scl (Ex. 72). B6: LH all in II. B6b-8: 5/3 scl; LH: 4/4. C sec.: all in I (RH & LH). C2 & 6: pat. C4b: pat.

Black Joke   Key: G major   Form: AAB

Also known as *Black Jack*. This tune is 22 measures long including the repeat, instead of the usual 32.

Patterns, etc.: A1-2: seq. A3-4: seq. B1, 3: pat. B5: ouch (sorry!). B7-8: seq. LH: B1a, 3a: in I. B2 & 4: 4th note in I. B5: 3rd note in I.

The Grand Slam: Fifty Dance Tunes

Drowsy Maggie

Key: E Dorian Form: AAB(C)

Once when I was tired, I mixed up consonants and called this tune *Draggy Mowsie!* To make it 32 bars long for a contra dance, it's played AAAABC, but in jam sessions it's usually only AAB.

Patterns, etc.: A1, 2b, 4b: pats. A 2nd ending: *Pet*. B1, 3 & 5: Ex. 28. B7: Ex. 7. C1 & 3: Ex. 88. C7: seq. LH: A1: low notes in I. A4: shift to I on 6th note (A4b: pat.).

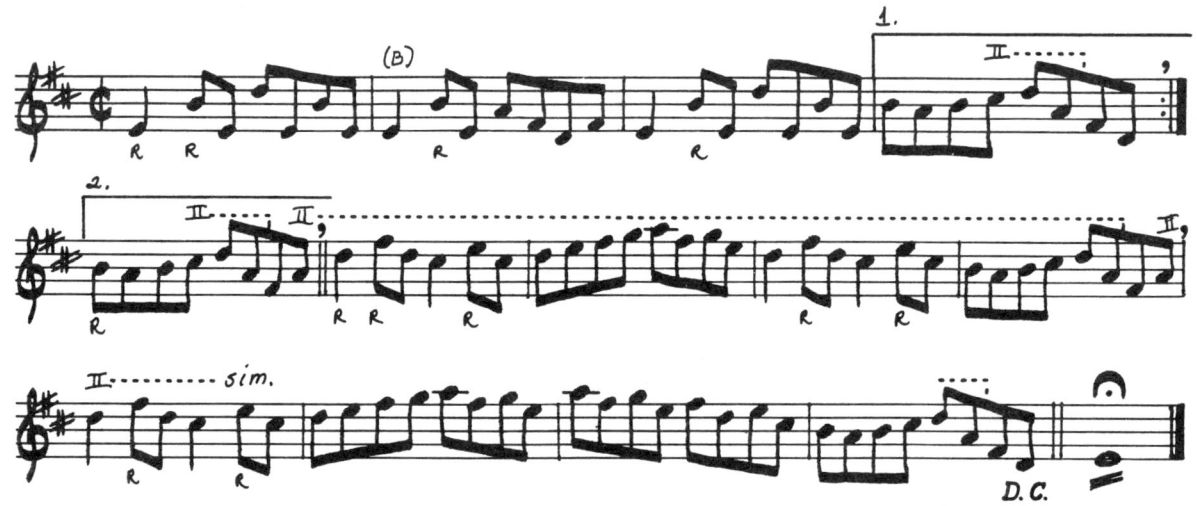

C section (optional):

*originally:

Draggy Mowsie!

Striking Out and Winning!

The Flowers of Edinburgh Key: G major Form: AABB

The Scots call the town *Edinburruh*. (My Scottish country dance teacher would want you to know that!)

Patterns, etc.: pu + A1: Ex. 92 (desc. & asc. triplets optional). A2a: pat. A4: big reach to 3rd note; LH: in II). A6a: pat; LH: 4th note in I. A7: scl. Bpu: Ex. 89. B1-2: seq. B4a: LH all in II. B5a: pat; LH: 3rd note in II; 5th note in I or II. B6: scl; LH: 3rd note in II. B7: scl; LH: 1st note in II.

Larry O'Gaff Key: G major Form: AABB

Can't think of a better tune to end with! This is the second tune I played on *Shadrach* (my first dulcimer) when it arrived at my home one rainy July 14, 1978. Why this tune? I opened a book, and there it was!

Patterns, etc.: Apu: Ex. 91. A2b: pat. A3: seq. A4: 3/4 scl; LH: 4/3. B1b-2a & B3b-4a: pat. B6: pat; RH may play 3rd & 4th notes in I if desired; LH: shift to I on fourth note.

The Grand Slam: Fifty Dance Tunes

Conclusion (or, Where do you go from here?)

You now have a sizeable list of tunes. Keep playing them while you add to your play list. Many of the tunes here are well known to contradance and bluegrass musicians, so if you haven't yet become part of a group that plays together even occasionally, find or start one. It's not only more fun, it makes playing the dulcimer easier. (If you're still shy about group playing, try playing along with my cassette, *Tunes Plus You*.)

Besides dance tunes, what's next? Chords to back them up with! *The Hammered Dulcimer A-Chording to Lucille Reilly* will explain it to you from the beginning (with the help of the triants, who you met on pages 144 and 152), and gives the chords to all 50 tunes in this book. (Find a group to play with if you plan to go this route. Chords played alone don't sound real exciting.)

How about arranging hymns, carols, classical or popular music? I'm already planning to publish instruction on this subject. Until it's available, the advice on page 175 is an excellent start in that direction.

I've got to get back to performing. (I enjoy writing, but the itch to play is too strong!) I hope this book has helped you understand the dulcimer and music better. Thanks for reading, and may you strike out joyfully!

The End!

Appendix

Appendix

Music symbols in this book

Fig. A-1 *Jingle Bells* (chorus)

1. Staff—the five lines and four spaces on which music is written
2. G clef—shows where the note G is on the staff (the center of the clef encircles the second line, designating G)
3. Key signature—shows which tones need to be sharped (#) or raised one half-step, or flatted one half-step (♭; see Fig. 3-5a & b, pp. 26-27)
4. Time signature—the top number (2) shows the number of beats per measure; the bottom number (4) tells which note value receives one beat (the quarter note, or ♩)
5. Measure—a group of beats, as shown by the top number of the time signature; also called a *bar*
6. Bar line—marks beats of music into measures
7. Accent—places emphasis on a note
8. Repeat sign—go back to the beginning and play again. Also ‖: (the facing repeat sign, seen often in the B sections of dance tunes)—return to this point and repeat
9. First and second endings—play music to :‖ and repeat; the second time, skip the first ending and play the second ending instead
10. Double bar line—the music ends here

Other symbols

¢   cut time (a time signature the same as 2/2 time)

D. C. al fine   go back to the beginning and repeat the music to the word *fine* (Italian for *end*)

D. S.   (*dal segno*, or "from the sign) go back to the sign 𝄋 and repeat the music from that point

,   phrase mark (generally appears every four measures)

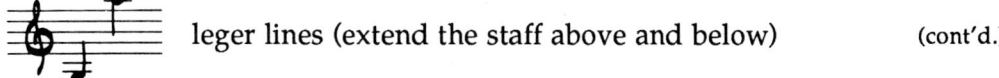 leger lines (extend the staff above and below)   (cont'd.)

Striking Out and Winning!

:|| repeat over and over until you have the feel of the melodic pattern

⌒   fermata; two meanings:
1. hold the note longer than its value (not applicable here)
2. end here the very last time through a tune

♪ 𝆑   multiple-bounce strokes

♪ 𝆑   two-stroke rolls

♪ ♪   one-stroke rolls (jigs only)

⌣   two meanings:
1. tie; combines two notes of the same tone into a longer note
2. slur; connects two or more different tones (not applicable)

Position symbols

I   first position (right side of the treble bridge; generally understood but appears occasionally in written music)

II······:   second position (left side of treble bridge)

B······:   bass position (the bass strings)

(II), (B)   optional; play in this position or in first

L, R   left, right stroke

[bracket; shows which notes of a double stop are in the position shown

A complete explanation of usage appears in Chapter 1.

Note values

This chart shows only the note values used in this book.

in 2/4, 4/4 and ₵:

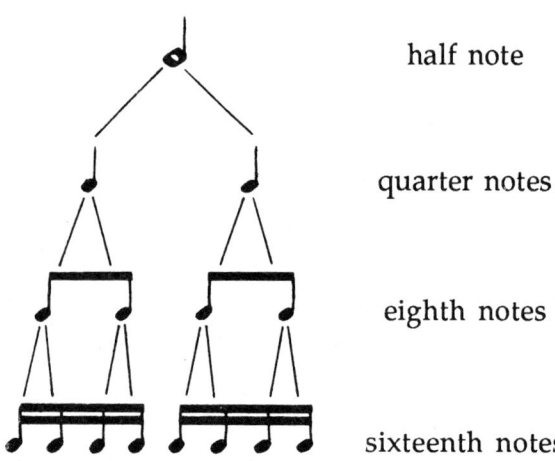

half note

quarter notes

eighth notes

sixteenth notes

Appendix

in 6/8:

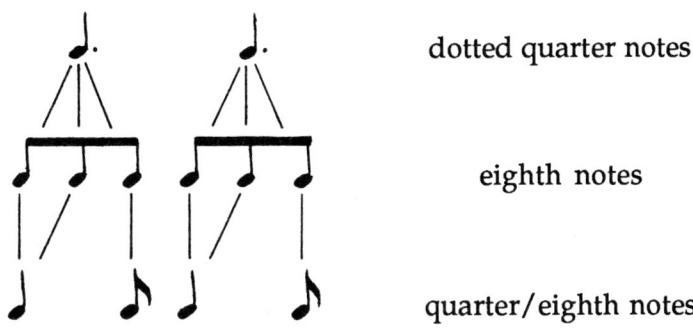

dotted quarter notes

eighth notes

quarter/eighth notes

A dot following a note increases the value of that note by half:

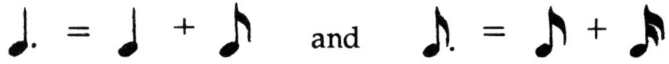

Triplets:

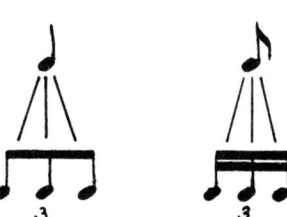

Addendum to Fig. 1-4a

I explained in Chapter 2 how the curved handle design in Fig. 1-4a prevents swing and a full sound, but it doesn't have to! Swiss *hackbrett* players (and some English dulcimer players) use hammers of similar design and produce the same full, pure sound by holding them between the *index and middle* fingers!

Use the same hold as shown on pages 15-16. Make sure the thumb pad is still on top of the middle segment of your index finger. Then slip the handle in so it sits on the middle flange of your middle finger. Swing the hammers before you play and compare it with the swing from a thumb/index hold. It's the same as the swing from a flat handle sitting on your index finger! There's quite a difference in sound, too; however, this handle would work even better if the curves were shorter (Fig. A-2). The long curve allows the handle to wander on the middle finger.

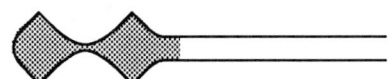

Fig. A-2 A handle with a short curve more suitable for an index/middle-finger hold

(cont'd.)

Striking Out and Winning!

You can play every technique in this book with this hold. For rolls, you must still point your thumbs to produce multiple-bounce strokes, despite their lack of contact with the handles (that's why thumb placement is still important).

About the lettering on page xiv

You may be wondering why I wrote "DUH-kuh-duh-kuh DUM" so strangely at the bottom of page xiv. It's written in International Phonetic Aphabet (IPA), a system of sound representation I learned in college so I could sing in Swahili if I had to. (That still hasn't happened, but Hindi has come up!) A typeface for IPA symbols isn't available, so I had to write the syllables in "longhand" in Chapter 4; the "spelling" on page xiv, however, is the spelling I use when I teach.

Chapter 3 diagrams

Unisons

Unisons occur on steps 5 and 6 of each major scale. Every third pair of courses is not a unison; they are one half-tone apart.

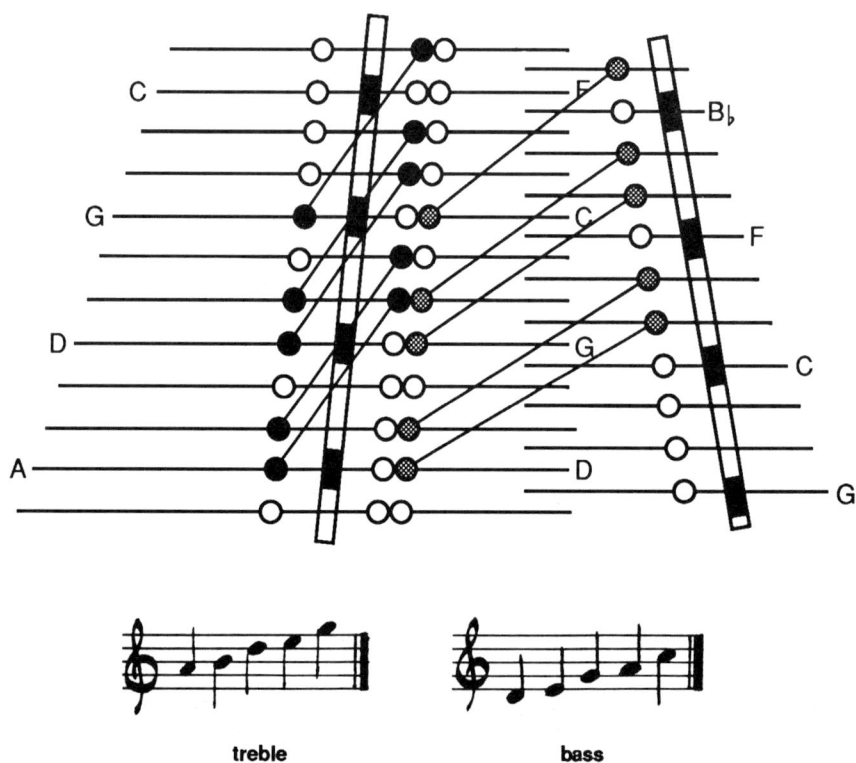

Fig. A-3a Unisons on the 12-11 dulcimer

The tone A appears in three places on the 12-11 dulcimer.

Appendix

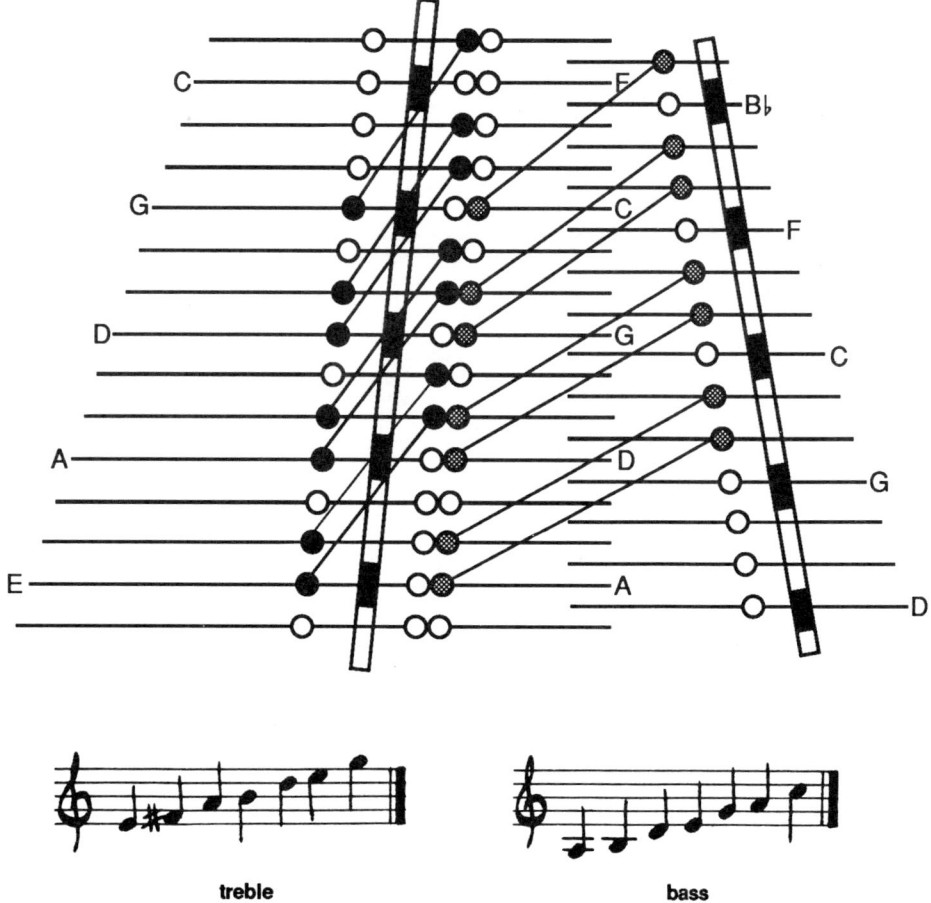

Fig. A-3b Unisons on the 15-14 dulcimer

The tones A and E appear in three places on the 15-14 dulcimer.

Striking Out and Winning!

Octaves

In neighboring positions

Octaves spanning two positions occur more consistently than unisons do.

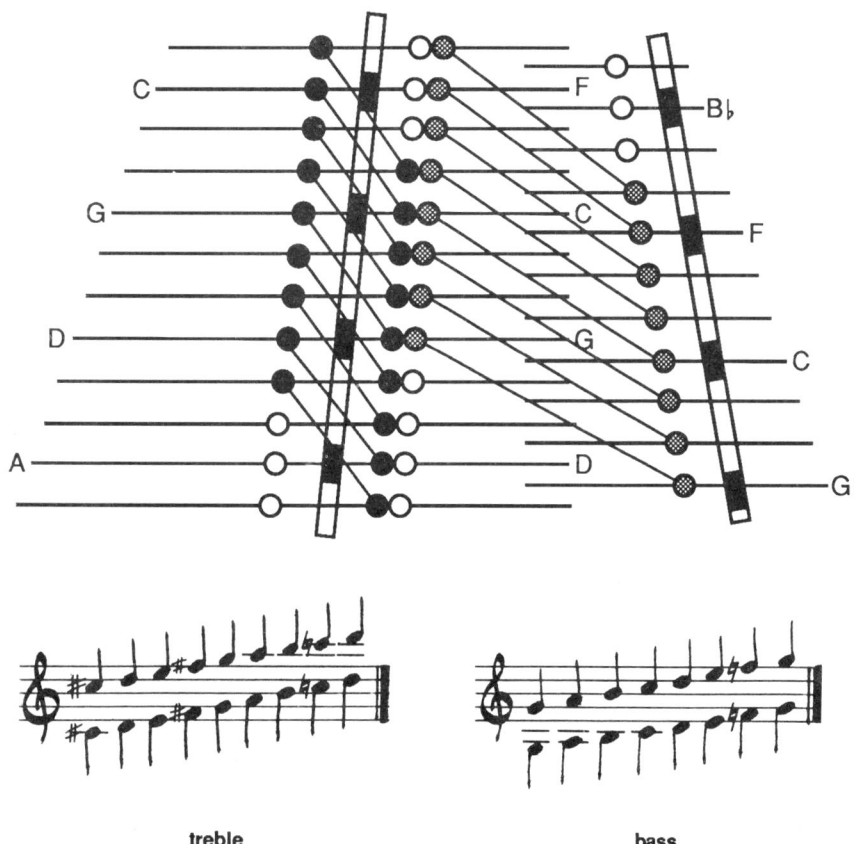

Fig. A-4a Two-position octaves on the 12-11 dulcimer

The 12-11 has 5 two-octave intervals:

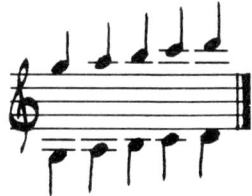

Fig. A-4b Two-octave intervals on the 12-11 dulcimer

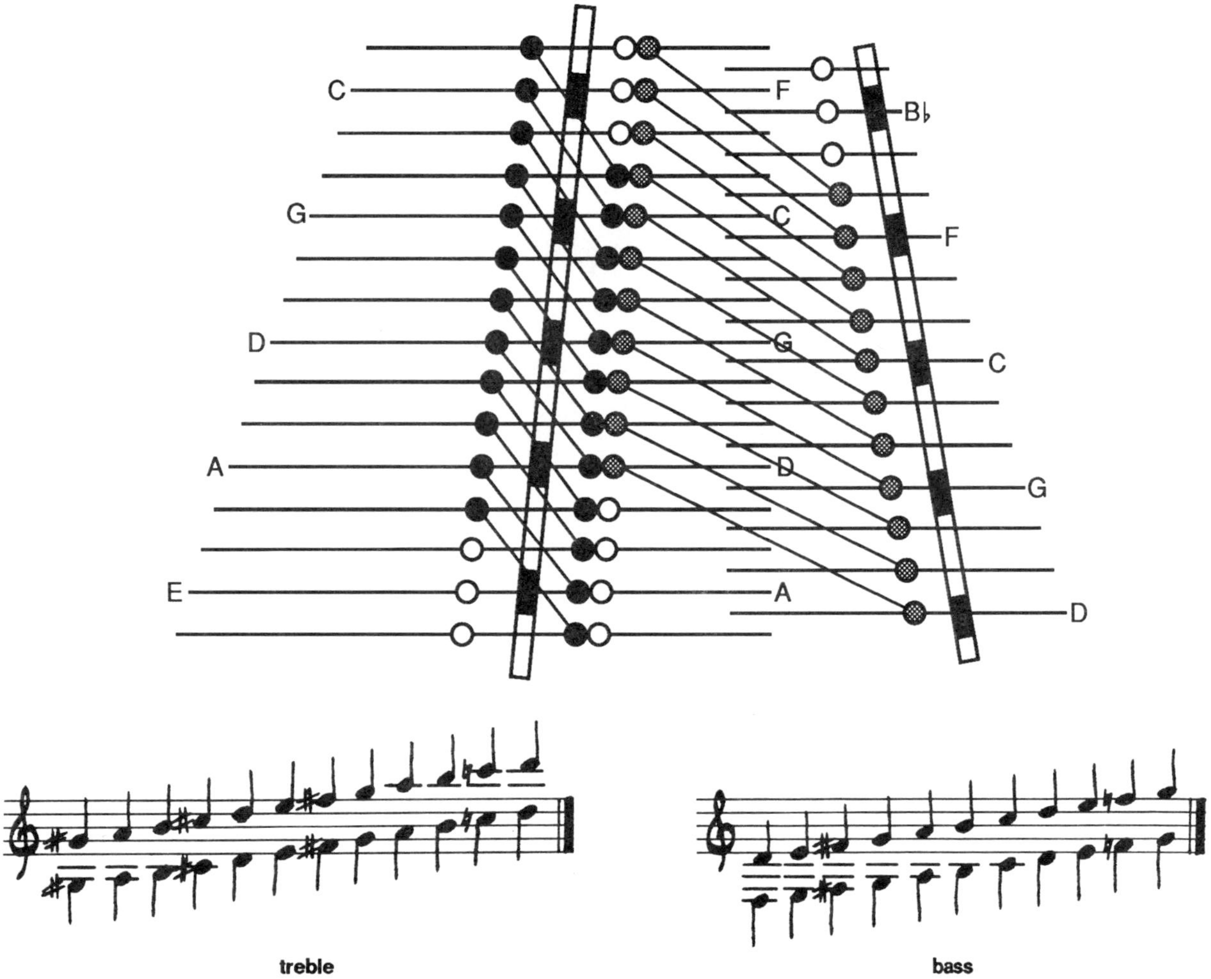

Fig. A-4c Two-position octaves on the 15-14 dulcimer

Some players think the seventh octave they strike (C♮) is incorrect. That's because they've been listening to the scale they've been playing (which isn't major) more than the *intervals*.

The 15-14 has 8 two-octave intervals...

Fig. A-4d Two-octave intervals on the 15-14 dulcimer

...and one three-octave interval (next page):

165

Striking Out and Winning!

Fig. A-4e The only three-octave interval on the 15-14 dulcimer

Spanning second and bass positions

Octaves are shown in the next two diagrams. Any bass- and second-position course pairs that don't produce octaves sound an interval one half-tone larger.

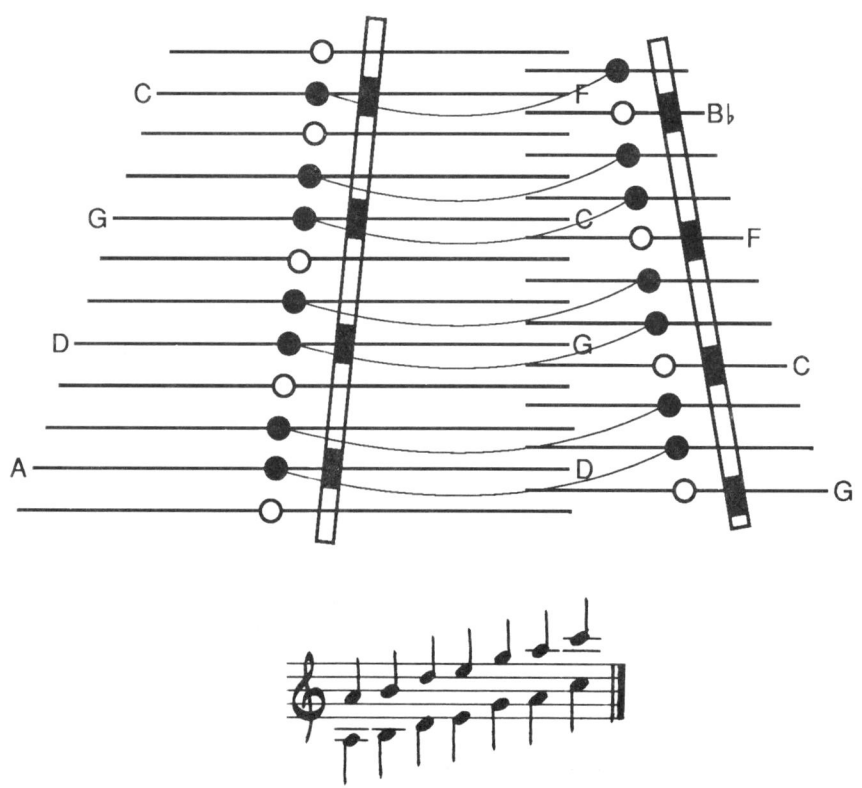

Fig. A-5a Bass/second-position octaves on the 12-11 dulcimer

Appendix

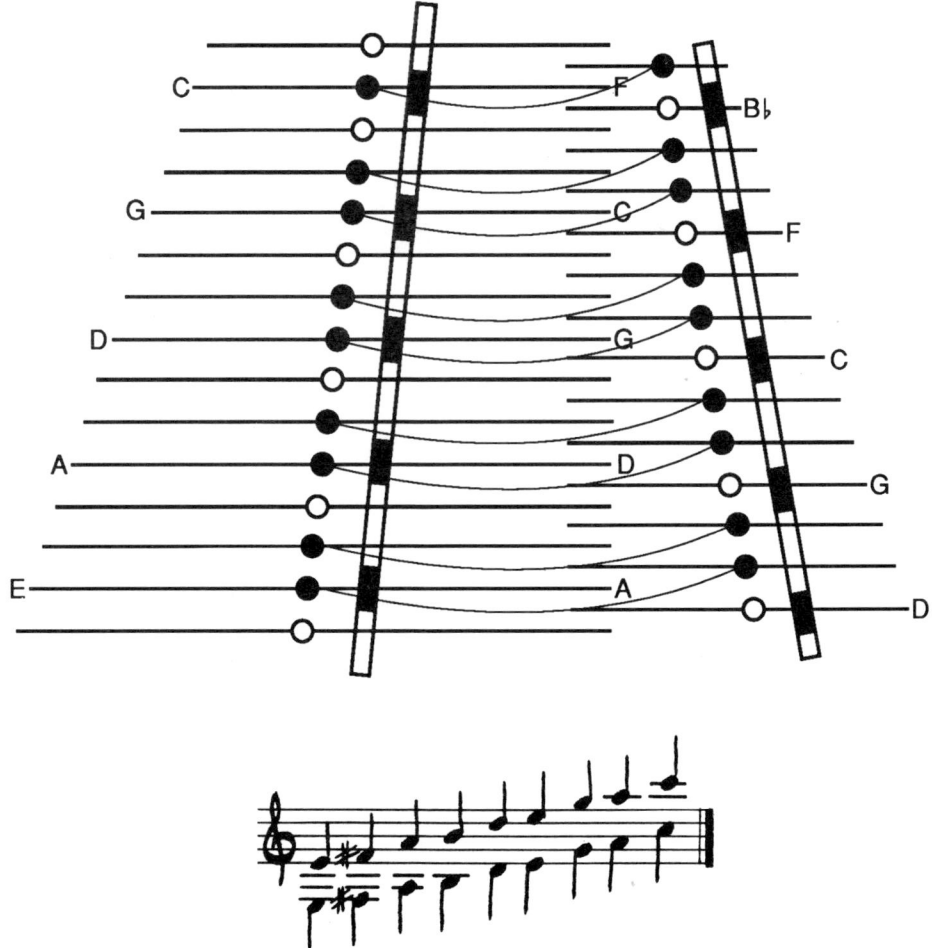

Fig. A-5b   Bass/second-position octaves on the 15-14 dulcimer

Striking Out and Winning!

In one position

Shown in the next two diagrams. Any one-position course pairs that don't produce octaves sound an interval one half-tone smaller.

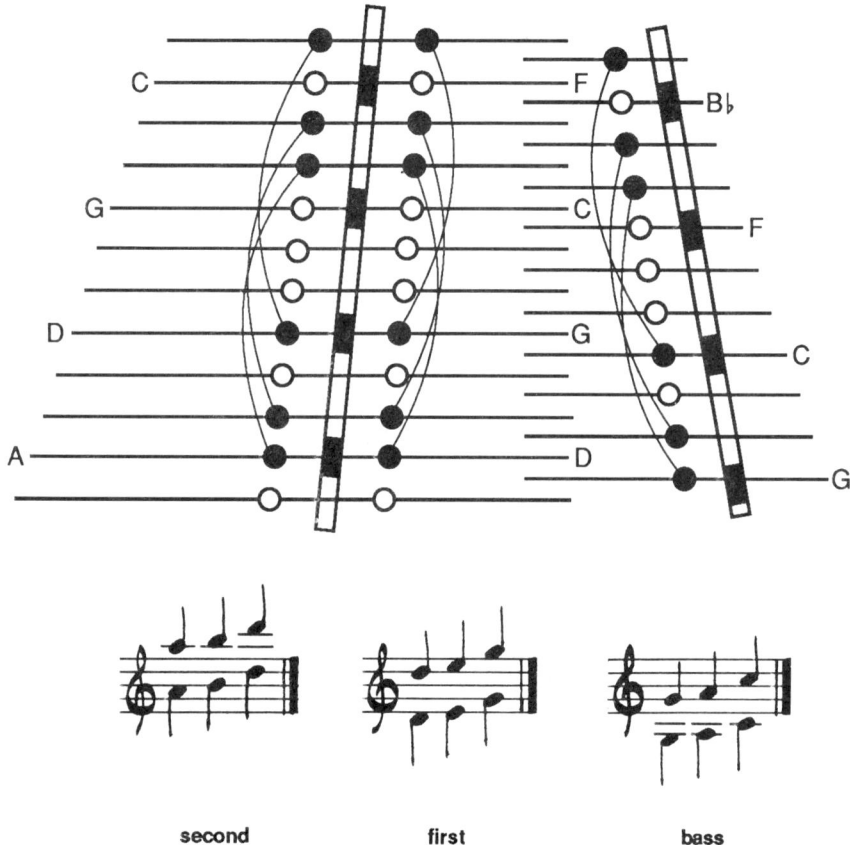

Fig. A-6a One-position octaves on the 12-11 dulcimer

Appendix

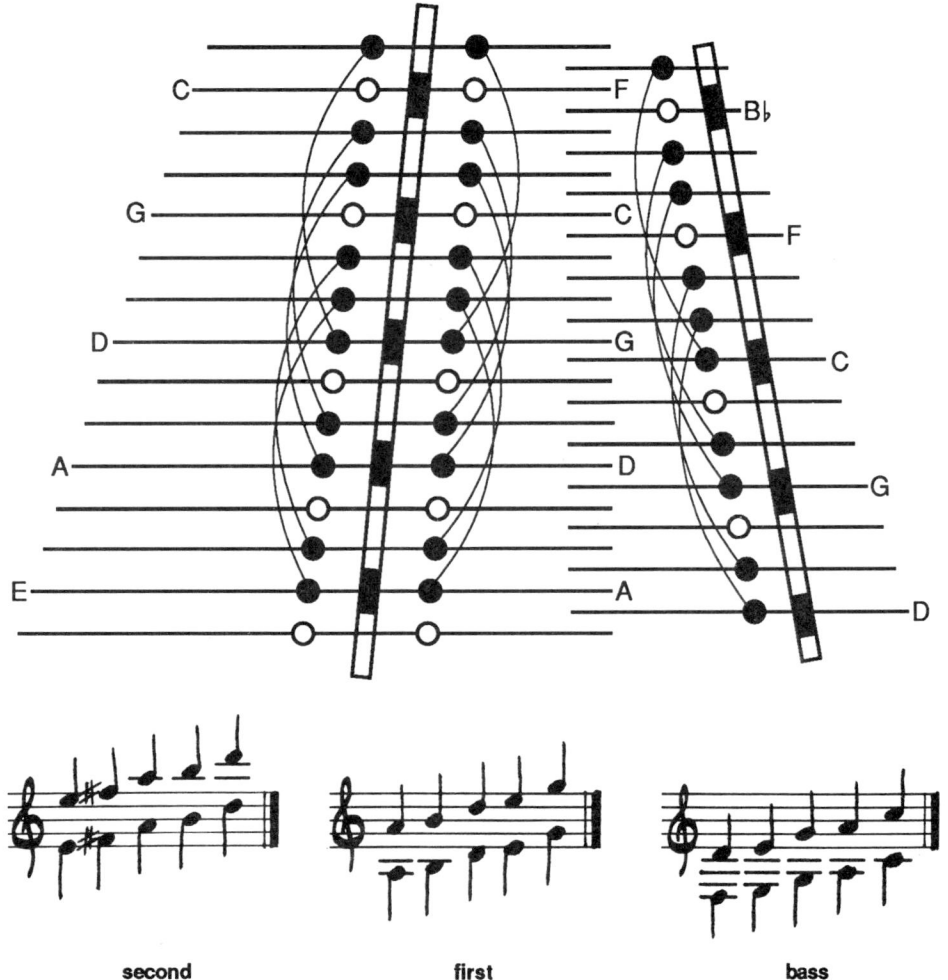

Fig. A-6b   One-position octaves on the 15-14 dulcimer

Striking Out and Winning!

Answers to *A Challenge*, page 35

Here are three more ways to play the D major scale by alternating strokes without crossing hammers:

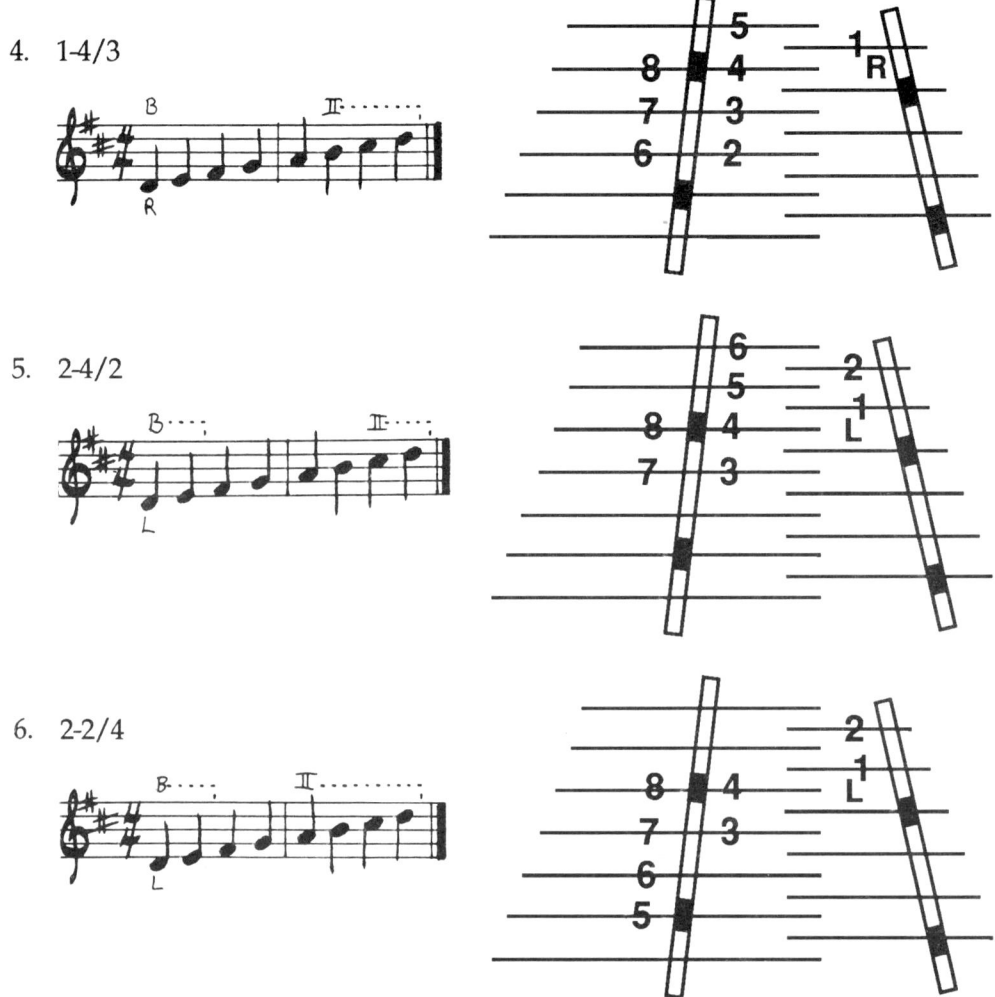

4. 1-4/3

5. 2-4/2

6. 2-2/4

All six scale patterns are also possible in G major, and for 15-14 dulcimers, A major.

An A major scale is possible on 12-11 dulcimers in the 2-4/2 pattern, as is an E major scale on 15-14 dulcimers.

Appendix

How to count measures

Musicians often refer to measures by numbers.

Measures in music (notes grouped into beats by bar lines) come in two forms: *complete* and *incomplete.* Complete measures have the same number of beats (not notes) shown in the time signature. Incomplete measures have fewer than the specified number of beats.

When a tune begins with a pick-up (1-4 notes before the first bar line), the first full measure (abbreviated "m.") is measure 1, as shown below. A pickup in a tune always makes the last measure incomplete; m. 4 below has 1½ beats. Add this and the half-beat of pickup together and the sum is two beats, the number of beats for a complete measure in the tune.

Fig. A-7 *Arkansas Traveller* (excerpt)
showing complete and incomplete measures

Measures are written in the text as m. A1 or B5. A and B tell you what section the measure is in. If the A section begins with a pick-up, the B section probably will, too; m. B1 is the first full measure of the B section.

When an "a" or "b" follows a measure number (B6a, A2a, B5b, etc.), it refers to the first or second *beat* of the measure respectively.

How to find the first note of a tune

You've sung *Soldier's Joy*, patted its rhythm, and you're ready to play. You know the first note is in first position, but *where?* Find out by asking yourself these questions:

1. What is the key? (D major.)

2. In what position is the first note played? (First.)

3. Is the first note on a line or space on the staff? (A space.) If you count the spaces (or lines) from the bottom to the top, which of the four spaces is it on? (The first space.)

4. Turn to Fig. 3-5a or b on pp. 26-27. Find the D major scale and the note on the first space of the staff. What scale step is it? (Step 3.)

5. Now find the D major scale on your dulcimer and count up to the third course in that scale. There's the first note!

Note: If a tune starts above the scale shown on page 26 or 27, count the last note of the scale as 1, then count lines *and* spaces up to the note. If the first note is below the scale, call the first scale step 8 and count lines and spaces backwards to the first note of the tune.

Striking Out and Winning!

Form

Form is the analysis of identical, similar and different phrases or sections in music.

Form is illustrated by a series of letters shown with each tune in this book. Each letter represents a new or repeated section of music, generally eight measures long.

Let's take a close look at the form of *Kitty McGee*.

Kitty McGee   Key: D major   Form: AABB

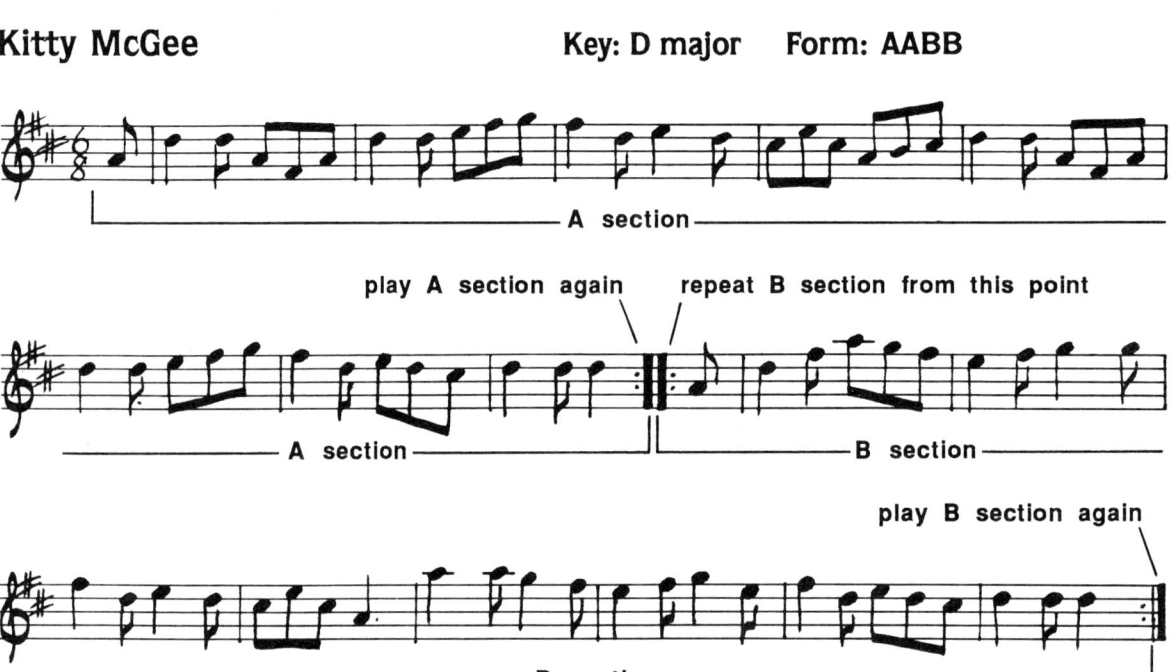

The first A represents the first eight measures of music. At the end of m. 8 is a repeat sign (:|) telling you to repeat the A section, so now you have AA. After the repeat, you go on. The next section of music is different from the first, so call it B. At the end of the tune is another repeat sign, but this time you go back to the facing repeat sign (|:) at the beginning of the B section and play the B section again. You've now played the tune in AABB form, also known as *binary form*.

Not all of the tunes in this book are AABB. *Keel Row*, page 138, is only AB. You can guess now what to do for AAB. But how about AABB´? B´ (called "B prime") means the music is almost like the B section with a small difference somewhere, usually at the end of the tune (see *Golden Slippers*, page 128 and *Smash the Windows*, page 137).

Some tunes also have C sections, signalling another change in the melody. Sometimes the C section is marked off with a secondary double bar line (||) as in *Galopede*, page 129, but sometimes not, as in *Maggie Brown's Favorite Jig*, page 152. In the latter case, count eight measures into the B section and you'll find the C section beginning at the phrase mark (') over the music.

Appendix

Why aren't the chords with the tunes?

Several readers have asked this question. I left the chords out because right now you need position symbols more. The chords would have added visual clutter. However, you'll find the chords to all 50 tunes in the "sequel" to this book, *The Hammered Dulcimer A-Chording to Lucille Reilly*, with complete instructions on how to play them. Get it from your local music shop or use the *Order Form* on the last page to order direct.

Position shifts for Ex. 23, page 67

No strokes are shown. (I'm assuming you know what they are by now!)

About the footnotes with the tunes

Some notes in the original versions of certain tunes either weren't on the dulcimer or involved an awkward reach. I substituted those notes with more "normal" ones and showed the original note in the footnote, just in case you'd prefer that one instead.

More frequently I edited long notes down to two to four shorter ones (example: ♩. is written ♪ 𝄾 ♪) because the long notes die away on the dulcimer, leaving "holes" in the tune. The short notes help you "hold" the long notes long enough and make the tune "jingle," as a fiddler friend of mine says. The music footnotes (notes alone or on a staff) tell you that they appear as one long note originally. This is particularly important to know, because any edited notes should be played to *sound like* the original long notes. To "fake the sustain," as I call it, play the first note at the normal volume and the remaining notes more lightly. Singing the original versions will help you know when to lighten up.

I wanted to show you how to fake the sustain in detail in this book, but decided you have enough to think about for now. Watch for a how-to in another book. Meanwhile, see *Tunebook sources* on page 176 to find a tune, the whole tune and nothing but the tune in its original format.

Striking Out and Winning!

How to transpose a melody

When you transpose a melody, you play it in a different key.

Some tunes are known in two keys; one key or the other may be preferred. *Temperance Reel*, page 149, is a G major tune, but I'm sure I heard it first in D (which has more depth on the dulcimer). *Larry O'Gaff* is a G major tune in the USA, but a D major tune in Ireland. In the East we play *Golden Slippers* in D, but it's a G major tune in the Midwest.

Transposing tunes to other keys on the dulcimer is simple as long as the dulcimer has that key and its range allows it. For example, if you want to transpose *Temperance Reel* from D to G major, begin the tune in D major. *Do not look at the written music,* as this will confuse you. Notice where the tune begins *in relation to the bridge marks* in D (Fig. A-8), then find that same bridge-mark relationship in G major (four courses up). Play the tune in the same patterns in this new key.

12-11

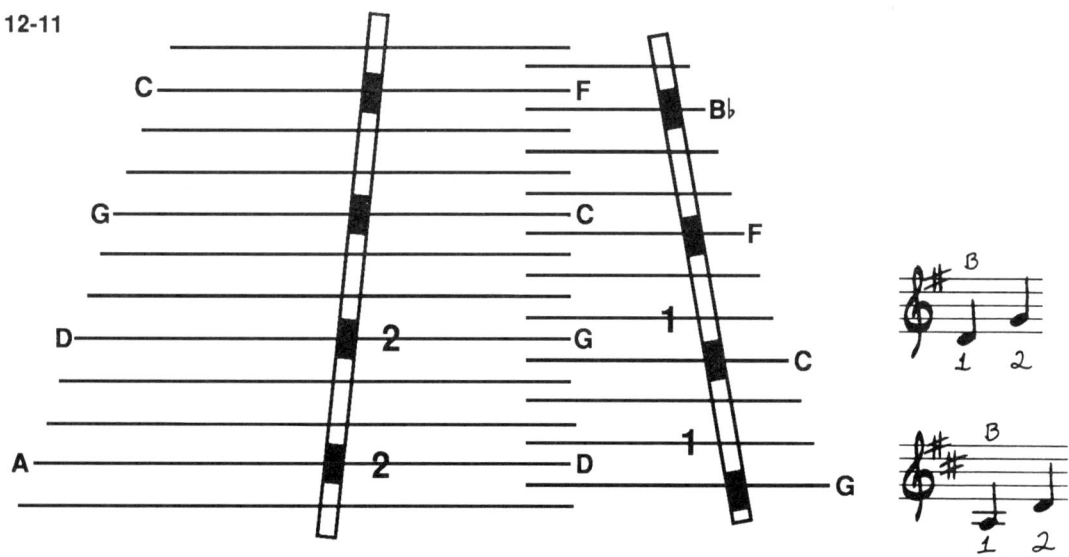

Fig. A-8 The first two notes of *Temperance Reel* on the dulcimer in D and G major

Now, if the band decides to play *Hull's Victory* in F, go find a partner and dance!

Going beyond: Creating variations of tunes

Adding notes to an existing tune can really liven things up for you and your listeners, especially the tenth time around! Although this subject needs its own space, here is what you can do to prepare yourself:

1. *Know the tune cold.* That means upside-down, backwards, in your sleep, etc. Play it a lot; it's the only way.
2. *Be able to sing the tune.* Is your *voice* turned on when you play?
3. *Know your dulcimer's tuning cold.* Again, play a lot.
4. *Your stroke order must be* impeccable! I couldn't spin out variations if my stroke order was haphazard and my lead kept switching hands. Get your hands on "automatic pilot," because you won't have time to think about right and left strokes. Your energy must be directed towards your brain and ear. Remember: A strong-hand lead is your best friend.
5. *Keep going despite mistakes.* Mistakes? What mistakes? They often inspire my best licks. If you play relaxed, you'll be able to turn the unexpected into an ornament without batting an eye. Group playing will encourage you to keep going no matter what, and is great fun besides.
6. *Listen to other musicians who play off the cuff.* They don't have to be dulcimer players. In fact, jazz and renaissance musicians can be just as inspirational as folk musicians. (My recordings *At Last!* and *Tunes Plus You* are full of ideas to get you going, too.)
7. *Time.* Never a factor when joy is involved.
8. *Send in the Order Form in the back of this book and express your interest in this subject.* These days I'm teaching the art of variation at festivals and in classes. Documented instruction could be forthcoming, and it'll happen sooner if I know this is the direction you want to take.

The history of the dulcimer

If you'd like to know more about the hammered dulcimer in the United States and around the world, here are two sources worth checking into:

Groce, Nancy, *The Hammered Dulcimer in America,* Smithsonian Institution Press, Washington, D. C., 1983.

Sadie, Stanley (ed.), *The New Grove Dictionary of Music and Musicians,* MacMillan Publishers Ltd., London, 1980. See the *Dulcimer* entry.

Striking Out and Winning!

Tunebook sources

These books contain the original versions of most of the tunes in this book, along with others worth adding to your tune list. They are well known among contra-dance musicians if you can't find them locally.

Keller, Kate Van Winkle and Ralph Sweet, *A Choice Selection of American Country Dances of the Revolutionary Era 1775-1795*, Country Dance and Song Society, Northampton, MA, 1976.

Kennedy, Peter, *The Fiddler's Tune Book* (I & II), Hargail Music Press, Saugerties, NY, 1954.

Miller, Randy and Jack Perron, *New England Fiddler's Repertoire*, Fiddlecase Books, Peterborough, NH, 1983. (Note: The pickups were left out at the beginning of many tunes so the bar lines could be drawn easily. Check these versions with knowledgeable dance musicans.)

Sannella, Ted, *Balance and Swing*, Country Dance and Song Society, Northampton, MA, 1982.

Sweet, Ralph, *The Fifer's Delight*, published by the author, revised 1981.

Tolman, Newton F., and Kay Gilbert, *The Nelson Music Collection: Selected Authentic Square Dance Melodies*, Rivercity Press, Leyden, MA, 1969.

Glossary

bass position—the courses on the bass bridge.

bridge—a long wooden support holding the strings off the dulcimer's soundboard so they can vibrate. The treble bridge on the dulcimer divides each string into two different vibrating lengths, resulting in two different tones.

bridge mark—a light or dark colored reference mark on the bridge showing where each major scale begins on the dulcimer.

chromatic dulcimer—a diatonic dulcimer having extra courses tuned to chromatic tones to fill in its range with more half-tones. It is more chromatic but not necessarily *completely* chromatic.

course—a group of strings tuned to the same tone.

diatonic dulcimer—a dulcimer tuning system based on the whole- and half-tones of several major scales.

double stop—two courses struck at the same time (see page 6).

double strokes—two notes struck by the same hand (RRLL).

15-14 dulcimer—a dulcimer having 15 treble courses and 14 bass courses.

fifth-interval dulcimer—a dulcimer with the treble bridge placed so the resulting interval is a perfect fifth (the first two tones of *Twinkle, Twinkle Little Star.*) *Fourth*-interval dulcimers (the first two notes of *Here Comes the Bride)* are also found in the United States.

first position—the strings on the right side of the treble bridge.

gauge—measurement of the thickness of string wire.

ginger snap—an alternating-stroke technique producing staccato sounds.

hitch pin—a stationary pin in the dulcimer's pinblock around which a string is anchored.

hornpipe—a "hopping" dance tune characterized by the dotted rhythm: ♩. ♪♩. ♪; also known in Scottish dance circles as a *strathspey*.

interval—the distance between two tones.

jig—a "jumping" dance tune in 6/8 time.

legato—smooth-sounding, connected notes.

lift—the continuous, upward motion between hammer strikes.

mode—a scale composed of a prescribed set of whole- and half-tones (pp. 38-41 and *The Hammered Dulcimer A-Chording to Lucille Reilly*).

multiple-bounce stroke—one arm stroke with a firm hammer hold that causes the hammer to bounce on the strings more than once.

octave—an interval whose tones are eight scale steps apart, such as steps 1 and 8 of the major scale. Both tones have the same letter name.

phrase—a musical sentence, generally (but not always) four measures long. A *half-phrase* is usually two measures long.

pinblock—the long, thick, usually laminated piece of wood set into either or both sides of the dulcimer, anchoring the tuning and hitch pins.

playing distance—the combination of how high the dulcimer is set and how far one stands or sits from it to play (see page 11).

position—on the hammered dulcimer, one of 2-3 (and sometimes more) vertical playing areas of either treble or bass courses (see page 1).

reel—a "running" type of dance tune in cut time (¢) or 2/4 time.

roll—two or more "overlapping" multiple-bounce strokes, producing one long "vibrating" sound.

second position—the courses on the left side of the treble bridge.

sequence—a short melodic motif repeating up or down along a scale.

single stroke—one strike of the hammer on the strings.

staccato—short, detached notes.

staff—the five lines and four spaces on which music is written.

syncopation—the emphasis of a normally unaccented part of the beat.

transpose—to play a tune in a different key (see pages 20 and 174)

tuning pin—a threaded pin which can be turned to raise or lower the tuning of a string.

unison—identical tones appearing in different places on the dulcimer (see pg. 29).

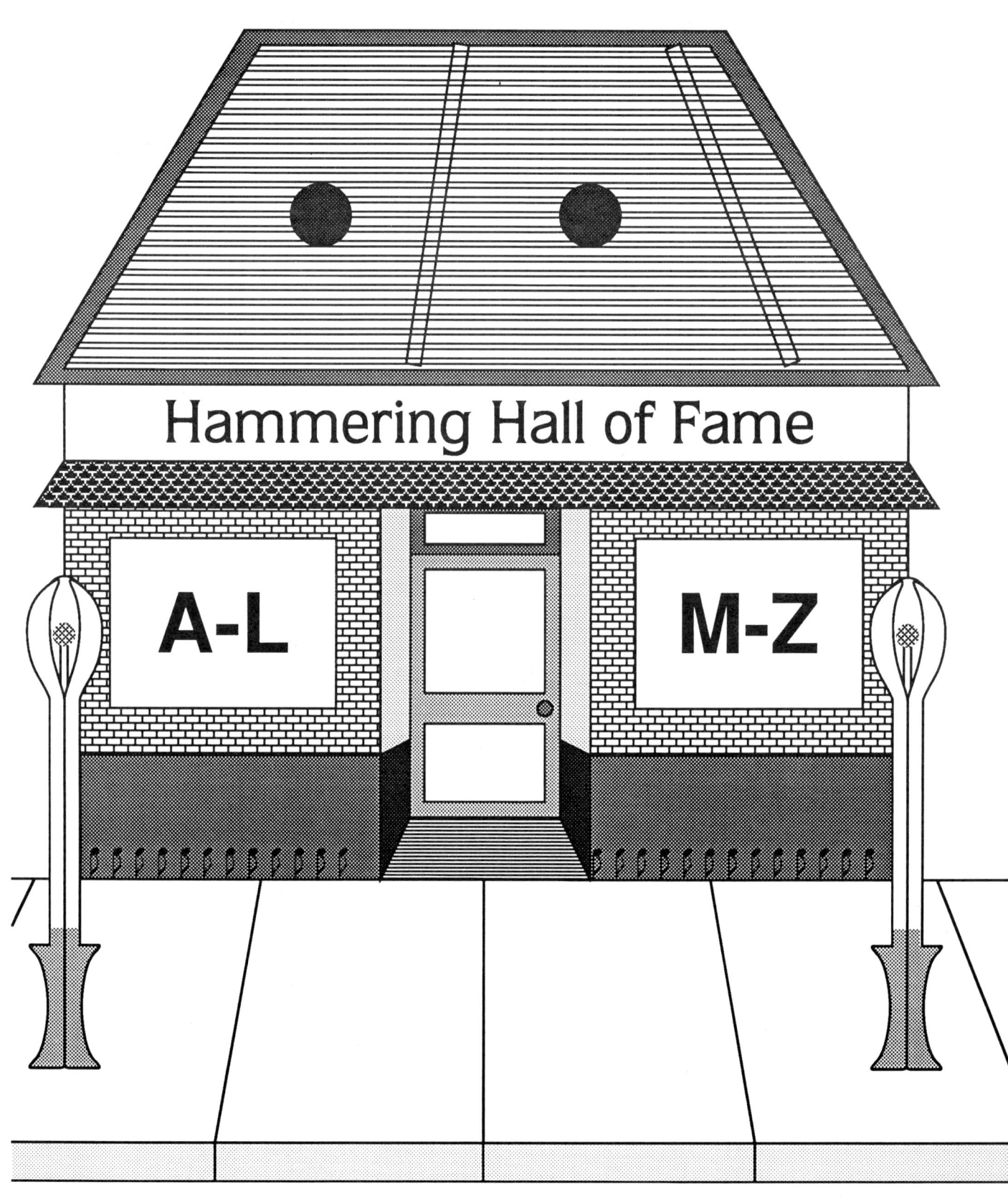

Index

Index

May you find what you seek here! Page references in *italics* refer to tunes. If you're encountering difficulty with any aspect of playing, the entry called "Troubleshooting" may just have a solution.

Accent, 96, 98, 159
  ringing sound of, 97
  waltz vs. jig, 97
Accuracy, in playing, 46, 50, 53, 127
Alternating strokes, 44-59
  in bass and second position, 45
  bouncy, *see* Ginger snap
  on "dump, dump, dump," 66
  in "going up," 62
  in hornpipes, 111
  how to sing, 46
  in jigs, 96-99, 102
  negative effects of, in rhythm, 69-70, 94, 105
  in reels, 44-54, 62
  vs. same-hand strokes, 55
  in syncopation, 93
Alphabet, musical, 26
Ambidexterity, 44
AND, 26
arc, Who built the, 92
Arching, 50, 53, 56, 68, 88, 91, 111
  in jigs, 100
Arkansas Traveller, 58, 89, 90, 134, *171*
Arm (*see also* Forearm, Upper arm)
  in chicken wing, 18, 75
  frozen, 53
  inactive:
    bounce of, 91
    in ginger snaps, 84-85
  loose, 13, 18, 49, 96, 112
  "open,", 11
  "rocking," 67, 103
  symmetrical, 17
Automatic pilot, 43, 64, 70, 127

Badaladalump, 82
Bar line, 159
  double, 159
  secondary double, 53
Bass fiddle, 85
Bass position (*see also* Position)
  playing in, 20
Beat, steady, in rhythm, 62
Beats, 118
berUMP, 82, 87, 88, 89
Black Joke, 154
Blackberry, 61, 66
  in reverse, 74

Bounce:
  function of, 49
  height, 13, 18, 63
  of inactive arm, 91
  in jig pick-ups, 99-100
  lack of, 19
  multiple (*see* multiple-bounce stroke)
  silent, between strikes, 48, 49
  of strong hand, 109
  single, of hammer, 18
  two, of hammer, 18
  of weak hand, in rhythm, 63
Boys of Bluehill, The, 110, 111, *139*
Bracket, 6, *141*, 144 160
Brakes, pumping, 62
Breakdown, The, 141
Breathing, 63-64, 65 (*see also* Lift, Motion)
  hammer, in rhythm, 63-64
  in jigs, 96
  with one hand, 66, 104
  striking without, 66
  with two hands, 63, 64, 65, 66
  to start playing, 64, 104
  when to avoid, 66, 104
Bridge, xii, 1, 176
  bass, xii
  caps, 118
  "closed," xii, 120
  mark (*see* Bridge mark)
  "open," xii
  saddles, x
  treble, xii
  adjusting of, 119
Bridge mark:
  on dulcimer, ix, xii
  how to use, 12, 20, 21, 23, 28, 52
  temporary, x
"Brush" stroke, 79, 112
Bubble gum, 77

C section, *129, 152, 154, 155, 172*
Case, 7
Chair, 9-10 (*see also* Playing distance)
  position of, 17
"Chestnut," 132, *143*

Chord, 52, (*see also* Visual pattern)
   lack of, in tunes, 173
   tone, 117
Choreography, dance-tune, 72
Cincinnati, 56, 57, 58-59, *127*
   about end of A section, 74
Circle (*see* Motion)
College Hornpipe, 84, *146*
"Comparison shopping" (♣), x
Constitution, USS, 143
Course, 176
   individual, 117
   vs. string, xiii
Crescendo, 81
Cut time (¢), 159

D. C. al Fine, 159
D. S., 159
Dance tune (*see* Hornpipe, Jig, Reel, Tune)
Dancer and music, 62, 67, 102, 108
Devil's Dream, The, 143
DOG, 26
Dorian mode, 40-41, *138*, *140*, *148*, *151*, *155*
   how to find, 40
   alternate patterns for, 40
   two-octave, 41
Dotted rhythm, 109
   confusion of, with syncopation, 109n
   stroking of, with triplets, 111
Double bar line, 159
Double stop, 6, 141, 176
Double strokes, 102, 105, 176
   in hornpipes, 111
   in jigs, 102
Double tonguing, 46
"Double whammies," 3
Downbeat, 44 (*see also* Accent):
   how to start playing on, 66, 96, 110
   rhythm, 74
   rolls, 91
Drowsy Maggie, 155
DUH-kuh, 46, 49 (*see also* Syllables)
   IPA symbols for, xiv, 162
Dulcimer, 176
   affixing letter names to, x
   chromatic, ix, 176
     bridges on, 1
   diatonic, 176
   fifth-interval, 176
   fourth-interval, 176
   history of, 175   (cont'd.)

Dulcimer (con't.)
   learning tips, about, x
   "mirror" effect of, 14
   parts of, xii-xiii, 1
   set-up of:
     standing, 9, 10
     sitting, 9-10, 11
     at home, 123
     on a table, 4
   stand (*see* Stand)
   storage and transport of, 123
   teaching, about, xi
   "thud," 3
   tuning, ix, x (*see also* Tuning by ear)
   "voice" of, 70
   volume of, 13, 18

8-4-2-1, 14
Ending, first/second, 159
Elbow:
   as arm guide, 46, 54
   dangling, 13
   function of, 13, 18
   loose, 12, 13, 17, 46, 52, 59, 78, 79, 99, 112
   position of, 11, 12, 17
   rocking, 103, 104, 108
   shuttling, 46
   strong, in lift, 77, 93
   test for relaxed, 13n
   weak:
     in descending triplets, 113
     in lift, 75-78
Exercise, 43, 125
   "bottomless," 54, 57-58, 66, 67, 69, 97, 98, 111
   "topless," 97, 103-104

Feel of playing, 43 (*see also* Motion)
fermata (⌒), 127, 160
Fifth-interval:
   dulcimer, 176
   how to adjust, 118
Fingers (*see also* Hand, Thumb):
   position of, 15, 16
   test for relaxed, 15
   use of, to see course patterns, 12, 53
First position, 1, 177 (*see also* Position)
Fisher's Hornpipe, 114, *140*
Flashlight, 78
Flowers of Edinburgh, The, 115, *156*
Fly swatting, 96

Index

Forearm (*see also* Arm, Upper arm):
  alignment of, with hammer, 17
  angling of, on rise, 75
  function of, 13, 18, 19
  in ginger snaps, 84-85
  in multiple-bounce strokes, 78
  pivoting of, 20, 52
  position of, 10, 12
  twisting of, 45
Form, (binary, etc.), 172

G clef, 159
Galopede, 51, 66-67, 83, *129*
Gaspé Reel, 148
Ginger snaps, 84-87, 177
  and rolls, 87
  when to play in tunes, 86-87
Going up, 61-65, 76-77
  in ascending triplets, 114
  how to sing, 66
  in rolls, 80
  scooping of, 62-63
  variants of, 66, 89
Golden Slippers, 87, *128*, 174
Gravity, 10, 46

Habits, changing old, xi, 15, 43
Hackbrett, 161
Hammer, 2-3
  alignment of:
    with forearm, 20
    with thumb, 16
  angle of, when playing, 18, 77
    incorrect, 75
  balance of, 3, 19, 79
  bounce (*see* Bounce)
  "buzzing," in rolls, 79
    in descending triplets, 112
  control, 18
  crossing, 27, 86
  design, 2-3
  "double whammies," 3
  drooping, 77
  emergency, 3
  as extensions of forearms, 17
  handle:
    about, 2, 19, 161
    placement of, on index finger, 16
  handle-less, 2, 16
  hold, 14-18, 161
    firmness of, 16
    unsteady, 21
    use of other, 19
  leather-backed, 3, 7   (cont'd.)

Hammer (cont'd.)
  level of, in playing, 18, 75
  mallet, about, 2, 3
    wood vs. leather-backed, 3
  parallel, 17
  pigeon-toed, 17
  position of, in second and bass
    positions, 20
  readiness of, over dulcimer 18, 20
  rigid, 18
  shaft, about, 2
  sliding:
    in ascending triplets, 114
    in descending triplets, 112-113, 115
  storing, 7
  swing, 16, 18
  unsteady, cause of, 21
  woods for, 3
Hammered dulcimer (*see* Dulcimer)
Hand (*see also* Arching, Motion,
    Stroke order):
  bouncing, 13, 14, 18, 20, 44, 45, 50, 52,
    65, 84, 85, 87, 91
  drooping, 77
  higher, in jigs, 103
  level, 18, 75, 96
  limping, 109
  position of, 14, 15, 16
  stopping, 62
    cure for, 65
  strong:
    determining, 44
    in hornpipes, 111
    in rhythm, 61, 62
    and lift, 93
    lead (*see* Lead)
    strokes, series of, 55, 87
  weak:
    "building up" of, 44
    cheating of, in rolls, 80
    in rhythm, 62, 63, 65, 109
    in syncopation, 92
    lead (*see* Lead)
    for one-stroke rolls, 108
    in hornpipes, 109
    restoring motion of, 45, 67
    sitting, 93
    strength of, 65
    withdrawal of, in *going up*, 68
Handshake, 18
hiccups, 72, 100, 110
Hitch pin, xiii, 177
Hornpipe, 109-111, *138-139*, 177
  breathing hammers in, 110 (cont'd.)

Striking Out and Winning!

Hornpipe (cont'd.)
   converting reels into, 109
   how to sing, 110
   lift in, 110
   triplets in, 111
Horse, posting on, 77
Hull, Cpt. Isaac, 143
Hull's Victory, 143, 174
Humidity:
   and dulcimer, 118
   and pitch pipe, 117
Humpty Dumpty, 102

International Phonetic Alphabet
   (IPA), 162
Interval, 177
   fifth, 176 (*see also* Fifth Interval)
   fourth, 177
      rising, 115
   octave (*see* Octave)
   two-octave, 32, 164, 165
   three-octave, 32, 166
Irish ornaments, 112 (*see also* Triplet,
   ascending and descending)
Irish Washerwoman, The, 99-100, 135

"J," 93
Jamming, 73, 157
Jellyfish, 15
Jig, 96-108, *135-138*, *150-154*, 177
   how to start, 96, 102, 104
   incorrect stroking of, 99
   pattern changes with lead in, 98
   rhythm, 102-106
   rolls, 106-107
Jingle Bells, 159

Keel Row, 110, *138*
Key signature, 35, 36, 159
Kitty McGee, 104, 105, *136*, 172
Knees, 9, 77, 45
Knuckles, "slope" of, 16

La Bastrangue, 147
Ladder climbing, 104
Larry O'Gaff, 114, *156*, 174
Lead, 44, 60, 70, 73
   in jigs, 96
   positive effects of, 70, 73, 125
   in reels, 60
   switching of, to oppositie hand:
      causes of, 105
   negative effects of, 51, 53, 56, 57, 68,
      94, 98   (cont'd.)

Lead (cont'd.)
   in variations, 70, 175
   in weak hand (jigs), 96, 98
Leaning (*see* Motion)
Leaps, large, 20
Left-handed playing:
   instructions for, 43, 125
   in right-handed players, 52, 56, 57,
      68
Legato, 67, 85, 177
Leger line, 159
Liberty, 68-69, *131*
Lift, 63-65, 75-78, 110, 177 (*see also*
   Breathing, Motion)
   in ascending triplets, 114
   activating, 65
   in dance tunes, 86
   factors preventing, 70, 94
   height of, 63, 64
   in jig rhythm, 100, 103
   before pick-ups:
      in jigs, 99-100
      in reels, 63-64
   in rolls, 80, 81, 82, 107
   and scissors, 72
   in strong hand, 93
   and tempo, 77, 103
   in weak hand, 63-65, 75-78
   whole-arm, 75-78

"M," 53
MacIlmoyle Reel, 57, *144*
MacPherson struts, 45
Maggie Brown's Favorite Jig, *152*
Mallet, hammer, 2, 3
Measure, 159, 171
   abbreviation, 47n, 125, 171
   counting, 171
Melodic pattern, (*see also* Sequence,
   Visual pattern)
   isolating, in tunes, 51
   "seeing," 50
   use of, when playing tunes, 50
Metronome, 127
Mirror, 7, 14, 46
   dulcimer as, 14
Mistakes:
   cause of, 14
   cures for, 46, 53, 58
   as inspiration, 175
   on purpose, 58-59
   usefulness of, 20
   in variations, 175

Index

Mixolydian mode, 38-39, 97-98 *146*
  how to find, 38
  three-ocatve, 39
  two-octave, 39
Monopod, 4
Mode, 38-41, 177
  Aeolian, 41
  Ionian, 41
  Dorian (*see* Dorian mode)
  Mixolydian (*see* Mixolydian mode)
Momentum, 43, 64, 65
Motion (*see also* Breathing, Lift)
  arc (*see* Arching)
  arm swing, 94
  body, 12, 62, 77
  circles:
    backward, 63-64, 104, 106, 114
    clockwise, 88
    counterclockwise, 88
    forward, 94, 104
    "hot-dog," 112
  continuous, 13, 14, 18, 50, 53, 93
  effects of, on sound, 13, 18, 19, 65
  "J," 93
  in jig pick-ups, 99
  lack of, 65, 111
  leaning, 12, 13, 20, 23-24, 25, 28, 47, 50, 54, 62
  in lift, 62-65, 75-78
  "M," 53
  and music vs. notes, 65
  pivoting, 12, 20, 24, 45, 68, 91
  in reels, 62, 64
  restoring, in weak hand, 71
  rocking, 67, 103
  and speaking, 66
  swaying, 12, 46, 50, 57, 67, 69, 115
  symbols in music for, 43
  "U," 94, 103
  vertical, 64
Movement (*see* Motion)
Multiple-bounce stroke, 78-79, 112-115, 160, 177 (*see also* Roll)
  how to play, 78-79
  incorrect use of, in reels, 81
  as a roll in jigs, 107-108
  in rolls, 80
  special uses for, 112-115
Mummer's Parade, 128
Music:
  making, vs. notes 43, 52-53, 56, 57, 65, 67, 68, 69-70, 94, 95, 105, 111
    (*see also* Sound, Stroke order)
  memorizing, about, 48-50, 70 (cont'd.)

Music (cont'd.)
  translated to visual patterns, 50 (*see also* Visual Pattern)
  visualizing, importance of, 50, 55
  written, how to use, 3-4, 48-50
My Love Is But a Lassie Yet, 67, 83, 84, 86, 87, *129*

Nail, hammering, 64, 66
Note:
  finding the first, of a tune, 171
  long, break-up of, 173
  names:
    on dulcimer, x
    on music, 50*n*
  short, 46
  values, 160-161

Octave, 31-34, 164-169, 177 (*see also* Interval)
  in bass and second positions, 33, 166-167
  how to find, 31, 33, 34
  in neighboring positions, 31-32, 164-165
  in one position, 34, 168-169
Old Grey Cat, 91, *148*
Old Rosin the Beau, *153*
On the Road to Boston, 85-86, *133*
Over the Waterfall, 89, 90, *133*
Overtonitis, 62
Ornaments, Irish, 112 (*see also* Triplet, ascending and descending)

Paint-brush stroke, 79
Pattern:
  melodic (*see* Melodic pattern, *Petronella*, Scale, Visual Pattern)
Patterns, etc., about, 125
Patting (*see also* Rhythm, Stroke order):
  to learn tunes, 49
  of tricky passages, 59
Petronella, 70-71, 83, *132*
  pattern, 70, 85, 105, 108, 114
Phrase, 55, 177
  mark, 159
  types, 55
Piano, 38, 59
Pick-up, 171
  four-note, *144*
  rolls (jigs), 107-108
  two note:
    in jigs, 99-100   (cont'd.)

Pick-up (cont'd.)
    in reels, 61-62
Pickles, 112-113
Pigeon-toe (*see* Hammer)
Pin, tuning (*see* Tuning pin)
Pinblock, xiii, 118, 177
Pistons, 44
Pitch pipe, 117
Pivoting (*see* Motion)
Playing:
    accuracy of, 4, 46, 127
    cause of difficult, 14
    convenience in, 51, 52, 68
    distance (*see* Playing distance)
    by ear, 3-4, 19-20
    horizontal, 53
    improving accuracy and speed, 127
    loose, 13, 14, 18, 20, 45, 46, 53, 62, 64, 73, 96
    "stop-and-search," 13, 59, 110
    without music, 46
    uneven, 59, 110
    vertical, 52, 53-54
    via written music, 48-50, 56
Playing distance, 23-24, 25, 36, 38, 51, 57, 177
    changes in, 12
    determining, 11-12
Position, 1, 177
    bass (B), 1, 160, 176, 177
        playing in, 20
    first (I), 1, 5, 160, 177
        playing in, 17
    of five- or six-note scale passages in tunes, 51
    optional, 5, 57, 160
    patting in, 49
    second (II), 1, 177
        playing in, 20
    shift, 51, 101, 125
        without crossing hammers, 67-68
        for left-handed players, 43, 56, 125
        logic of, 51, 52, 53, 54, 56, 57, 67-68, 86, 101, 173
        symbols, 5-6, 160
    third (III), 1
Potatoes, four, 61
Practice tips, 48-50, 51-54, 55, 58-59
Pretty Little Dog, 142

Quaker's Wife, The, 105, 153

Red-Haired Boy, 146

Reel, 44-95, *126-135, 140-150, 155-156,* 177 (*see also* Rhythm)
    played as a hornpipe, 109
Reel de Montréal, 145
Relaxation in playing, 14, 45, 46 (*see also* Breathing, Elbow, Lift, Repetition, Shoulder)
Repeat sign, 159
    secondary, 53, 160
Repetition:
    about, 43, 127
    importance of, 43, 51-54, 55
Rhythm:
    alternating strokes in, 62, 69
        negative effects of, 73, 94, 105
    downbeat, 74
    feeling of, 43 (*see also* Lift, Motion)
    how not to play, 61, 69-70, 71, 94, 99, 105
    how to start playing, 63, 66
    in jigs, 99, 102-105
    with or without lift (*see* Lift)
    patting, 49
    in reels, 60-74, 92-95
    repetitive, in tunes, 55
    plus scissors, 68
    singing of (*see* Singing, Syllables)
    spaces in, 64, 72, 103, 111
    stroke order of (*see* Stroke order)
"Right" notes, 49, 59
Rising fourth interval, 115
Rocking, 67, 103 (*see also* Motion)
Roll, 78-84, 87-90, 107-108, 177
    adding to reels, 82
    with alternate hand hold, 162
    on "and" of beat 1, 82-84
    on "and" of beat 2, 88-89
    over bar lines, 88-89
    cheating the weak hand in, 80
    crescendo in, 81
    in dance tunes, 81
    downbeat, 91
    effects of, on dancers, 88
    four-stroke, 91
    with ginger snaps, 87
    within going up, 83
    in jigs, 107-108
    notation for, 5, 55, 81
    one-stroke:
        incorrect, in reels, 81
        in jigs, 107-108, 160
        played with wrist, 79
    rapid-fire, 89-90
    scoop in, 80, 82   (cont'd.)

Roll (cont'd.)
  singing of, 82, 88
  plus single stroke on a different course, 88, 89-90, 91, 108
  substituted with a single stroke, 55
  three-stroke, 91
  two-stroke, 78-84, 87-90, 107
  warmups to, 80-81, 90, 91
Rose Tree, The, 91, *134*

St. Anne's Reel, 56, 59, 72, *132*
St. Louis, 50, 52
Scale (*see also* Mode), 23
  A major, on 12-11 HD, 170
  alternate patterns of major, 170
  E major, on 15-14 HD, 170
  five-note, 12-13, 45, 46, 64-65, 104
  key of, how to find, 26
  major, 23-29
    bass, 24-27, 28
    treble, 23-24, 26-28
  minor, 35-37
    key signatures of, 35
    relative, 35-36
    step #1, how to find, 35-36
  patterns:
    1-4/3, 170
    1-6/1, 37
    1/7, 39
    2-2/4, 170
    2-4/2, 170
    3/5, 40
    4/4, 23-27
    4/5, 47
    5/3, 27-28, 40
    5/4, 47
    6/2, 28, 37
    7/1, 37, 39
    8/0, 28, 36, 38
    three-octave Mixolydian, 39
    two-octave major, 28-29
  in sequences, 49
  in tunes, 47
    how to use, 35, 47
Scissor strokes, 44
  in ascending triplets, 114
  in descending triplets, 113
  in jigs, 96-99
  and lift, 72
  in rolls, 79
  when to play, 87
Scotch snap, 112
Scoop, 59, 62, 70, 80, 114
  in rolls, 82

Second position, (*see* Position)
See-saw, 18
Sequence, 48, 109, 177
  "aerobic," 68-71, 104
  "bottomless," 54, 58, 66, 67, 69, 97, 98, 111
  pattern consistency of, 51
  "topless," 97
Shadrach, 156
Shaft, hammer (*see* Hammer)
Shandon Bells, 151
Shoes, effects of, on playing, 10
Short notes, 46, 84-87
Shoulder
  in lift, 62, 75
  jiggling, 45
  loose, 13, 17, 46, 59, 79, 96, 99, 112
  position of, 45, 79
Simile (sim.), 5
Singing, 6
  of alternating strokes, 46
  function of, 19, 20, 48-50, 55
  ginger snaps, 84-86
  hornpipes, 110
  incorrect, of rolls, 82
  jigs, 97, 100, 104, 107
  legato, 86
  reels, 46, 66, 74, 93
  relationship of, to playing, 46, 84, 86
  rolls, 82, 88
  staccato, 85
  syncopation, 93
  voice range for, 49
Single stroke (*see also* Alternat-ing strokes, Ginger snap)
  as warmup to rolls, 80-81, 90
Sitting to play, 9-10, 11
Skipping rhythm:
  in hornpipes, 109-111
  in jigs, 102-106
Slant (*see* Upper arm slant)
Slur, 160
Smash the Windows, 104, *137*
Sneeze, 93, 95
Soldier's Joy, 51-55, 82, *126*
soprano, 49
Sound:
  bright, 55, 67, 85
  "buzzsaw," 18
  compromising, for convenience, 68
  and dulcimer stand, 3-4
  "flat," 70, 77, 81, 94, 111
  legato, 85   (cont'd.)

Sound (cont'd.)
   nasal, 19, 79
   overtones in, 14
   "pulling" of, 77
   resonant, 13, 19, 53, 65
   rigid, 21
   staccato, 84
   singing, 63
   tests, 21, 45, 68, 69-70, 77, 79, 85, 94, 99, 105, 111
   2D, 77
   3D, 75-78
Staff, 159, 177
Speaking while playing, 61, 62, 74, 80
Staccato, 67, 84, 177
Stand, dulcimer, 3-4
   height, 10, 12
   temporary, 4
Standing to play, 12
Staten Island, 69, *131*
Strathspey, 112*n*
"Stop-and-search" playing, 13, 110
String:
   crossover point of, 1, 9, 13
   broken replacing, 119-122
     equipment for, 7, 119
   cleaning, 123
   loop-end, 122
   plucking individual, in one course, 117
   where to strike, 1, 9, 13
Stroke:
   alternating (*see* Alternating Strokes)
   brush, 79, 112, 113
   double (*see* Double strokes)
   mark (*see* Stroke mark)
   multiple-bounce (*see* Multiple-bounce stroke)
   order (*see* Stroke order)
   scissor (*see* Scissor strokes)
   sliding, 114
   "soft," 79
Stroke mark, (R, L, etc.), 5, 6, 43, 160
   left-handed, 43, 125
   how to interpret, in music, 5, 49
Stroke order, 43-115, 125 (*see also* Lead and individual dance tunes)
   about changing, x, 49
   confusion, causes of, 68
   and dancing, 67
   and musicality, 43
   and lift, 70   (cont'd.)
   and rhythm, 43, 70, 73, 94, 99, 105, 111 (*see also* Sound)
Stroke order (cont'd.)
   in hornpipes, 109, 111
   incorrect, 61, 69, 81, 94, 105, 111
   in jigs, 96-106
   left-handed, 43, 125
   logic of, 51, 52, 57, 68, 69-70, 86, 87, 94, 99
   memorizing, to play tunes, 70
   in one hand, 55
     vs. ginger snaps, 87
   principle of:
     for reels, 44
     for jigs, 96
   in reels, 44, 60, 84, 92, 112, 114
   relationship of rhythm to, 72
   for rhythm, 44, 45, 60-61, 74, 92, 96, 102, 109, 111, 112, 114
   in syncopation, 92
   in variations of dance tunes, 175
Strong hand (*see* Hand)
Success tips (★), about, x
Successful Campaign, 67, 86, 88, 89, *130*
Sustain, "faking," 173
Swallowtail Jig, 106, *138*
Swaying (*see* Motion)
Swallowtail Reel, 113, *140*
Swing, hammer, 16, 18
Swinging on a Gate, 57, *147*
Syllables for singing, 46, 49, 66, 71, 85-86, 97, 105, 110
Symbols:
   "★" and "♪," x
   position (*see* Position symbols)
   motion, 43
Syncopation, 92-95, 177
   vs. dotted rhythm, 109*n*
   and rolls, 94
   sneeze in, 93

Tempo:
   controlling factor in, 65
   and lift, 64, 77
   four potatotes and, 61
   for new players, 13
Temperance Reel, 91, *149*, 174
Tenpenny Bit, 105, *151*
Tension:
   excess physical, 9, 12, 13-14, 19, 21, 49, 52, 53, 58
   effects of, 65, 66-67
   cause of, 62, 99
   good, about, 14*n*

tentacle, 96
"Thud," 3, 77
Thumb:
   adverse effects of, 19
   angled, to hammer, 21
   "button" on, 16
   "hinge" on, 16, 44
   hooked, 18, 78
   loose, 16-17, 18
   in multiple-bounce strokes, 78
   pad, 15, 18, 78
      on hammer handle, 16
   placement of, on hammer handle, 16
      incorrect, 16
   pointing, 78, 79, 113
   "pressure point," 16
   in rolls, 80
   tension in, 21
   test for relaxed, 16
   weak, in descending triplets, 113
   weight of, 18
Tibet, 102
Tie, 160
Time, about, 175
Time signature, 159
Tire, pumping air into, 84
Tobin's Favorite, 136
Top of the Cork Road, 98, *150*
Transposing a melody, 20, 174
   defined, 177
Triad, 52, 53, 56, 71, 101, 110, 113
Triangle, 16, 53
Triple tonguing, 97
Triplets, 111-115, 161
   ascending, 114-115
      "faking," 115
      scooping to play, 114
      warmup to, 114
      when to use, 115
   avoiding lead switch in, 111
   descending, 112-113
      strong hand and, 112
      uses, for, 112
      warmups for, 113
   in hornpipes, 111
Troubleshooting:
   arms are frozen or stiff, 45, 53, 66
   arms look like chicken wings, 10, 11
   arms, neck and back ache, 12
   bent wrists, 17
   "buzzing" sound, 18
   can't lift, 65
   hammer bounces twice, 18
   hammer feels unsteady, 21   (cont'd.)

Troubleshooting (cont'd.)
   hammer bounces once in rolls, 79
   hammers pigeon-toe too much, 17, 18-19
   hammers won't bounce, 18
   hammers won't swing, 18
   lead switches hands 49, 63, 105
   mistakes, 20, 46, 53, 54, 56, 58-59, 71
   multiple-bounce stroke bounces once, 79
   "nasal" or tinny sound, 9, 19, 21, 45, 79
   no continuous hand/arm motion, 63
   playing feels difficult, 13, 69-70
   rolls don't zing, 81
   rolls fall apart, 79, 80
   stroke-order confusion, 61, 62, 63
   strong hand stops between strikes, 53
   thumbs grip hammer tightly, 18
   weak arm won't move, 45
   weak hand won't lift, 69-70
Tune (*see also* Hornpipe, Jig, Reel and individual tunes)
   determining stroke order of, 72
   editing of, 173
   footnotes with, 173
   how to learn, 48-50
   songs used as, *135, 136, 150, 153*
   sources, 176
   "tough," about, 71
   in two keys, *145*
   variations of, 70, *137,* 175
   in what mode?, *142*
Tuner, electronic, 7, 117
Tuning:
   by ear, 117-118
   maintenance of, 118
Tuning chart, ix, 117
Tuning fork, 7, 117
Tuning pin, xiii, 177
   how to turn, 118
   slipping, 118
   removing string from, 119
   winding new string onto, 120
Tuning wrench, 7
Turkey in the Straw, 94, 95, *135*

"U," 94, 103
Unison, 29-31, 162-163, 177
   function of, 31
   how to find, 29-31
   regularity of, 162
   in tunes, 57
Up, going up, 66

Upbeat, 62
Upper arm (*see also* Arm)
  slant, 23-24, 45, 47, 93
    how to maintain, 17
  in jigs, 103
  and large, vertical reaches, 68
  in lift, 75
  position of, 11
  in syncopation, 93

Variation, dance tune, 70, 137, 175
Visual pattern, 12, 52, 54*n*, 56-59, 68, 69, 70-71, 72
  changing, with lead in jigs, 98, 106
  consistency in, 51, 101
  jumping notes as, 71
  and lift, 65
  playing music via, 50
  references to, 125
  triangle, 52
  vertical, 46, 47, 48, 52, 53, 54, 56, 58
Voice:
  of dulcimer, 70
  singing, 6, 175
Volume, 13, 18

Washington, George, 130, 134
water, bailing, 62
Waterfall, 74
  how to sing, 74
Watermelon pits—yuck!, 91
Wave, 77
Weak hand (*see* Hand)
Weather, and the dulcimer, 117, 118
When Daylight Shines, 69, *154*
Whiskey Before Breakfast, 69, *150*
White Cockade, The, 145
Wire, music, 119, 122
Wrist:
  in accents, 96
  adverse effects of, 19
  bent, 17, 45
  and energy, 77
  function of, 13, 17
  loose, 17, 18, 20, 59, 75, 77, 96
  relaxed, 20, 77
    test for, 18
  stiff, 18
  "straight," 17
  taking over action, 66

Notes

ORDER FORM

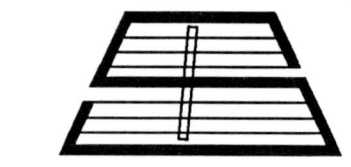

SHADRACH PRODUCTIONS
P. O. Box 49
Basking Ridge, NJ 07920

(PLEASE PRINT CLEARLY)

NAME _____

ADDRESS _____

CITY _____ STATE _____ ZIP _____

☐ Please add me to your mailing list for the first word on forthcoming books, recordings and workshops.

☐ Send me your catalog of dulcimers, gourmet hammers and stands, etc. (Sent with every order; if you want the catalog only, enclose SASE.)

☐ Please send the following item(s). My check or money order is enclosed.

	QTY.	PRICE
Striking Out...and WINNING! Book $35^{00}	____	____
Set of *three companion cassettes* (includes all tunes and exercises played exactly as written) $32^{00}	____	____
The *companion video,* showing everything in living color! See your music dealer or write us for more information.		
The Hammered Dulcimer A-Chording to Lucille Reilly $27.95	____	____
Tunes Plus You, a *play-along* cassette for <u>both</u> *Striking Out* and *A-Chording:* $12.95 each	____	____
At Last! The hammered dulcimer as celebrated by Lucille Reilly (includes selected tunes from *Striking Out).* Cassette: $9.98	____	____
SUBTOTAL		____
NJ residents: Please add appropriate sales tax		____
Shipping: $2.50 for first item; 75¢ each additional item		____
TOTAL		____

Comments (tell us what subjects you'd like to see in print, too): _____

_____

_____

_____

_____

THANK YOU!